DIGITAL TRANSFORMATION USING EMERGING TECHNOLOGIES

A CxO's Guide to Transform your organization

Fawad A. Khan

Jason M. Anderson

COPYRIGHT

DEDICATION

Dedicated to my beautiful wife and lovely children Ehan and Aleeza.

Fawad Khan

FOREWORD

Fawad and I have worked together for a few years, and in those few years Fawad has had a front row seat in not just observing but helping drive on the most amazing product transformation stories at Microsoft: the story of how we transformed a set of on-premises, monolithic "CRM" and "ERP" applications into modern, composable, intelligent SaaS applications, that today are growing faster than any of their competitors in their respective domains. In this short span, we not only transformed traditional CRM and ERP applications, but we also introduced a new class of data-first, insights applications as well as mixed reality applications built on HoloLens to really help drive transformative experiences and significant outcomes for our customers.

When Fawad first approached me and mentioned he was putting together a book to help business leaders think strategically about the next wave of digital transformation, I thought it was a great idea. Fawad is an expert voice in this space, given how close and how core he has been to what we have achieved in the business applications space in such a short period of time, incorporating the best of what the full Microsoft Cloud has to offer, and how close he has been to our community of passionate partners and committed customers in helping them with their transformation. And, I think the timing is ripe for this type of book: the world of technology and innovation has evolved at break-neck pace in recent years, all the while disrupting businesses across all industries and creating new opportunities for business leaders to truly transform. And yet on the heels of all this change, we're only now at the dawn of the next major wave of digital transformation.

"Despite all this rapid change in the computing industry, we are still at the beginning of the digital transformation." – Satya Nadella

This book clearly lays out the fundamental building blocks of the next wave: cloud computing, machine learning, artificial intelligence, Internet of Things (IoT), and blockchain.

At its heart, this book is really about Microsoft Cloud, and cloud has made things we never could have dreamed about before imminently possible. Microsoft Power Platform and Dynamics 365 are both built on Azure, and Dynamics 365 sits on top of Power Platform – enabling unparalleled capability and extensibility. Within the Dynamics 365 space, we're able to do things today that were never possible before – in a large part, due to cloud computing, and also by weaving in the advances in AI, machine learning, and IoT and wearables.

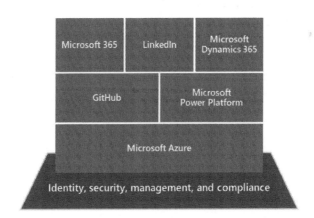

This next wave of digital transformation will be truly data-led and cloud-based. Data is now coming from everywhere and data is coming first, from customers interacting with your brand on social sites, to telemetry data being emitted real time and continuously through increasingly connected products, to observational data captured through cameras and videos – and these are just a few examples. All of this is a new class of data and an exponential amount of data that wasn't available before. What was available before in on-premises systems was simply *transactional* data that organizations captured in their systems of records, which pales in comparison to the data being available today.

At the heart of unlocking true transformation is unlocking the value of this massive amount of data, coupled with transactional data by bringing it together (in the cloud, which offers limitless scalability), reasoning over it via AI to generate not just insights but what is the next best action to guide the end user on what they should do. Cloud-first, modern business applications are fast and easy to implement and augment your existing technology stack to bring you rapid business insights. You don't have to bring in IT or technology consultants to extend your business applications: anyone in your organization can take advantage of the Power Platform to easily build custom apps, automate workflows to replace time-consuming or manual tasks, or build intelligent bots with a no-code interface. And this is just the beginning. The opportunities to truly harness data to drive insights and actions across the business are only just emerging.

The question: is your business ready to successfully navigate this next wave of digital transformation, capture the opportunities ahead, and emerge a leader?

At Microsoft, we believe in hitting refresh, and for business leaders in today's era that means making the most of the opportunities created by technology. And now more than ever, that means taking a hard look at the possibilities the near future brings and taking steps to get ready.

For any CxO asking the questions of *what* these new opportunities really are, *why* they are real today (and not science fiction), *who* am I going to need to make this work in my business, and *how* they really work in practice – this book is for you. If you need to hit refresh and ground yourself with a basic understanding of various emerging technologies, including cloud computing, machine learning, artificial intelligence, Internet of Things (IoT), and blockchain – that's all covered in this book, and it's rich with customer stories, expert opinions, and industry statistics (we love data). If you want a quick primer on all of these new emerging technologies without getting lost in the weeds, then grab a cup of coffee and sit down with this book, or take it on your next flight. This is the fast read that will get you up-to-speed so that you can think about how your business is going to navigate the future.

Muhammad Alam
CVP Microsoft Dynamics 365

PREFACE

If you are in a CxO role (CIO, CTO. CDO, et. al) for an organization and are responsible for the digital transformation of your organization, then this book is for you. However, we don't want to limit the readership to just the CxO since we also believe that other IT roles such as senior directors, directors, IT managers and solution architects will also benefit immensely from this book.

This book is for a practitioner CxO and can be used as a reference guide by the CxO to understand the basic concepts of digital transformation along with the fundamentals of various key emerging technologies including **Cloud Computing**, **Machine Learning**, **Artificial Intelligence**, **Internet of Things (IoT)**, and **Blockchain**. The book provides examples of services and tools from Microsoft Azure Cloud to help you harness these technologies to enable your digital transformation scenarios. Although we have used Microsoft Azure Cloud to highlight services and tools and highlight customer stories, all these can be replaced with Amazon's AWS or Google Cloud's services and tools since all the top cloud providers offer compatible cloud services with some nuances.

Since this book was born from a graduate course that Fawad Khan teaches at the University of Washington, this book can also be used for a graduate level course in Information Technology/Information Systems/Information Management programs in a university or a college.

This book does its best to describe all the fundamentals of any topic that is discussed by including the *what, why, who* and the *how* elements of the topic at hand. To make this book relevant to our targeted readers, we have also created and brought in content which is appreciated by our focused audience. Throughout the book we have included industry statistics, expert opinions, business use cases and customer stories which we believe will be appreciated by the CxO readers.

The book is organized logically into the following chapters to help you learn in a systematic way:

Chapter 1: Digital Transformation

This chapter provides an introduction and overview of digital transformation including the *what, why, who* and the *how* of transformation via digital technologies. We also outline some of the best practices for proper and successful execution of your transformation initiative. In this chapter, we also review some key challenges and reasons for digital transformation failures.

Chapter 2: Cloud Computing

The importance of cloud computing can't be overemphasized enough and since most of the emerging technologies, which are driving digital transformation, are offered via the cloud providers a good understanding cloud computing is important. Thus, we have dedicated a full chapter on it. This chapter outlines cloud computing history, core concepts and benefits. Cloud deployment and service models are introduced and discussed in detail. Considerations for transforming legacy IT to cloud are discussed along with challenges around using cloud computing. The chapter concludes with cloud computing trends and the future.

Chapter 3: Azure Cloud Services

This chapter dives specifically into Microsoft Azure Cloud and outlines the key services it offers. Understanding of the concepts and topics in chapter 2 are a pre-requisite for you to fully understanding this chapter. Basic Azure IaaS, PaaS and DBaaS services are introduced and discussed. Key and emerging cloud services including serverless, containers and hybrid cloud are described along with their benefits and business use cases.

Chapter 4: Machine Learning

This chapter introduces machine learning and its differences from AI and deep learning. Core concepts around data, algorithms, models along with how to build, train, and deploy the models are described. Azure Machine Learning tools and services are discussed to help you understand how you can use them to realize your machine learning digital transformation scenarios. This chapter also looks at the challenges and the future of machine learning.

Chapter 5: Artificial Intelligence

This chapter explores artificial intelligence, it benefits and business use cases. Azure AI platform and the offering available are explored such as Azure Cognitive Services, Bot Services, Cognitive Search services and Databricks services. AI challenges section looks at primary business and AI domain specific hurdles and issues. The chapter concludes with an outlook of AI with discussion around AI governance, responsible AI, technical advancements, and AIOps.

Chapter 6: Internet of Things

This chapter reviews the fundamentals of Internet of Things (IoT), its business value, and use cases. Various Azure IoT offerings and services are explored to get you started with it. Azure IoT SaaS solution, IoT Central, is reviewed to see how it can be utilized to build a no-code IoT solution. Azure IoT Hub and Digital Twins can be used to create complex and customized IoT solutions. The chapter concludes with an overview of IoT challenges and the future development of this technology.

Chapter 7: Blockchain

This chapter provides an overview of blockchain, and its possible business uses for various industries. Enterprise blockchain is discussed in detail and how Microsoft Azure Blockchain can be used for these enterprise scenarios. The chapter also explores various challenges this technology is facing as you consider it for your organization along with where this technology is going in the future.

We would like to thank a few people who have helped us with the review and copy editing. Special thanks to Pat Altimore[1] for helping us review the chapters and providing professional edits and recommendations. Two of my students, Kulraj Singh Kohli[2] and Manas Tripathi[3], at the University of Washington helped with the book review and for making edits. Along with that I am also very thankful to Asfandyar Azhar[4] , my mentee at Eindhoven University of Technology in Netherlands, for reviewing the chapter on machine learning.

Note:
This book is published both as a paperback and as an eBook at the same time. Thus, we have made sure that the content includes links for the e-version readers but also the complete URLs, spelled out in the footnote of the pages where the links were shown, for those who have a paper copy and still wanted to visit those links. Although we have double-checked all the links in this book but because of the nature of the Internet, some of the links may be broken when you read this book and try to get to those links.

---

[1] https://www.linkedin.com/in/pataltimore/
[2] https://www.linkedin.com/in/kulrajkohli/
[3] https://www.linkedin.com/in/tripathimanas/
[4] https://www.linkedin.com/in/asfandyarazhar/

We have provided many examples of tools and services from Microsoft's Azure Cloud. Microsoft is continuously evolving its tools and services and by the time you read this book, some of the tools or services we have mentioned in the book, may not be available or alternative and additional services/tools have been made available. Any significant changes and corrections to the book will be provided online[5]. We are also planning to update the book in the subsequent editions to make sure we keep it as current as possible.

Thank you and we sincerely hope that you enjoy and learn from our book and go tackle and solve tough problems in your organization by utilizing the knowledge gained from this book!

Best Regards,
Fawad Khan
Blog[6] | LinkedIn[7] | Twitter[8]

Jason M. Anderson
LinkedIn[9]

---

[5] http://digitalfawad.com/dxemergtechadd/
[6] http://digitalfawad.com/
[7] https://www.linkedin.com/in/fawadakhan1/
[8] https://twitter.com/DigitalFawad
[9] https://www.linkedin.com/in/jasonmanderson/

Table of Contents

CHAPTER 1:

DIGITAL TRANSFORMATION

DIGITAL TRANSFORMATION OVERVIEW

On January 26th, 2021, in a press release Satya Nadella, CEO of Microsoft, referred to Digital Transformation in today's age of COVID-19 as "the dawn of a second wave of digital transformation sweeping every company and every industry."

"Digital transformation" has been the industry buzzword for more than a couple of years now. According to an IDC report[10], it is predicted worldwide spending on the technologies and services that enable the digital transformation of business practices, products, and organizations will reach beyond $1.3 trillion beyond 2020. In this chapter, we will explore the fundamentals of Digital Transformation, understand the primary reasons for organizations adopting it, they key stakeholders and how to go about executing it.

---

[10] https://www.idc.com/getdoc.jsp?containerId=prUS46377220

As we live through the COVID-19 pandemic, it has become more critical than ever for companies to go digital to survive in these difficult times. COVID-19 has accelerated the adoption of digital technologies by several years for the long run globally. According to a McKinsey report[11], the three top areas of digital technologies adoption acceleration included remote work/collaboration, online purchasing/services and operations.

Understanding the basics

Digital transformation is the utilization of digital technologies into areas of a business resulting in changes to how business operates and delivers value to customers via its products, services, and experiences. Digital transformation can be the digitization of business processes, both internally within an organization or externally. It is the integration of digital technologies which ends up providing value to the customer at the end of the day. In other words, making "customer focus" as the core of what drives you to digitize your processes and operations. Digitization will help you improve your products, services, processes, and offerings to improve customer experiences and satisfaction. These changes will in turn help you evolve your business and business models.

---

[11] https://www.mckinsey.com/business-functions/strategy-and-corporate-finance/our-insights/how-covid-19-has-pushed-companies-over-the-technology-tipping-point-and-transformed-business-forever

Expert Opinion

"Too many leaders equate digital transformation with investments in new technology and miss its mission-critical goal of transforming the business, culture, and operations. Every business must evolve its target markets, products, services, culture. and operations for a global, digital world where customer experience is a differentiator and becoming data-driven an essential organizational capability. Yes, digital transformation requires technology and data investments, but using new tech aimed to optimize today's business will not achieve a transformation. Transformation requires a vision on where the organization must compete over a multiyear horizon, and it requires a change to a smarter, faster, experimenting culture."

Isaac Sacolick[12], President of StarCIO[13], and author of Driving Digital[14]

Industry Statistics

70%

Organizations either have a digital transformation strategy[15] or are working on it.

---

[12] https://www.starcio.com/isaac-sacolick
[13] https://www.starcio.com/
[14] http://driving-digital.com/purchase
[15] https://www.zdnet.com/article/survey-despite-steady-growth-in-digital-transformation-initiatives-companies-face-budget-and-buy-in/

Industry Statistics

7%

Organizations have fully implemented[16] their digital transformations.

Contrary to the misled perceptions digital transformation is not about technology but rather how technology will evolve your business and business models at the end of the day. Technology does, however, play a huge role since it is an enabler that helps you to execute your digital transformation strategy, but it is not the core of what you are trying to achieve for your business at the end of the day.

Digital transformation does require a huge investment into technology. A report from the World Economic Forum suggests the value of digital transformation for both society and industry could reach $100 trillion by 2025.

Why should you do it?

Top factors triggering organizations to digitally transform include revenue & growth opportunities, customer expectations and competitive pressures. COVID-19 has acted as a catalyst and forced many organized into accelerated adoption of digital technologies. A report from the State of Digital Transformation[17] research also confirms these factors,

---

[16] https://www.clickz.com/digital-transformation-2019-primer/224247/
[17] http://insights.prophet.com/the-state-of-digital-transformation-2018-2019

along with others, as the top three reasons for why organizations are transforming.

Industry Statistics	**27%**
	Organizations say digital transformation is a matter of survival[18]

Industry Statistics	**55%**
	Organizations without a digital transformation believe they have less than a year before they start to lose market share[19]

Business model evolution with revenue generation opportunities

Digital technologies are enabling scenarios which are helping organizations to rethink and evolve their business models to offer new products and services leading to additional revenue generation opportunities.

---

[18] https://digitalmarketinginstitute.com/en-us/blog/17-08-16-the-what-why-and-how-of-digital-transformation
[19] https://www.progress.com/docs/default-source/default-document-library/landing-pages/dach/ebook_digitaltransformation_final.pdf

Industry Statistics

60%

Organizations that have undergone a digital transformation have created new business models[20]

Expert Opinion

"Digital transformation must be fundamentally aligned to business transformation and not treated as a purely technology solution. Successful digital transformation initiatives have made sure that the business model and business process is first looked at too see how they need to be transformed to deliver better value to various stakeholders engaged, typically a platform led transformation approach to create platform based business models have led to greater success than siloed technology led approaches, obviously all such initiatives can never forget the leadership, people and change management dimensions which are critical to ensure long term success. Microsoft's vision of creating holistic integrated technology platforms should definitely accelerate and future proof technology investment strategies of companies that have a holistic long term digital transformation agenda."

Srikar Reddy[21] - MD & CEO Sonata Software

---

[20] https://www.ptc.com/en/products/plm/capabilities/digital-transformation-report
[21] https://www.linkedin.com/in/srikar-reddy-676986/

Higher customer expectations

Customers nowadays are expecting enhanced experiences along with more options from their products and services. To provide such enhanced customer experiences, organizations will need to use emerging digital technologies such as Artificial Intelligence (AI), Machine Learning (ML), Blockchain, Fifth Generation (5G) and Internet of Things (IoT) etc. to live up to their customers' expectations and to improve their overall satisfaction with your products and services.

Industry Statistics

35%

of the respondents reported improvements in ability to meet customer expectations[22] because of digital transformation.

Market and competitive pressures

Digital transformation projects are often a way for large and established organizations to compete with nimbler, digital-only rivals. In today's age of open-source software and ubiquitous availability of infrastructure resources and services from cloud providers, smaller organizations have an edge in being agile and using these technologies to come out with products and services much quicker than their large established counterparts. Because of this, you want to make sure that you jump on this agility bandwagon to either stay lockstep or ahead of your competitors with a culture of innovation and experimentation in your organization.

---

[22] https://www.ptc.com/en/products/plm/capabilities/digital-transformation-survey

Industry Statistics

36%

of the surveyed executives said that they saw improvements in faster time to market[23] because of digital transformation.

Key stakeholders

Have you heard the adage that it takes a village to do it? That holds true in case of digital transformation too but with a slight variation - it takes a whole village to do it including the village chiefs! Traditional digital transformation may start from the top with the CEO and CIO driving it initially, but you will have to have your whole organization bought into it for it to be successful. This will include your complete C-suite working together to make it successful including the CIO, CFO, CMO, CISO and CDO to name a few. In most cases, digital transformation will also mean a major shift in the organizational culture. Almost all successful digital transformations will require a top-down effort by the C-suite of the company along with a bottoms-up approach. **16%** of the companies surveyed in the State of Digital Transformation[24] report said that their C-suite is involved in some capacity in digital transformation.

IT leads the way

In recent years, there has been a fundamental shift happening for the role of IT unit in an organization. CEOs increasingly want their CIOs to help generate

---

[23] https://www.ptc.com/en/products/plm/capabilities/digital-transformation-survey
[24] http://insights.prophet.com/the-state-of-digital-transformation-2018-2019

revenue for their organizations. Almost two thirds (**64%**) of the respondents to the 2017 Harvey Nash/KPMG CIO Survey[25] of more than 4,600 CIOs say their CEO wants the IT organization to focus on revenue generation, rather than the traditional edict for IT unit to save costs. **85%** of companies surveyed in the State of Digital Transformation[26] report say that their digital transformation efforts have expanded beyond IT into organization wide initiatives. That said, IT unit continues to lead most of the digital transformation initiatives. The top 5 digital transformation focus areas, according to the State of the Digital Transformation report, are:

1. IT
2. Customer Service
3. Operations
4. Innovation
5. Marketing

Bring the village along with you!

At the end of the day, it will take the whole organization working together as a well-oiled machine for digital transformation initiatives to succeed. In some cases, you may have to work on changing the organization's culture to bring in critical success factors such as customer focus, agility, innovation, experimentation, and a collaboration to be successful with your transformation.

Collaboration will have to work at all levels of the organization from working with others in a team, to peer teams to different units within an organization. Agility will help with rapid experimentation and go-to-market strategies to gain an edge over your competition with

---

[25] https://www.hnkpmgciosurvey.com/
[26] http://insights.prophet.com/the-state-of-digital-transformation-2018-2019

quick introduction of new products, services or improving customer experiences.

Innovation will also have to be encouraged at all levels of the organization from frontline teams to the senior leadership teams. Microsoft is a prime example of company where CEO Satya Nadella has changed Microsoft's organizational culture from being a closed and marketing-based company to an engineering-focused, collaborative, agile, and customer-centric culture. Digital transformation is not just all about the C-suite believing in it and working together but rather it is a combination of both top down and bottoms-up approaches where all teams and units also must live and breathe a culture of collaboration, innovation, experimentation, and customer focus.

According to the State of Digital Transformation[27] report, organizational buy-in remains a top challenge for those leading digital transformation with cultural issues posing a notable threat to successful digital transformation (**26%**) execution.

---

[27] http://insights.prophet.com/the-state-of-digital-transformation-2018-2019

THE 'HOW' OF DIGITAL TRANSFORMATION

In this section, we will dive deeper into how to go about accomplishing digital transformation in your organization. We will discuss how culture and people play an important role, what key technologies are enabling and accelerating the transformation, role of experimentation & innovation, and the importance of tracking analytics to assess the ROI of your efforts.

Transform the organizational culture

Culture is considered one of the key factors for successful digital transformation, as you start thinking about how you are going to go about digitally transforming your organization. Organizational buy-in remains a top challenge for those leading digital transformation with cultural issues posing considerable threat to successful digital transformation efforts. Buried under the covers of culture are key factors including customer focus, collaboration, top down and bottoms-up support for digital transformation, agility, innovation, and experimentation.

Industry Statistics	**70%**
	Digital transformations fail[28], most often due to resistance from employees.

Traditionally, engineering and technically focused organizations have made decisions on their products and services they create without involving or engaging the customers throughout the product life cycle. These organizations will have to change their paradigm and should start building products that are continuously driven by customer requirements and feedback.

To truly make digital transformation initiatives successful, all layers of management from the top senior leadership to the first line managers will have to believe and support it to make it successful.

Although, most of the work and engagement may start and come out of the IT unit of the organization, it will for sure require involvement and engagement from other units within the organization. All teams and units in an organization will have to partner with each other to complete different aspects of the digital transformation projects. Internal collaboration must be built into the DNA of the organization for successful transformation completion.

---

[28] https://www.forbes.com/sites/carstentams/2018/01/26/why-we-need-to-rethink-organizational-change-management/#571fb86ee93c

Another major part of the cultural change will be how the organization uses agility to stay ahead of the competition with new and improved products, services, and customer experiences. Agility becomes more critical for large corporations which may have too many processes and rigid hurdles to accomplish projects and key initiatives in a timely manner. Startups and smaller digital-only companies on the other hand are much nimbler and can get products and services out in the market before their competitors. Amazon Web Services (AWS) is an example of a large corporation which has been able to work in a startup mode, living by the principles of agility, and has been able to crank out many successful cloud services at lightning speed.

Microsoft, which has transformed its organizational philosophy, is living and breathing a culture of agility in many of its units including Microsoft 365, Azure, and Dynamics 365 and launching services very similar to Amazon Web Services.

Pick the right technologies

Industry Statistics **93%**

Organizations consider innovative technologies as necessary[29] to reaching digital transformation goals.

---

[29] https://news.sap.com/2019/03/forrester-survey-intelligent-technology-digital-transformation/

Digital transformation is about incorporating digital technologies in all aspects of business to build customer-centric products, services, and experiences leading to evolved business models. Thus, it is important to choose the right technologies to help you transform your business. With easy access to technology, open-source software availability and free evaluations available from technology companies you can evaluate and decide on the proper technology stack which will help you change your business models and build customer-centric products, services, and experiences.

Industry Statistics **68%**

Global business leaders believe the future of business involves humans and AI working together[30]

Cloud, cyber security, ML/AI and IoT led the way in technology investments for the enterprises in 2019 according to the State of Digital Transformation[31] report. IDC[32] forecasts that enterprise AI solutions and applications will deliver over $52B in global market revenue by 2021, attaining a compound annual growth rate (CAGR) to **46.2%** through 2021.

---

[30]https://www.fujitsu.com/global/about/resources/news/press-releases/2018/0712-01.html
[31] http://insights.prophet.com/the-state-of-digital-transformation-2018-2019
[32] https://www.idc.com/getdoc.jsp?containerId=US44403818

Customer Story

Target is an example of an organization which has transformed themselves via digital technologies to stay competitive. They added new technology in their stores, introduced online ordering and increased their social media, web presence and online sales to increase their market share.

Read the entire story[33]

Industry Statistics

60%

Executives believe connected technology and the Internet of Things will play an important role[34] in their company's digital strategy.

Another technology on the horizon is blockchain and it will enable various business scenarios, specifically around supply chain management and the finance industry. We will cover blockchain in chapter 7 of this book.

Harness the cloud

Amazon, Microsoft, and Google are the top three cloud service providers in the US right now. According to an IDC report[35] by 2022, the top four cloud "mega platforms" will host **80%** of Infrastructure as a Service (IaaS). By 2024, for Platform as a Service (PaaS)

---

[33] https://www.game-learn.com/7-examples-of-successful-digital-transformation-in-business/
[34] https://resources.idg.com/download/white-paper/2018-digital-business
[35] https://www.idc.com/getdoc.jsp?containerId=US44403818

deployments **90%** of global 1000 organizations will mitigate lock-in through multicloud and hybrid cloud technologies and tools.

Cloud computing has and will continue to play a major role as a catalyst for digital transformation initiatives. Cloud computing has become one of the top priorities and investment areas for many enterprises and especially during the COVID-19 pandemic where most of us have been forced to work remotely. Organizations which were already utilizing the cloud for their basic Software as a Service (SaaS) and Infrastructure as a Service (IaaS) business scenarios are now moving into hybrid cloud computing so they can fully leverage both their on-premises data centers resources and the public cloud together to enable advanced business use cases. Cloud is also moving the companies from capital expenditure (CapEx) to operating expenses (OpEx) model of spending. We will cover cloud computing in chapter 2 and then in chapter 3 we will do an overview of Microsoft Azure Cloud Services.

Expert Opinion "During Digital Transformation, you will need to run old and new systems, called digital twins in parallel for some time and that means greater investments. Having cloud (OpEx) based spend helps enterprises absorb the cost shock during transition period. Cloud is a no-brainer for creating systems, and it's a viable option for operating (same) systems in most cases."

Sarbjeet Johal[36]– Cloud Computing & Digital Transformation Expert and Strategist

---

[36] https://www.linkedin.com/in/sarbjeetjohal/

The beauty of utilizing the public cloud is that you can also consume emerging technologies like ML, AI, IoT, blockchain and big data from the cloud too. Most of the cloud providers are offering there emerging technologies and associated services along with core and traditional cloud services. All cloud services are available at reduced cost, pay-as-you use model, accelerated speed and unlimited scaling as your needs grow. Because of these advantages, organization, small and large, are adopting public cloud and using basic cloud services along with emerging technologies services.

Customer Story	Back in 2012, most people thought that Best Buy was dead. Even people within the company didn't believe it could survive against Amazon. But a new CEO and a fresh digital perspective transformed the electronics store from a place to buy CDs to a digital leader in technology by enriching their current potential lives with the help of technology. Along with that they moved 90% of their advertising media from mail to all digital._Read the entire story[37]

Depending on the scope, nowadays using the cloud, you can take your idea to implementation in matter of days whereas the same might have taken you weeks or months. With cloud you can get your minimal viable product (MVP) out in the market quickly and become the trailblazer for your market. The pay-as-you use cloud model has made it a perfect place to experiment and

---

[37] https://www.forbes.com/sites/blakemorgan/2019/07/21/7-examples-of-how-digital-transformation-impacted-business-performance/?sh=33fccdc51bbe

innovate without investing huge capital upfront, which you had to do for doing any experimentation using your on-premises data center. Availability of almost unlimited and scalable infrastructure, variety of software from the cloud marketplaces, and core cloud services has made cloud the playground for many innovators. You can use the cloud by provisioning the required resources, experiment as needed, and then de-provision the resources once done. You can come back and repeat this cycle whenever needed to do any additional experimentation.

Make the right decisions for the people, technology, and processes

As you adopt newer digital technologies, you should inventory your in-house skillset and retrain or re-skill your workforce to make sure that they can efficiently utilize and manage the newer digital technologies. With new technology comes new sets of processes which will also have to be adopted both internally and externally when working with the customers.

For certain digital transformation initiatives, you may be required to seek external expert help in the earlier phases of adoption and utilization of newer technologies because of lack of the required skill-set in-house. You can bring in external experts and consultants as needed with specialization and expertise in your industry and in the digital technologies you are planning to utilize.

A key advice in most of the scenarios of transformation would be to not discard all the older technologies just because you want to use the new shiny digital technologies. Carefully reevaluate your products, services, and customer experience scenarios with both the newer and older technologies to assess if a hybrid approach of using old and new technologies is an option. Another approach may be to introduce the newer digital technologies in phases. With budget constraints, hybrid and phased approaches may work out better than sinking huge investment into a newer digital technology and completely discarding the older technologies.

Customer Story	Home Depot has transformed themselves from a hardware store to both physical and online presence with an investment of $11 billion of over the period of three years. They invested heavily in their IT department along with modernizing the customer experience, via visual & voice interfaces and analytics, across multiple channels. Read the entire story[38]

Whatever approach you take, make sure that you carefully consider customer experience changes, learning, and adoption. Adopt agile and structured project management approaches to manage all the digital transformation initiatives with proper communication to stakeholders with findings, results, and next steps for both experimental and production projects. As stated before, follow agile approach to creating new customer experiences, products, or services with minimal core functionality and then iteratively improving and enhancing it after customer feedback. Bringing change in phases and via iterative processes is a better option for

---

[38]https://www.forbes.com/sites/blakemorgan/2019/07/21/7-examples-of-how-digital-transformation-impacted-business-performance

large scale digital transformation projects than creating a 3-year project plan. You should clearly layout both the short and a long-term plan for your transformation projects.

Utilize data and analytics to assess your progress

As you kick off your digitization projects, make sure that you are utilizing data and analytics to examine the results and then making proper business and technical decisions. Data analytics will not only help you with making data-driven decisions but will also assist you in calculating the ROI of your effort. For a 360-degrees view of your transformation projects, utilize all relevant data sources from your systems, apps, and customers. Data analysis should be performed periodically throughout the transformation to assess the progress, understanding what is working, and what needs to be changed to get to the results you are desiring.

Calculate the ROI to show the true value

Calculating the return on investment is one of the key challenges of digital transformation. You want to make sure that you have a set of key metrics you are tracking to calculate the ROI. These metrics should be defined upfront before starting your digital transformation projects with proper agreement and support from senior leadership and key stakeholders.

Industry Statistics

56%

CEOs say digital improvements have led to increased revenue[39]

Tracking those metrics and periodically calculating the ROI from those to show the value and results of digital transformation will be the key to the overall success of your transformation initiatives. Some typical key metrics include customer-base growth, revenue and profit growth, customer satisfaction improvements, and high Net Promoter Scores (NPS).

Industry Statistics

24%

Executives who track revenue as one of the key success metrics[40] of digital transformation.

Industry Statistics

23%

Executives who track Net Promoter Score (NPS) as one of the key success metrics[41] of digital transformation.

---

[39] https://www.gartner.com/en/newsroom/press-releases/2017-04-24-gartner-survey-shows-42-percent-of-ceos-have-begun-digital-business-transformation
[40] https://www.genesys.com/resources/the-us-customer-experience-decision-makers-guide-2018?cid=7010B000001Sctw
[41] https://www.genesys.com/resources/the-us-customer-experience-decision-makers-guide-2018?cid=7010B000001Sctw

ROLE OF A CIO

A CIO plays a critical role in digital transformation and although she is not the only C-suite executive engaged in digital transformation initiatives, she is one of the most active and key leaders during the transformation. Granted that digital transformation is not just about the new technologies and using them, it is usually the IT department under the CIO's leadership which is responsible for evaluating, trying, deploying, maintaining, and supporting any new digital technologies in the organization. Thus, it is important to understand the role of a CIO in depth, for digital transformation.

Industry Statistics **28%**

In 2018 and 2019 digital transformations were led[42] by the CIO.

---

[42] https://insights.prophet.com/the-state-of-digital-transformation-2018-2019

The number above has trended similarly in 2020 and 2021 with CIOs leading the charge on most digital transformations. A CIO who wants to survive digital transformation in their company needs to have certain traits and characteristics. This section discusses some of those key characteristics that will make the CIO come out as a victor during and after the transformation.

Offers technical leadership

As expected, one of the key roles of the CIO is to provide technical leadership. She is expected to have deep knowledge of the industry and typically comes with a breadth of technical experience. She and her team are expected to choose and try out new emerging technologies and assess the impact of those technologies on improving or building products, services, and customer experiences. In today's age of innovation and experimentation, she and her team should be looked on as the authority within the organization on emerging and trending technologies (Cloud, IoT, Blockchain, 5G, Artificial Intelligence, Machine Learning, *et al.*) and provide any required technical assistance in experimenting with them. A CIO can help orchestrate innovation and experimentation within the whole organization by providing technical resources and experts from her team.

Expert Opinion	"This CIO role is key to any successful transformation. The organization is looking to the CIO to shepherd the organization through all the difficult technical architecture to ensure what the organization is investing in and meets company's uses cases, produces measurable results, is secure, scalable, in some cases reusable (such as services/microservices) and provides relevant business outcomes. This might be the hardest part of the transformation to obtain. If not achieved, delays, cost overruns and future expansion of capability is in jeopardy."

Doug Saunders[43], CIO and VP Advanced Disposal Services

Provides business leadership

A CIO not only needs to be a technical leader but also should have deep business understanding and acumen. Digital transformation can't just pivot around the IT unit's traditional cost savings mantra. It is about customer centricity, revenue generation, and competing in your market while innovating and experimenting for continuous improvements in products, services, and customer experiences. A good business leader in today's age understands the importance of agility and innovation to live up to the ever-high customer expectations. A CIO understands the business models and has a vision on how they will evolve because of the digital transformation initiatives within the organization. They have the data analytics and make data-driven, balanced, and prioritized

---

[43] https://www.linkedin.com/in/dgsaunders/

decisions. Such profound business thinking, and practices will lead to organizations with evolved business models, revenue growth possibilities, and competitive advantages.

Acts as the master of ceremonies

A CIO should be an exceptional communicator. She should be able to simplify complex technical scenarios and translate those into key business messages to her senior leadership team around business value, competitive analysis, business model evolution opportunities and revenue generation prospects. Along with communicating with senior leadership, she should be able to clearly articulate the vision and the strategy of the organization's digital transformation top down to make sure that she can influence all layers of the organization. This will help in getting buy-in from majority of the employees in various units of the organization. Such influence and employees' understanding will lead to success of the transformation initiatives. Getting buy-in across all layers of her organization, her peers and their respective units will help the initiatives which span multiple units of an organization.

Industry Statistics **71%**

Leaders say the workforce is important[44] in supporting their digital transformation strategy.

---

[44] https://www.industryweek.com/talent/interactive-report-workforce-enablement-missing-link-digital-transformation-strategies

---

Cultivates collaboration across the organization

A CIO should be a master collaborator who works across all units of the organization. Building partnerships and bridges across all units will help in overall success of initiatives spanning across multiple units in the organization. Close partnerships with the leads from all the units will be a must if the digital transformation is going to cover multiple parts of the organization. CIO's IT unit alone cannot be successful in the transformation efforts if there is dependency on other units in the organization. While they may have the deep technical expertise to understand how the technology works, they absolutely will need the subject matter experts from the related units to successfully execute on all transformation scenarios. This deep dependency on other units makes the CIO's role critical and essential in building partnerships and working closely with the leads from the other units.

Expert Opinion	"Forward thinking organizations are quickly learning what forward thinking CIOs already know. The CMO and CIO are allies in digital transformation. The other thing that is becoming crystal clear is that alignment with the business, customer goals and creating great customer experience is everyone's job. IT has a role in marketing and marketing has a role IT. In order to evolve we must align."
	Jo Peterson[45], VP Cloud & Security Services at Clarify360

---

[45] https://www.linkedin.com/in/jopeterson1/

Takes care of the people

People are key to a successful digital transformation in any organization. A CIO should understand the impact of the transformation on her unit and other units in the organization. She should recognize how change brings in resistance, fears, and doubts in employees' minds. She should clearly and succinctly communicate the goals and reasons for the transformation and help people in her and other units understand the impact of the transformation. She should carefully assess the impact of the transformation and make decisions on getting external consulting help (if needed), retraining, teams' consolidation and hiring. In some cases, digital transformation may lead to job eliminations, but it will also at the same time create new jobs, roles, and opportunities.

Industry Statistics **37%**

Organizations say digital transformation helped them create[46] new jobs.

---

[46] https://futurumresearch.com/futurum-2018-digital-transformation-index/

Expert Opinion	"This might be the most obvious objective but it's tricky. You want to provide the current IT/Digital organization the company objectives, roadmaps and articulate how their current roles might need to change. Offering training and skill enhancement is paramount. The other tough choice is when to make change in the org structure to achieve needed capability. Most companies are not keen on just adding new headcount. They want responsible headcount management along with the delivery of new capability. It's a delicate cultural balance to replace staff, while training current staff and maintain a positive culture within the IT department. You must be prepared for "ups and down" during this process and be ready to over communicate." Doug Saunders, CIO and VP Advanced Disposal Services

Provides executive sponsorship and oversight

CIO's sponsorship and oversight during the execution phase of this transformation is critical to the overall success of the transformation journey. It is great to have a vision and strategy for your transformation but not paying attention to the execution phase of the transformation can lead to the overall failure of the transformation. Ideally, the CIO should be one of the executive sponsors or the main sponsor of the digital transformation initiatives.

She can nominate or assign a key person from her leadership team to have overall oversight and accountability for the initiatives. As the sponsor, the CIO should become an advocate of the initiatives and continue to help the people in the organization understand the digital transformation initiatives and their overall importance to the organization. It is important to make sure that the CIO and her team stay deeply engaged in budget, schedule, and resources discussions of the initiatives. She should remove any hurdles during the execution phase of the initiatives to make sure they are making progress and are going to deliver within budget and on time.

INNOVATION AND EXPERIMENTATION

Innovation and experimentation are an important part of any digital transformations journey. This section provides high level recommendations on building innovation and experimentation framework in your organization along with high-level guidelines for leading successful digital transformation experiments.

Both innovation and experimentation will help you move closer to the digitization of processes, creation of products and services, and enhanced customer experiences. According to the State of Digital Transformation[47] research, innovation is ranked as one of the top five areas of focus for companies which have embarked on a journey to transform.

Emerging and open-source technologies have opened new frontiers not only for the startups but also for well-

---

[47] http://insights.prophet.com/the-state-of-digital-transformation-2018-2019

established large enterprises in trying and experimenting these technologies for their business scenarios. Emerging technologies such as Cloud, 5G, Machine Learning, Artificial Intelligence, Internet of Things, and Blockchain are going to lead the way in technology investments for the enterprises in 2021 and beyond.

Cloud computing is and will continue to play a key role as an enabler and a catalyst for innovation and experimentation. Numerous cloud services from multiple providers are helping organizations to run experiments, using various emerging technologies, to try and test new business transformation proof of concept ideas before making huge investment on scaling these ideas into production systems. One of the key advantages of cloud computing is getting your MVP out in the market as quickly as possible, thus, gaining competitive edge in the market.

Regardless of what technology you are using to innovate and experiment, it is critical to keep the customer as the center of focus. It all starts with creating a MVP, taking it to the customers for feedback, coming back and improving the product/service/experience with that feedback and then taking it back again to the customers for reevaluation. Repeat this cycle multiple times till you see huge customer adoption and positive feedback. This iterative process will lead to customer approved products, services, and experiences which your customers will love and will continue to use along with becoming an advocate of your products/services and organization.

As you get ready to socialize innovation and experimentation in your organization, it helps to create a framework with the following key elements:

- Build a cross-organization innovation council which has membership from all business units.
- Create a structure to generate ideas and initiate experimentation from all business units.
- Create a governance model to ensure smooth review, approval, and execution of all approved ideas.
- Evangelize and encourage innovation and experimentation throughout the organization.
- Make customer centricity and product/service/experience improvements as the core component of all experiments.

All initiated experiments should be carefully evaluated against a set of core criteria including possible business model changes, improving customer experience, increasing the customer-base, gaining competitive edge, or creating revenue generation opportunities.

As teams and individuals from different units in your organization start to innovate and experiment on business and customer scenarios, here are some guiding principles to follow for achieving successful experimental initiatives:

Solve a business or a customer problem

Before you start an innovation or experimental project, make sure that you have clearly identified a business or a customer problem you are trying to solve. Don't just innovate or start an experiment just for the sake of doing one or just because everyone else is doing it. Basically, don't put the horse before the cart where you are doing an experiment for the sake of experiment and not really filling a business void or solving a problem. A business problem can be a creation or improvement of a product, service, or a customer/partner experience. Creating a technically advanced product, service, or experience, as part of your experiment, will not go anywhere if it is not solving a business or a customer problem in your specific industry.

Define a niche for your product, service or experience

For all your experimental projects, make sure that you differentiate your product and service from your competitors by building a niche for your product/service so you can compete with other similar ideas in your industry. This means that you will have to research upfront and perform a competitive analysis that you are not recreating the wheel and the product/service/experience doesn't already exist in your industry.

Use inexpensive and existing technologies & services

Experiments usually don't have any budget associated with them and thus you are forced to scavenge and use either existing resources available to you or anything else you can find at no or minimal cost to create your proof-of-concept product/service/experience. Taking a minimalistic approach will help you set up your experiment without waiting for any budget allocations. Cloud services, existing software and infrastructure, free open-source software and time limited free evaluation products and services from other vendors are some of the ways you can start and complete your experiment without asking for any budget.

Create an MVP, gather feedback and iterate

This is where you need to remember that you are not looking for perfection when you are experimenting but rather you should aim for agility to get the minimal viable product out the door as soon as possible. Build your MVP, take it to core set of loyal customers, have them use it and provide feedback and suggestions. Go back and use the feedback to make improvements to the MVP. Once your experimental product/service/experience has gone through various iterative customer feedback cycles and improvements along with getting acceptance, you will be ready to scale your product/service/experience and obtain resources and budget to create a production version.

In today's agile startup environment, bringing nimbleness to your innovation and experimentation process is key to you getting the products and services to the market and gaining competitive edge over the rest of the players in your industry.

> **Expert Opinion**
>
> "One of the benefits of the new digital world we are in is that trying and failing can be far less costly and tested quickly; spin up AWS, use vast compute to test something out at low cost and spin it down, without large financial and time commitments."
>
> Ian Moyse[48], Chief Revenue Officer - OneUp Sales

Obtain sponsorship

Getting sponsorship and support from your top management is extremely important for the long-term survival of your experimental project. You will need this support so that you can continue to iterate and gradually improve your product/service/experience without your management resetting your priorities. With the backing of your unit's leadership, you have higher chances of your innovation/experiment seeing the light of the day and possibly being considered for a scaled production system. Your leadership will be able to get you any required resources and budget and may also get you any required help from other business units in your organization.

Build partnerships across different units

No one builds a product or a service in any organization on their own. For large enterprises, it almost always takes multiple units to build, create, or improve a product/service/experience. In most of the cases, you will have to collaborate with others in your unit or

---

[48] https://www.linkedin.com/in/ianmoyse/

across other units in your organization to successfully complete your experimental project. A product/service/experience built with cross-collaboration partnerships across different units of an organization will generally be much more successful due to the input and different perspectives considered for it. It will also be fully balanced and can also potentially be used across various units in your organization due to the input you received from various stakeholders in different units.

Communicate, communicate and communicate

Communicate the progress and status of your innovation and experiment up and down and across the stakeholder and management chain. Explicitly highlight the business or customer problem you are solving along with the ROI of the experiment and how your initiative will potentially help the organization with product/service/experience creation or enhancements and that in turn will result in the organization obtaining a competitive edge, increase in customer-base or in potential revenue growth.

CHALLENGES AND PITFALLS

Digital transformation has many challenges which you may have to tackle. In this section we will review some of the challenges such as lack of vision & strategy, dysfunctional culture, absence of executive sponsorship, inadequate budget, and lack of required talent.

According to a 2019 survey of directors, CEOs, and senior executives[49] by the Wall Street Journal Digital Transformation, risk is their #1 concern yet 70% of all Digital Transformation initiatives[50] do not reach their goals. $1.3 trillion was spent in 2017 on digital transformation and it is estimated that $900 billion went to waste. So, the question at hand is, why do some transformation efforts succeed, while others fail? Let's try to analyze and understand some key factors which lead to Digital Transformation failures and how to avoid them.

---

[49] https://blogs.wsj.com/riskandcompliance/2018/12/05/businesses-predict-digital-transformation-to-be-biggest-risk-factors-in-2019/
[50] https://www.forbes.com/sites/forbestechcouncil/2018/03/13/why-digital-transformations-fail-closing-the-900-billion-hole-in-enterprise-strategy/#4f74e9207b8b

Nonexistence of a cohesive vision and strategy

In today's culture of startups of building and pushing MVP out to your current and potential customers, is creating a culture of accelerated innovation and experimentation. At the same time, it is leading to different teams and units within an organization doing their own thing without understanding the company's digital transformation vision and strategy. This leads to wastage of resources and effort and eventually leads to failure. While accelerated innovation may produce great ideas and MVP, it may not get the broader exposure that it otherwise could receive if it is aligned with the overarching digital transformation strategy of the organization.

Your digital transformation strategy should evaluate your current processes, customer experiences, products, and services and understand how you can improve all those to retain and increase your customer base. Your strategy will also impact your business models so those also need to be assessed as a part of the discussion and understood as to how they will evolve as you go through the transformation.

A common misconception that should be clarified as part of your strategy discussion upfront is that Digital Transformation is not about using the latest and greatest technologies.

Expert Opinion	"Digital Transformation is not about technology and should not start with technology, but with people engagement, mindset shift and processes. Leaders who can answer the question *"why" will be more apt to *bring their businesses along*. We are going through this process to remain competitive, improve efficiency and productivity, bring superior customer experience, and push us towards innovation — this is all about the 'why'."

Antonio Figueiredo[51], RVP Salesforce

Your strategy should absolutely consider new and emerging technologies but only to improve your products, services, and customer experiences, thus making it all about the customer and not the technology.

Lack of a cohesive vision and strategy will lead to many initiatives in different parts of your organization, but they will never see the day of the light due to the misalignment with the top-down digital transformation strategy. It is imperative that any initiatives started as part of digital transformation are communicated properly both top down and bottoms up and have the support of the senior leadership to have any chances of success.

Dysfunctional organizational culture

One of the key challenges of digital transformation which has led to many organizations failing at it, is its culture or its ability to change its culture. An organizational culture which is based on collaboration,

---

[51] https://www.linkedin.com/in/afigueiredo/

agility, and innovation is surely set up to succeed with its digital transformation efforts compared to a culture where different units are unwilling to work with each other.

Collaboration between all units within an organization will guarantee the success of any company-wide digital transformation initiatives. Innovation and agility to create and enhance products, services and customer experiences will help your organization compete in today's world of startups which are cranking out products, services and enhancements at unprecedented speeds compared to larger legacy organizations.

Fear also plays a critical role in the failure of digital transformation initiatives. Many organization personnel fear the possibility of potential loss of their jobs due to the digital technologies partly or completely replacing them. This may lead them to be unwilling to help or being non-collaborative with others working on transformation initiatives.

Expert Opinion	"When we are truly honest, we must admit that Digital Transformation is the wrong title for what we want to achieve. The real transformation takes place between people and processes. The digital tools are no more and no less than the vehicles that support this transformation, and to some extend even enable the transformation. Transformation processes fail when the tools become more important than the goals, and digital transformation is no exception."
	Johannes Drooghaag[52], CEO Spearhead Management

---

[52] https://www.linkedin.com/in/johannesdrooghaag/

While loss of certain job roles is inevitable with digital transformation within an organization, most of the jobs can be saved with proper personnel retraining and changed job functions to work with newer digital technologies. Again, clear, and succinct communication about your digital transformation vision and strategy to all the units in the organization will help you alleviate fears that most of the personnel may feel.

Lack of executive engagement and sponsorship

Most of the time executive and senior leadership will not have the deep knowledge of the technologies being utilized in the digital transformation initiatives. For overcoming the lack of digital technologies literacy of your senior leadership, digital transformation owner or the key stakeholder needs to educate them. Help them understand how technology can assist transform the business models, products, services, customer experiences and thus the whole business.

Some of the most innovative and customer-centric initiatives within a company fail to make it to the surface because the senior leadership in your company were not aware of them. This is a very common scenario in large enterprises where you may have dozens of initiatives simultaneously being worked on at any time.

If you are an owner of one of the digital transformation initiatives in your organization, then at minimal, get buy-in from your immediate manager and then work with her closely to have her help you get the required exposure for your transformation initiative in the organization. You should regularly communicate the progress, status and ongoing results and impact of the project across the organization.

Your communication should concentrate on how the digital technologies are being utilized to build or improve customer-centric products, services, and experiences rather than on the technologies themselves. You also want to make sure that your communication clearly spells out how your digital transformation initiatives will potentially change the business model leading up to improved customer satisfaction and increasing the prospects of revenue growth. This kind of messaging will get senior leadership's attention and build their interest in your initiative and its success.

Insufficient budgets

Overall budget spend for digital transformation has gone up in 2019. Gartner report[53] in 2018 projected a **3.2%** increase in IT spending to $3.8 trillion in 2019. A Spiceworks annual survey[54] from last year also found that **89%** of the organizations were expecting to grow or keep steady their digital transformation and IT spending.

Due to Covid-19, we have also seen a decrease in overall IT budgets in organizations for both 2020 and 2021. While some companies have halted their digital transformation taking a financially cautious approach, others have accelerated it. The later organizations are the ones who believe and see the pandemic as an opportunity to offer virtual services to their customers to replace the pre-pandemic physical experiences. Some organizations

---

[53] https://www.gartner.com/en/newsroom/press-releases/2018-10-17-gartner-says-global-it-spending-to-grow-3-2-percent-in-2019
[54] https://www.spiceworks.com/marketing/state-of-it/report/

also have provisional budgets that they also may decide to use for the transformation.

The question then is - How do you maximize your budget allocation and align with the overall digital transformation strategy? First and most important thing is to understand your core customer scenarios. You should consider utilizing the existing software, hardware, and infrastructure you own, in your digital transformation scenarios, rather than completely discarding them and starting from scratch.

Another option to consider, is to take an iterative approach on products, services and customer experiences creation and improvements, by creating an MVP and then getting customers and partners to provide iterative feedback as you continue to improve it. This approach will probably work better than investing completely into a full fledge long term project. Cloud services and emerging technologies (AI, ML, IoT, Blockchain, etc.) offered by the cloud providers are key here to help you with creating products, services, and experience prototypes/MVP with minimal budget investment.

Shortage of talent

With the growing global and USA tech economy, there is a shortage of technical expertise which is directly impacting digital transformation initiatives.
IDC's Worldwide CIO Agenda 2019 report predicts that **30%** of high-demand roles for emerging technologies will remain unfilled through 2022. Availability of technical talent is one of the top obstacles in achieving business goals for many organizations. The biggest organizational skill gaps are found for ML, AI, big data, analytics, and information management.

But if you think it's tough to find great talent now, <u>new research from the Korn Ferry Institute</u>[55] suggests that things are only going to get even worse and the global talent shortage could reach **85.2 million** people by 2030—costing companies trillions of dollars in lost economic opportunity.

Other factors that contribute to this shortage include need for specialized expertise as more and more companies start to consider and use emerging technologies like AI, ML, IoT and blockchain et. al as part of their digital transformation strategy. It is becoming harder and harder to find technical talent in these technology domains. Competition is another key factor that is leading to the widening of this gap between supply and demand of the technical talent. Your competitors are also in the market to nab the same technical talent that you are looking for and this makes your job much harder to attract and retain the talent.

As an alternative to hiring, you can bring in external consulting firms to fill the demand in the short term while you continue to search for the required talent in the background and start to reskill your current personnel with the required skills.

◆ ◆ ◆ ◆ ◆ ◆ ◆ ◆ ◆ ◆ ◆

---

[55] https://www.kornferry.com/challenges/future-of-work

WHY TRANSFORMATION FAILS

While many factors can play into digital transformation failures in an organization, there are five key areas of concern for you to consider before and during your digital transformation journey.

Key reasons we will discuss in this section will be not remembering the fundamentals, overcomplicating the initiatives, vendor sourcing, technology choices and initiatives oversight and management.

Forgetting the fundamentals

Lack of a cohesive vision and strategy will lead to digital transformation disaster. Never forget the basics - It is all about the customer (external or internal). Concentrating on the technology and not on the customer or how the products/services/experiences will help the customer will lead to nowhere. Business model implications should be considered upfront when creating your digital transformation vision.

Customer Story	In 2012, Procter & Gamble set out to become a digital transformation phenomenon. The company was already leading the industry competitively when it decided to take things to the next level with its digital transformation effort. However, its wide goals led to broad initiatives that lacked purpose or substantial ROI. Their digital transformation for the sake of transformation, without a clear direction, failed and the CEO was soon asked to resign by the board. Read the entire story[56]

As mentioned before several times, organization culture plays a key role in digital transformation success. A collaborative and agile work culture goes a long way in ensuring the long-term success of digital transformation initiatives in any organization. Digital transformation cannot be successful without bringing agility to your processes and operations and having a collaborative environment in your organization.

---

[56] https://www.forbes.com/sites/blakemorgan/2019/09/30/companies-that-failed-at-digital-transformation-and-what-we-can-learn-from-them/?sh=6610e3c3603c

Customer Story	In 2014, Ford Motors tried digital transformation with their new business unit, Ford Smart Mobility. This was Ford's attempt to digitally enable their vehicles. This unit was not fully integrated into the rest of the company along with being remotely located from the rest of the company. Lack of collaboration and partnership with the other units of the company led to the failure of this transformation with huge loss of capital. Read the entire story[57]

What ties everything together is collaboration between all units within the company. To build long-term success innovation and experimentation should be encouraged at all levels in your organization. This will help you to come up with new and improved ways of creating and offering targeted products/services/experiences to your customers. For you to show the business value and benefits, always make sure that you are measuring and communicating the progress and ROI of your new or improved products/services/experiences offerings to all stakeholders.

---

[57] https://www.forbes.com/sites/blakemorgan/2019/09/30/companies-that-failed-at-digital-transformation-and-what-we-can-learn-from-them/?sh=6610e3c3603c

Expert Opinion

"Communication is critical, especially to your internal customers. It is important to communicate a clear and concise message around what is changing and how the change will impact their work processes, etc. In a previous delivery, we had representative stakeholders from all functionally impacted groups attend a bi-weekly communication update meeting to ensure everyone received consistent messaging and was kept abreast of progress."

Shane Fogle[58], Principal Delivery Leader

Trying to take over the world

Starting digital transformation within a large enterprise can be a monumental initiative and depending on the scope it maybe an impossible feat to accomplish. Instead of taking on a colossal initiative approach across the whole organization it may be prudent to take an incremental or a phased approach.

For internal organization digital transformation, try it out for one unit of the organization instead of across all units. You can scale across all units or abandon depending on the results of the pilot with the first unit. For external transformation efforts you can pick a single product/service/experience to introduce or improve for your external customers using an MVP approach. With taking on digital transformation in one big swoop, you do run the risk of budget shortfall before completion along with spreading your resources too thin to be effective.

---

[58] https://www.linkedin.com/in/shanefogle/

Customer Story	Back in 2011, GE initiated a major initiative to go digital and in 2015 started a new business unit called GE Digital. With more than 1000+ employees, the transformation failed. Key reasons for failure included focus on quantity vs. quality and traying to take on too much at one time without a clear vision and strategy.

Read the entire story[59]

Not picking the right vendor

Many enterprises use out-sourced vendors for many of their initiatives. If your digital transformation efforts are going to use an out-sourced vendor, you want to make sure that you go through a proper procurement process and consider multiple vendors with relevant experience in your technologies and industry. If appropriate, always consider having the potential and short-listed vendors to build a proof-of-concept product/service/experience as a part of your vendor selection process.

Some organizations put their blind trust in certain vendors they have worked with previously and do not consider any other factors in selecting them for the transformation initiatives. Selecting them maybe the natural and easy choice, considering the already built relationship with them, it may not work in the long run due to the nature of the initiative and the vendor's inability and inexperience to deliver it successfully.

---

[59] https://www.forbes.com/sites/blakemorgan/2019/09/30/companies-that-failed-at-digital-transformation-and-what-we-can-learn-from-them/?sh=6610e3c3603c

Not having rigor around the out-sourced vendor selection has led to digital transformation disaster at Hertz, where Accenture was hired without a rigorous procurement and vendor selection process. Along with that Hertz allowed Accenture to run wild and didn't have tight initiative oversight. End all is that earlier in 2019 Hertz sued Accenture[60] for $32M.

Completely throwing out the older technology

Transformation initiatives should not consider swapping out all the older technologies for completely newer technologies. Rather adopt an experimental methodology and take a hybrid approach of using old and newer technologies together for your transformation scenarios. Consolidate technologies as much as possible. Many digital transformation efforts have failed due to the digital transformation initiatives which didn't consider the existing software, hardware, infrastructure, or resources but rather tried to replace all with newer technologies. Co-operative bank is an example of this where it sunk £300M before the bank decided to cancel its transformation initiative in 2013.

Lack of project management rigor and oversight

While having a great vision and strategy is important to have, not having a good execution plan will not move the initiative forward along with not leading to the desired

---

[60] https://www.adweek.com/agencies/hertz-sues-accenture-for-breach-of-contract-over-seriously-deficient-web-design-work/

deliverables. All digital transformation initiatives should have proper checkpoints, milestones, communication plan and deliverables clearly defined. Along with that, there should be proper oversight of the initiatives to make sure that the desired goals are being achieved and deliverables are being produced on time.

Expert Opinion	"Assigning an executive-level Program Manager from the customer needs to be in place, to compliment the vendor(s) assigned Project Management role(s). This role is vital to the success of the program to ensure that appropriate executive-level sponsorship is maintained throughout the delivery of the program as well as to ensure vendor commitments are being met."

Shane Fogle[61], Principal Delivery Leader

Not having proper oversight led to BBC scrapping their Digital Media Initiative (DMI) and they had to write off around £100 million. They had chosen Siemens as the vendor for this transformation initiative and let it continue without proper executive oversight.

---

61 https://www.linkedin.com/in/shanefogle/

SUMMARY

Driving a successful transformation within your organization requires much more than just using the latest and greatest digital technologies, just because others are using it. It is about customer centricity, customer's high expectations, staying competitive in today's business landscape and about evolving your business models.

To execute on your digital transformation, you may be required to change your organization culture to encourage innovation and experimentation, collaborate across various units of the organization and bring agility to your operations.

It is about communicating the vision and strategy across the organization and garnering support at all levels of the organization so that you can bring all the people at all layers of the organization along for this journey. This will significantly improve chances of success of your transformation initiatives. At the end of the day, it does take a whole village to accomplish a successful digital transformation.

In the next chapter, we will review cloud computing basics, benefits, history, evolution, challenges, and the future of this technology. Understanding the fundamentals of cloud computing is essential before you learn and understand the emerging technologies which are offered by the cloud providers. Emerging technologies including AI, Machine Learning, IoT and blockchain are going to be explored further in this book. As discussed in this chapter, these emerging technologies are key to many of the digital transformation initiatives which have been initiated in many organizations.

CHAPTER 2:

CLOUD COMPUTING

CLOUD COMPUTING BASICS

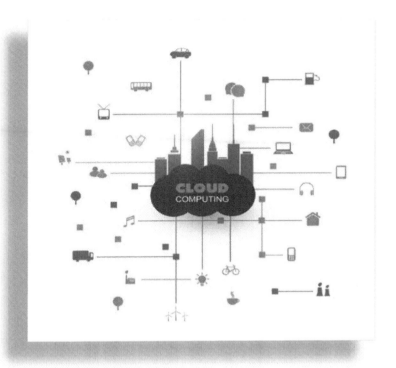

The importance of cloud computing can't be overemphasized enough and since most of the emerging technologies, which are driving digital transformation in many organizations, are offered via the public cloud providers such as Amazon, Microsoft, and Google, a good understanding of cloud computing is important. Thus, we have dedicated a full chapter on it.

Cloud computing is the availability and usage of network, storage, compute, and application resources in on-premises or public data centers. These resources can be provisioned and de-provisioned automatically via a self-serving portal and scaled as needed. This concept, when it exists in the on-premises data centers, is referred to as a private cloud.

The same concept, if it exists in the public data centers or the Internet, is referred to as the public cloud. Key vendors such as Microsoft, Amazon, Google, IBM, Oracle et al. have global data centers and provide infrastructure, storage, compute, and application resources for everyone to use via their public global data centers on the Internet. The cloud providers also offer self-serve portals (such as Azure portal for Microsoft cloud services), automation in provisioning and scaling of these resources. Other key characteristics along with automated provisioning and scaling includes broadband network access, service usage measurement and metering, and real-time monitoring and statistics. These providers also offer customer technical support for their customers for their provisioned resources. Customers of cloud services from these providers follow the pay-as-you use operational expenditure (OpEx) model that all the providers offer compared to the capital expenditure (CapEx) model that they may have followed for setting up their own on-premises data center.

Cloud computing was fueled by and was the natural evolution of virtualized computing that happened in the 2000s. Compacting of network and server devices with automation and self-serving portals led to the birth of both private and public clouds.

Currently, the top three public cloud providers are Amazon's Amazon Web Services (AWS), Microsoft's Azure Cloud Services, and Google's Google Cloud Platform (GCP). Other key cloud providers include VMware, Oracle Cloud, IBM, and Alibaba. As of the writing of this book, Amazon's AWS is the top cloud provider and started way back in 2006 whereas,

Microsoft Azure was introduced in 2010 and stays as the second-best cloud provider with deep roots in the enterprises. Google Cloud Platform was introduced in 2011 and takes the number three spot among the top cloud providers. Google Cloud has struggled to catch up with both AWS and Azure in its cloud offerings and customer attach rate. A yearly State of the Cloud Report from Flexera[62] compares AWS, Azure, GCP, and other cloud providers in the market.

Cloud computing has become an enabler for many organizations that want to evolve their business models as a part of their digital transformation. Previously, they couldn't enable many of their business transformation scenarios because of the infrastructure or the compute resources needed. Costs and resources required for acquiring and setting up the infrastructure or getting the needed compute power was a big hindrance for small to large businesses to move forward on enabling many of their business scenarios. Public cloud computing has solved this problem now. There are now multiple cloud providers out there now with global data centers and massive compute power. It is now possible for companies of all sizes, from small to large enterprises, to tap into that compute capacity and scale it on demand for their requirements globally.

All the cloud services are typically subscription-based where you pay a monthly fee depending on the service and usage of a service. This model is completely different than the traditional model of paying for software licenses and upgrades. Most cloud providers also support Bring Your Own License (BYOL) scenarios where you can use your already existing software

---

[62] https://info.flexera.com/SLO-CM-REPORT-State-of-the-Cloud-2020

licenses, which you may have obtained for your on-premises use, for the same services in the public cloud.

Key advantages of cloud services

There are several advantages that cloud services offer that you should fully understand before you start utilizing them. The following sections will provide an overview of the several features that you get when you start using cloud services.

Free trials

Most of the cloud providers offer a free trial account/subscription with a certain credit amount for a limited amount of time or free cloud services forever. It is typically a good idea to try the cloud services out before you sign up for a production subscription. Any power user in your unit or organization or someone from the IT unit can help you sign up for a cloud subscription. Microsoft Azure free account, for example, offers a free access to its most popular services for 12 months, along with $200 credit to explore Azure for 30 days, or always have access to 25+ cloud services forever.

Cost savings

Cloud services costs are considered an operating expenditure (OpEx) instead of the traditional Capital Expenditure (CapEx) costs of procuring similar kind of services within your own on-premises data center or another private cloud. Thus, the advantage of cloud services is that you don't have to put up the capital upfront to provision the cloud services in the cloud provider's data centers. This scenario is useful for your company if you experiment and innovate with different proof of concept ideas and require infrastructure, virtual machines, application platform, database, and other similar services only for a limited amount of time. You can provision the needed resources for a limited amount of time - setup, configure, and utilize them and then deprovision them after that. With this scenario, you do not pay any CapEx or upfront costs but only the costs for the actual time you were utilizing the provisioned cloud resources. Most of the cloud providers also offer tools and utilities to help you manage costs for all your cloud resources and services you are consuming.

Expert Opinion	"Digital Transformation begs faster experimentation which is also economically viable, and cloud brings both agility and economics (CapEx to OpEx) factors together. Only due to cloud, a six people company was sold for $1 billion!" Sarbjeet Johal[63], Cloud Leadership

Security

Security has and will stay as one of the top concerns for the cloud adoption and utilization. When considering migrating to the cloud, organizations should understand the fundamental differences between their on-premises data center and application/data security vs. how the security looks like when you end up choosing one of the cloud providers. Moving into the cloud means that you are now dependent on the cloud provider for making sure that their data centers are secure and have proper identity and access management systems, physical security, personnel security, infrastructure and devices/server security, and privacy measures in place.

---

[63] https://www.linkedin.com/in/sarbjeetjohal/

You, as an organization, still own the responsibility of making sure that for your cloud resources, data security is intact as you start utilizing the cloud services. The onus of protecting your data, applications and other cloud resources is not only on the cloud provider but also on you, thus making it a shared responsibility between you and the provider. As organizations adopt the cloud, the data and application security scenarios maybe simple. But as we move into the future and large enterprises start implementing complex hybrid scenarios for splitting up their data and applications between their on-premises data centers or private cloud and the public cloud, the data and application security scenarios are also going to get involved.

It is critical that the current best practices and policies, which you may already have in place for your on-premises data and applications security are tweaked and made suitable to be applied to your data, applications and other cloud resources that reside in the public cloud or are part of the hybrid setup. Cloud providers also offer security tools to help you properly configure your cloud services along with analyzing your services and making recommendations on any possible security issues it may see with your cloud services. We will review various security tools and services which are available from Microsoft Azure in chapter 3 when we do an overview of core Microsoft Azure Cloud Services.

Each cloud provider also has plethora of documentation that you can access to properly configure your cloud services following the best security practices. This is a good start for accessing the official Microsoft Azure documentation[64].

---

[64] https://docs.microsoft.com/en-us/azure/

Expert Opinion	"The burden of possessing, managing, and maintaining the IT infrastructure has been the key challenge for financial sector. Banking with the cloud has definitely been a game changer. Many banks have already placed their less critical application to cloud computing as a low-risk exercise. The major benefits to the bank are: • No upfront capital costs and reduced technology costs • Faster implementation • High flexibility and scalability • Multi-channel reach." Ratan Jyoti[65], CISO - Ujjivan Small Finance Bank

Support for open-source solutions and services

Open-source software and solutions are and can be key enablers of your digital transformation initiatives along with helping you innovate and experiment with your proof-of-concept ideas. You can utilize open-source solutions to minimize infrastructure and development costs along with helping you reduce time to market leading to you gaining competitive advantage.

Key considerations when utilizing open-source software and solutions are to keep security front and center since some of the code may need to be modified to adhere to your organization's security framework. Almost all cloud providers provide support for enabling and deploying open-source solutions and resources. A prime example of

---

[65] https://www.linkedin.com/in/ratanjyoti/

open-source existence in the cloud is the Linux virtual machines that can be provisioned and deployed in the cloud. Microsoft Azure supports many common Linux distributions[66], including Red Hat, SUSE, Ubuntu, CentOS, Debian, Oracle Linux, CoreOS, and the list is growing every day.

According to one estimate, in late 2017, it is reported that **40%** of all customer-hosted virtual machines had Linux as its operating system. Another recent open-source product from Microsoft has been Azure Sphere, which is based on Microsoft's own developed Linux kernel, and is now widely being used in IoT devices to bring both hardware and software level security to IoT and edge computing devices. Other open-source solutions and services from both Microsoft and other vendors are available through the Azure Marketplace.

Cloud marketplaces for third-party solutions and services

Every cloud provider offers a marketplace, with solutions and services from themselves and third-party vendors, to offer to their customers. Microsoft Azure calls their marketplace Azure Marketplace[67]. It has around 17,000 Microsoft certified solutions and services available to anyone using Azure. All open-source cloud solutions are available via these cloud marketplaces.

GUI and CLI tools

Graphical User Interface (GUI) portals and Command Line Interface (CLI) tools are available for cloud administrators, architects, or developers to help them provision, deploy, configure, manage, maintain, and

---

[66] https://azure.microsoft.com/en-us/overview/linux-on-azure/
[67] https://azure.microsoft.com/en-us/marketplace/

troubleshoot their cloud services. GUI portals are available for cloud users with minimal IT skills and know-how to use and navigate in a web browser whereas CLI tools are available for experienced IT users, who may already be using the CLI tools in their on-premises data centers and private cloud. Azure provides the Microsoft Azure portal[68] as the GUI portal whereas CLI tools such as Azure CLI, PowerShell, and Linux Bash shell are provided for experienced IT professionals. Along with these tools, there are other tools available within the Azure portal that help you optimize your cloud services configuration, security, and utilization. Three of these key tools are:

- **Azure Advisor**: Azure Advisor tool analyzes your cloud services configurations and usage data and then offers personalized recommendations to assist you optimize your Azure resources.
- **Azure Cost Management tool:** This tool helps you analyze cloud costs, monitors your budget, and optimizes cloud cost with customized recommendations.
- Azure Security Center[69]: It is a security management tool that oversees the security of all your public cloud resources and across on-premises data center thus spanning your hybrid cloud infrastructure. It constantly assesses your environment, provider a bird's eye view of your cloud resources along with making recommendations to secure your resources against any threats.

Along with GUI and CLI tools to deploy and manage Azure Cloud Services, developer Integrated Development

---

[68] https://azure.microsoft.com/en-us/marketplace/
[69] https://docs.microsoft.com/en-us/azure/security-center/security-center-intro

Environment (IDE) tools such as Visual Studio and open-source Visual Studio Code is also fully supported with Microsoft Azure. Visual Studio Code is an open-source version of Visual Studio and is freely available for Windows, Linux, and Mac machines. This is yet another example of where Microsoft is fully embracing open source and making and supporting open-source technologies and tools compatible with multiple platforms and working with their Azure cloud.

Manual and automated provisioning

Once you have signed up for your cloud subscription, you are pretty much ready to start provisioning the required cloud services. Typically, you use the GUI portal from the cloud provider to sign up for one of the key cloud services such as deploying a virtual machine, setting up application platform service, or setting up a cloud database server. All these tasks can be managed via the GUI portals and typically take from half a minute to a couple of minutes at the most. For any complex deployments requiring deep customization and provisioning of bulk cloud resources at the same time, such as setting up 100 virtual machines in Microsoft Azure, you typically will use either PowerShell or Azure CLI tool. In some cases, there are also APIs available, from the provider, for you to connect to provision and deploy cloud resources.

Scaling Your resources

One of the defining characteristics of cloud computing is that it allows for elasticity and scaling of resources on-demand. Most of the cloud services resources can be scaled up or out depending on your needs.

Virtual machines, as an example can be scaled up, so they have enhanced hardware and more compute power.

Typically, this can be done even after you may have started with a VM with lower compute power and later decided that you need to enhance it to improve the performance of the virtual machine. As a simple example if you are running a web server and hosting a website on a virtual machine and it is slow, you can scale up the machine, which in turn adds more compute power to it by giving it additional processors, RAM, storage, and IOPS (Input and Output per second when working with storage devices).

Virtual machines can also be scaled out to handle more load or network traffic. Imagine you are a seasonal business and typically have more customers coming to your e-commerce website during the holiday season in November, December, and January. Typically, you would use virtual machines for frontend web servers to manage traffic to your site. By using the cloud services and automated configuration, you can set up triggers to bring in additional frontend web servers running on virtual machines to handle the additional traffic during those months. The virtual machines can be scaled down once the traffic load goes down.

Expert Opinion	"We live in a time where technology is affordable to all and the barrier is not size, costs or scale. cloud computing has flattened the options of choice. Legacy systems often required a large investment in infrastructure and installation making them prohibitive to the average firm. We had enterprise solutions and small business products from different vendors with different functions and benefits. Today innovation is rife, and a cloud solution can be for a global firm with 50,000 seats or used by a 5-user business, each paying a relevant monthly fee for their scale of usage. cloud has enabled AI., Big Data, IoT, Blockchain and more to be digestible to the small business. Anyone can utilize new technology to accelerate growth and breadth of customer reach."

Ian Moyse[70], Chief Revenue Officer - OneUp Sales

Maintenance & patching your resources

One of the key advantages of using cloud services is that you don't have to worry about patching your virtual machine or physical servers and other devices to the latest software. You will always have the latest and greatest software on your cloud resources. Since the cloud providers own the physical hardware and the infrastructure, they will be on point to do the required patching and security fixes on the entire infrastructure. You can, however, opt out of some software patching for your resources just in case the patching and updates do not affect your resources and applications.

---

[70] https://www.linkedin.com/in/ianmoyse/

DIGITAL TRANSFORMATION USING EMERGING TECHNOLOGIES

Backup and disaster recovery

Cloud providers also have options available to back up your resources and data. Typically, this is an additional cost to the cost of the resource itself. Common backup options include, backing up the resource in the same data center, another data center in the same region or to another data center in a different region. All core cloud services, such as applications, virtual machines, and databases have the options to be backed up. From disaster recovery and high availability perspective, you have the option to replicate your data in real time. Any disaster in one data center or region will fail over your services to another data center in the same or a different region.

Technical support, troubleshooting tools, and utilities

When an organization signs up for cloud services and starts moving their systems and workloads to the cloud, the internal IT support model will also evolve. Most of the technical support work that used to be done by the support personnel such as accessing the infrastructure, servers, and applications in the on-premises data centers will now be performed by the cloud provider's support and operational staff in their data centers. Since your provisioned servers, virtual machines and applications are now on the cloud provider's infrastructure it becomes their responsibility to manage and maintain those resources. Some cloud providers offer free technical support for certain services while others charge for their technical support through various technical support offerings. There is always free support that you can get from the provider's social media handles or from their community forums.

You as a cloud consumer will also have access to various tools, logs, and utilities to help you troubleshoot and maintain your resources on your own. There are various backend access tools and utilities provided by the cloud providers to help you troubleshoot and fix issues for your cloud resources. For common issues, there are also built-in self-serve utilities within the GUI portals to help resolve them on the fly. As an example, resetting the password for a virtual machine was a common question coming to Microsoft and now they have implemented the password reset feature right in the Azure portal for administrators to do it themselves.

Availability of key emerging technologies

All major cloud providers are offering key emerging technologies including machine learning, artificial intelligence, Internet of things, and blockchain et al. to help organizations move forward on their digital transformation journey. Companies like Amazon, Microsoft, IBM, and Google have "commoditized" these technologies and have made them possible to be in reach for organizations of all sizes via their cloud services offerings. We will view all these technologies in detail in later chapters of this book.

Cloud computing is fueling the fire on utilization of these key emerging technologies. The beauty of the cloud is that you can consume and utilize technologies like ML, AI, IoT, and big data at reduced cost, pay-as-you use model, accelerated network speed, and unlimited scaling as your needs grow. Because of these advantages, companies small and large, are adopting public cloud. Large organizations that have been using the public cloud for a while now are moving into the advanced stage of public cloud utilization with hybrid cloud scenarios. Hybrid cloud refers to connecting the on-premises data centers to the public cloud. Hybrid cloud will be covered later in this chapter and in the next chapter when we review the cloud computing offerings from Microsoft's Azure cloud.

CLOUD DEPLOYMENT MODELS

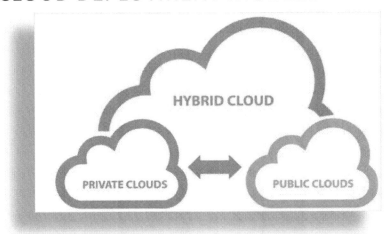

The cloud can be implemented in different ways, known as the cloud deployment models. We have already introduced private and public cloud in the previous section. In this section, we are going to review all popular cloud deployment models.

Public cloud

A public cloud is a cloud infrastructure operated and managed by cloud providers in their data centers. It provides a slew of cloud services categorized as service models: Software as a Service (SaaS), Platform as a Service (PaaS), Infrastructure as a Service (IaaS) and other service models. We will review these categories of services in the next section. A recent report from O'Reilly, in January 2020, shows that **88%** of the organizations were using the cloud infrastructure and many others plan to move to the cloud in the next year. Even though overall we saw IT budgets decreases in 2020 due to the COVID-19 pandemic, the cloud adoption rose as organizations used cloud-based services such as email, video conferencing, CRM, and ERP business applications to sustain their remote workforce and have business operations continuity.

Industry Statistics	**45%**
	Organizations reported that they expect to move **75%** or more of their applications to the cloud over the next year according to an O'Reilly report[71].

Customer Story	Walgreens Boots Alliance is using Azure's HealthCare Chatbot services from Microsoft Azure to help accelerate create chatbot during the COVID-19 pandemic to digitally help and provide customer services to its customers. Walgreens.com is using the Chatbot to provide COVID-19 risk assessment to its customers.
	Read the entire story[72]

Private cloud

A private cloud is a cloud infrastructure hosted on-premises or at a third-party datacenter for an organization. The cloud can be managed by the organization itself or a third party. Being a cloud, it has the characteristics of a cloud including availability of

---

[71] https://www.oreilly.com/radar/cloud-adoption-in-2020/
[72] https://customers.microsoft.com/en-us/story/812836-walgreens-boots-alliance-retailers-azure-bot-service-cognitive-services

network, compute, storage, scale elasticity, and self-management.

Hybrid cloud

A cloud infrastructure that includes private, on-premises infrastructure, and public cloud connected is referred to as the hybrid cloud. Most of medium to large enterprises with their on-premises data centers are moving to the hybrid deployment model as they connect their local data centers to the public cloud. According to State of the cloud Report from Flexera, 53%[73] of the surveyed organizations are using the hybrid cloud deployment model.

Many organizations that have been using public cloud services for a while are now trying out more advanced hybrid cloud scenarios now by connecting their on-premises data centers to the public cloud.

Industry Statistics

70%

of the enterprises will integrate all their private and public cloud via tools, technologies, and processes according to an IDC report[74]

---

[73] https://info.flexera.com/SLO-CM-REPORT-State-of-the-Cloud-2020
[74] https://www.idc.com/getdoc.jsp?containerId=US45599219

Expert Opinion

"A growing number of corporations have discovered the benefits of cloud solutions and digital transformation but are not willing to source critical processes and high value data to external service providers. Hybrid cloud can create the environment that serves these on-premises."

Johannes Drooghaag[75], CEO Spearhead Management

There are several strategic benefits and advantages to setting up hybrid cloud for mid-sized to large organizations. Ability to expand your organization's infrastructure and to start utilizing the public cloud services, without any capital investment upfront is one of the key reasons for using the public cloud. Organizations and their senior IT leadership see visible benefits of costs savings they can reap as they move from CapEx to OpEx model for their IT investments. They also realize that they don't have to take on any responsibility of managing or maintaining the public cloud infrastructure since the public cloud providers are on point for that. Public cloud is also perceived by the organizations as a fertile landscape for experimenting, innovating, and doing quick prototyping for realizing digital transformation scenarios. Some of the industry vertical organizations, such as healthcare, have traditionally shied away from the public cloud because of the various regulatory compliance around the patient data. That problem has also been solved now by the public cloud providers. Majority of them are now offering cloud services which have been certified for various national and international regulatory standards of

---

[75] https://www.linkedin.com/in/johannesdrooghaag/

many industry verticals. Azure is certified for a broad range of regulatory standards[76]. This has paved the way for the industry vertical organizations to start using the public cloud and extending their on-premises infrastructure to cloud to utilize it optimally. Worldwide availability of majority of core and important public cloud services has made it possible for global organizations to extend all their satellite on-premises networks to the public cloud to realize the full potential of the hybrid cloud.

Common hybrid business use cases

There are some use cases which lend themselves very nicely to the use of the hybrid cloud. Some of the common hybrid scenarios include:

- Moving your dev and test environments into the public cloud and keeping them connected to your private cloud or on-premises data centers.
- Segmenting your applications between the public cloud and the private cloud or the on-premises data center.
- Building cloud native applications that need access to resources in private cloud or the on-premises data centers.
- Creating a uniform sign-on experiences for your on-premises resources and the public cloud resources.
- Extending your on-premises infrastructure to the public cloud to access resources on your public cloud infrastructure.
- Enabling edge computing scenarios for processing close to the devices and connecting to the cloud when absolutely needed.

---

[76] https://azure.microsoft.com/en-us/overview/trusted-cloud/compliance/

- Managing the security plane of all your resources across the on-premises data centers, private cloud, and the public cloud.

In the following sections we review these common use cases in more detail.

Migrating non-business critical workloads
Non-critical workloads typically include dev and test environments and can be moved from the on-premises infrastructure to the public cloud. There are instances where your teams maybe experimenting and innovating as part of the digital transformation strategy and any quick prototyping and proof-of-concept ideas can also be done in the public cloud instead of using the on-premises infrastructure or the private cloud network. Such experimentation may include extending your private infrastructure into the public cloud.

Segmenting legacy applications
Traditional non-cloud applications which use logic, data, and presentation layers can be segmented and certain layer(s) can reside on the on-premises infrastructure and others can be in the public cloud. Most organizations have split up their applications and are hosting the presentation and logical layers in the public cloud whereas the data layer is still in the on-premises infrastructure. Main reason for this split is to maintain local access to the data and secure it through already existing on-premises infrastructure measures. This segmentation is also good for organizations to try out the public cloud for their existing application without relinquishing all control of their application and data.

Building cloud-native applications
For most of the startup organizations, it is an easy

decision to start with the cloud and build their systems and applications there rather than investing in building applications and deploying them on their on-premises infrastructure. For larger and mid-sized organizations however, it is always a decision-making scenario when they must decide on building and deploying a new application – to build and deploy locally to the on-premises data center or to use the public cloud? For organizations which have not yet ventured into the public cloud and building a non-business critical application, they may benefit from using the public cloud to utilize microservice architecture and build and deploy applications using serverless computing and containers.

Single sign-on experience across all connected infrastructure

One of the key issues Network Administrators, Developers and Systems Administrators must resolve when they connect two or more disparate networks is to provide a single sign-on experience to their users to connect across these different networks. Connecting public, private, and on-premises infrastructure is no different. You will have to solve the problem of having your users connect across these networks to access any resources or applications on these different networks. Azure provides the capability to use a single account to access all the resources and applications across all different kind of infrastructure.

Extending the on-premises infrastructure

One way to start using the public cloud is to first extend your on-premises infrastructure to the public cloud without setting up any resources. It is a basic first step to start using the public cloud and typically very easy to perform. Azure provides this capability with all the required security to make sure that end to end connection from the on-premises datacenter to the public cloud infrastructure is fully protected.

Enabling edge computing scenarios
Edge computing is when devices, which are typically installed on an organization's infrastructure, are generating data and this data needs to be processed close to the devices to reduce latency and improve performance. In pre-edge computing time, all this data was going all the way back to the public cloud to be processed and stored there. IoT is a prime example of edge computing and Azure is offering services and solutions now to enable these edge scenarios for IoT devices. Now with edge computing containers, virtual machines and data services can run close to the edge location rather than in the public cloud.

Utilize enhanced security tools
Connecting multiple disparate networks such as the on-premises networks, private networks, and public cloud is going to make the security landscape very complex and hard to manage across all of them. Cloud providers, such as Azure now provides tools, such as Security Center, which can help organizations to monitor and manage security across these different infrastructures.

There are various hybrid solutions available from cloud providers including IBM/RedHat, Azure, AWS, VMware cloud on AWS[77] and Google Cloud Platform. IBM/RedHat has IBM Cloud Pak, IBM Cloud Satellite, RedHat OpenStack and RedHat CloudForms. Azure offers Azure Stack[78] and Azure Arc[79] and we will dig deeper into those in the next chapter when we do on

---

[77] https://cloud.vmware.com/vmc-aws
[78] https://azure.microsoft.com/en-us/overview/azure-stack/
[79] https://azure.microsoft.com/en-us/services/azure-arc/

overview of Azure Cloud Services. Amazon offers <u>AWS Outposts</u>[80] to its customers interested in setting up a hybrid cloud. Google Cloud on the other hand is offering <u>Google Anthos</u>[81] as the solution for its hybrid cloud customers. In the next chapter we will discuss many hybrid cloud services from Microsoft Azure.

Challenges of hybrid cloud computing

There are several business challenges that you may face as an organization as you embark on your hybrid cloud journey. In this section, we will examine the most common challenges along with making recommendations for working through them and still making progress on your hybrid cloud strategy.

Complexity

One of the key challenges with the hybrid cloud is the multiple environments it has including the on-premises infrastructure, private cloud, edge environment, and the public cloud. Thus, making it highly complex to monitor, manage and troubleshoot in case of problems and outages. Another issue with this scenario is that you may be using different disparate tools and utilities to monitor and manage these environments which also makes the management of these environments very inefficient.

Primary recommendation here would be to spend on automation and integration tooling across these environments to get one view of all your digital estate. Azure offers various tools which can be used in combination to provide a unform view of your digital estate across private, public, and on-premises

---

[80] https://aws.amazon.com/outposts/
[81] https://cloud.google.com/anthos

environments. These tools include Azure Arc, Azure Defender, and Azure Sentinel.

Another recommendation would be to setup a cloud Center of Excellence (CoE) with representation from technical personnel from all units in your organization. The CoE can be responsible for building a cloud governance framework along with helping others in your organization by providing training and learning opportunities. Since you may be using multiple infrastructures, it is hard to find a single person who has expertise across both the on-premises network, private cloud, and the public cloud. You will have to retrain and reskill your IT workforce for multiple clouds. These IT personnel are the ones who are going to manage and maintain the hybrid cloud environment in the long run.

Costs control
According to the Flexera's State of the Cloud 2020 Report, **30%**[82] of the public cloud usage costs are wasted. If your organization is going to connect to the public cloud, as a part of your hybrid strategy, you want to make sure that you keep an eye on your cloud costs since hybrid cloud integration can lead to excessive cloud costs waste. If you have private cloud setup in your on-premises environment, then you want to control cloud costs across both private and public clouds.

This cloud cost waste challenge can be resolved by setting up a cloud governance framework across your organization along with costs management tools available from the public cloud providers and other vendors. For more complex hybrid environments, consider building a customized tool that works across the public cloud provider you are using. Cloud providers

---

[82] https://info.flexera.com/SLO-CM-REPORT-State-of-the-Cloud-2020

offer APIs which can be utilized to build such a custom tool.

Security
Hybrid cloud environment increases the complexity of your digital estate since now you must monitor, manage, and secure resources cross on-premises infrastructure, private cloud, edge environment, and the public clouds. According to the State of the Cloud report, **83%**[83] of enterprises indicate that security is a challenge when working with public cloud services.

Recommendation here is to setup a security governance framework for both your on-premises and cloud IT practices. Build and utilize security tools and utilities with built-in AI, machine learning, and threat intelligence. These tools will help with security threat detection, remediation along with recommendations to fix the vulnerability. Microsoft Azure offers Azure Defender and Azure Sentinel with these features to make sure you can monitor, manage, and secure your digital assets across the whole digital estate you own across your on-premises infrastructure, private cloud, edge environment, and multiple public clouds.

Monitoring & management
Monitoring, managing, and maintaining infrastructure and digital resources is a key part of any IT organization. A hybrid environment provides a unique and complex challenge where you must monitor and manage digital assets across multiple environments.

For monitoring and managing such a complex environment, you need tools which can work across the on-premises infrastructure, private cloud, public cloud,

---

[83] https://info.flexera.com/SLO-CM-REPORT-State-of-the-Cloud-2020

and the edge environment. Recommendation here is to either use any tools available from the cloud providers or build a customized tool to create a dashboard to get a uniform view of all your digital assets across your digital estate. Azure Arc is one example of such a tool which can help you in this situation. According to IDC IT industry 2020 predictions, **70%**[84] of the enterprises will integrate all their private and public clouds via tools, technologies, and processes by 2022.

Multicloud

Another permutation of hybrid cloud is the multicloud where organizations are starting to use multiple public cloud providers along with their on-premises data centers and private cloud. Majority of the global enterprises have a multicloud configuration and strategy in place. Typical reasons behind utilizing multiple public clouds are availability of certain required cloud services in your desired global region, compliance, costs of services, services availability for a certain cloud provider, and availability of IT talent for a particular cloud provider's services.

Industry Statistics

93%

Globally surveyed respondents have a multicloud configuration and strategy in place according to an Flexera State of the Cloud report[85].

---

[84] https://www.idc.com/getdoc.jsp?containerId=US45599219
[85] https://info.flexera.com/SLO-CM-REPORT-State-of-the-Cloud-2020

Virtual private cloud (VPC)

A variation of public cloud wherein a part of an otherwise public cloud infrastructure is dedicated to one customer, or an organization is referred to as the virtual private cloud (VPC). VPC offerings bring some of the price advantages of a large public cloud provider but with more customization, security, and isolation of VMs, storage, and networking. Most of the public cloud providers offer the option of VPC to its customers. Typically, organizations that are concerned about security and don't want to share their infrastructure with other public cloud customers, opt for this option. You can think of this option as having a small private data center within the public cloud.

CLOUD SERVICE MODELS

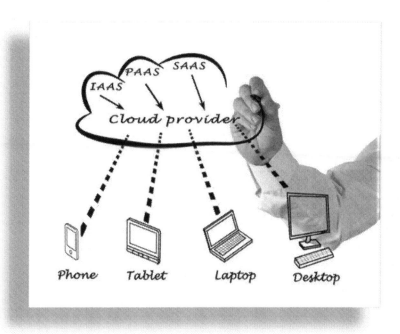

Majority of the cloud services generally can be categorized into three service models: Software as a Service (SaaS), Platform as a Service (PaaS) and Infrastructure as a Service (IaaS). These three models are primarily the basic building blocks of cloud computing and all the cloud services, offered by the cloud providers, are mapped to one of these models. As an example, if you are using Google Docs, which is part of Google Workspace, you are utilizing the Software as a Service (SaaS) model.

While SaaS, PaaS and IaaS are the three original and primary service models with majority of granular cloud services associated with them, there are other service models which are worth mentioning here too including Database as a Service (DBaaS) and Disaster Recovery as a Service (DRaaS). DBaaS provides the ability for users to provision and use cloud databases. Examples of DBaaS include Microsoft's Azure SQL database service and Amazon's RDS. DRaaS is the replication and hosting of physical or virtual servers in a remote site to provide fail-over to another regional cloud data center in the event of a natural or other catastrophe in the primary cloud data center.

Customer Story	**Paychex,** an organization specializing in human resources and payroll services via their app portfolio, was looking for a database solution to help them with reducing costs, meeting customer usage demands and high availability. They accomplished this by using Azure SQL database and elastic pools to meet customer demands with high performance and optimizing costs.
	Read the entire story[86]

For a traditional on-premises IT enterprise data center model, the IT department controls the whole technology stack from infrastructure, virtual machines, operating systems, storage, databases, application platforms, applications to application configuration.

The three service models define varying level of control the customers have to the different parts of the complete technology stack. The responsibility of managing these IT resources is now split between the cloud provider and the cloud customer. See **Figure 2-1**.

---

[86] https://customers.microsoft.com/en-us/story/paychex-azure-sql-database-us

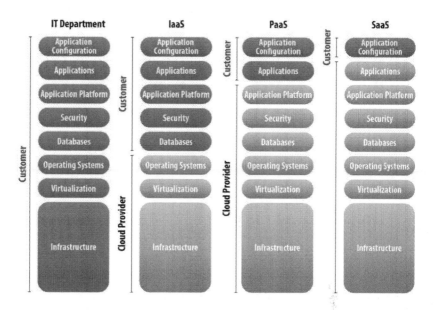

Figure 2-1

Cloud services in the SaaS service model offer cloud customers the ability to configure the provider's installed applications only. Services in the PaaS model offer customers the ability to configure the application platform and the developed applications hosted on the platform. IaaS cloud services allow for the customer to install and configure virtual machines, operating systems, databases, security, application platform, and developed applications.

As we live through this difficult time of the COVID-19 pandemic, cloud services from all the major cloud service models - SaaS, IaaS, and PaaS are actively being utilized to enable us to work remotely, be productive and keep the economy alive and running. Video conferencing, which is part of the cloud's SaaS offerings, is being heavily utilized by remote workers to communicate and collaborate to keep the businesses running. Gartner had initially predicted 116 billion revenue for cloud SaaS services in their report[87] back in late 2019 (See **Table 2-1**) but with the sharp and unprecedented increase in the cloud services utilization during the COVID-19 pandemic, this number surely is going to reach new heights in 2021 and beyond.

Overall we saw a decrease in IT spending in 2020, according to an IDC report[88], but the organizations are going to continue to invest in cloud adoption and usage to make sure that they can sustain the remote work model along with continuing to invest in mission critical systems.

Cloud Service Model	Revenue Forecast (Billions of US Dollars)		
	2020	**2021**	**2022**
Software as a Service (SaaS)	116 billion	133 billion	151.1 billion
Platform as a Service (PaaS)	39.7 billion	48.3 billion	58 billion
Infrastructure as a Service (IaaS)	50 billion	61.3 billion	74.1 billion

Table 2-1

---

[87] https://www.gartner.com/en/newsroom/press-releases/2019-11-13-gartner-forecasts-worldwide-public-cloud-revenue-to-grow-17-percent-in-2020
[88] https://www.idc.com/getdoc.jsp?containerId=prUS46268520

Cloud computing has saved the day for all of us, and we are able to work and be productive even when working remotely. Performance of the stocks of the top cloud providers including Amazon, Microsoft, and Google Cloud along with Zoom Video Communications Inc. during these uncertain times are a key indicator of how these companies are doing so well even in these uncertain financial times. All cloud providers have basically shrugged off the COVID-19 pandemic and posted huge revenues and profit[89]. While many smaller technical companies have frozen hiring during these times, large companies like Amazon, Microsoft, and Google continue to hire in their key cloud units due to the heavy demand of its cloud services.

Software as a Service (SaaS)

Of the three models, SaaS model offers the least amount of control to the customers but services in this model are easier to configure and use. Customers using cloud services from the SaaS service model can only configure applications which have been deployed in the cloud by the provider.

Most of the productivity tools and software are now available online from cloud SaaS providers, on subscription basis, and you don't need physical media to install and start using your software of choice. Examples of software as a service model includes office

---

[89] https://www.statista.com/chart/21584/gafam-revenue-growth/?utm_source=Statista+Global&utm_campaign=e051be2797-All_InfographTicker_daily_COM_PM_KW19_2020_Mo&utm_medium=email&utm_term=0_afecd219f5-e051be2797-303329113

productivity software such as Microsoft 365[90], Dynamics 365[91], or Google's Workforce[92].

Customer Story	Make-A-Wish is another example of an organization which is using both Microsoft 365 and Azure 365 cloud services in tandem to consolidate their IT operations and gain efficiencies. Read the entire story[93]

Basic advantages of using SaaS include automatic upgrades to the software and always getting the latest and the greatest version of the software. You don't have to worry about the upgrades and having your IT department plan it for weeks and months in advance for it. You get the latest version automatically when your cloud provider upgrades the software on their servers in their data centers. Cloud SaaS providers also offer different plans for businesses of all sizes along with for home users and students. As an example Microsoft offers Microsoft 365 plans for home users[94], students[95], small to mid-size businesses[96] and large enterprises[97]. Along with free lifelong upgrades, most of the SaaS cloud providers offer free or monthly fee-based technical support options.

---

[90] https://www.office.com/
[91] https://dynamics.microsoft.com/en-us/
[92] https://gsuite.google.com/
[93] https://customers.microsoft.com/en-us/story/811781-make-a-wish-foundation-nonprofit
[94] https://products.office.com/en-us/office-365-home
[95] https://www.microsoft.com/en-us/education/products/office/default.aspx
[96] https://products.office.com/en-us/business/explore-office-365-for-business
[97] https://products.office.com/en-us/business/enterprise-productivity-tools

Platform as a Service (PaaS)

PaaS service model cloud services is for developers and DevOps professionals and provide application platform application configuration to them. Customers using cloud services from the PaaS service model can only select their application platform, tweak it for their needs, host their applications on the platform and then configure their applications as needed.

PaaS is a great option for developers who want to create a standard web, API or mobile apps and don't need control of the underlying operating system or the virtual machine. Developers who opt for this service model are just looking for the availability of the application development platform and don't really care about the underlying operating system and infrastructure. Traditionally developers were also responsible for installing and configuring the operating system on the physical server or the virtual machine. Now, when you sign up for PaaS services with a cloud provider, they set up the virtual server, install the operating system on it and provide you the application platform of your choice so that you can start developing and then hosting your applications on this platform. PaaS compared to IaaS has limited customization or configuration options, but you don't need to manage and maintain the underlying operating system or the virtual machine. The cloud provider is responsible for that level of maintenance. The developer just chooses the proper cloud service from PaaS offerings, connects their favorite IDE to that service and they are on their way to building, publishing, and managing their apps in the cloud.

Infrastructure as a Service (IaaS)

With IaaS services, you can configure your virtual machine's operating system, install database servers & databases, configure security, setup application platforms, host developed applications, and configure your developed applications.

If you are an IT professional and want to set up a customized virtual machine or infrastructure, or a developer working on a highly customized application requiring operating system control, then you will probably use one of the cloud services from within the IaaS offerings from your cloud provider. IaaS provides you infrastructure, storage, virtual machines, or physical machines in the cloud provider's data centers.

Developers typically develop customized applications and then host them on these virtual machines. IT administrators maybe interested in deploying an infrastructure in the cloud and then extending their on-premises network to this cloud infrastructure to set up a hybrid environment. Developers and IT professionals, who opt for IaaS services, have full control of the virtual machines along with the responsibility for the updates and patching. This additional control of the infrastructure and the resources on it does increase the maintenance burden on developer/IT administrator.

Expert Opinion

"Cloud has democratized compute for everyone to create transformational platforms necessary for digital transformation with its elastic digital infrastructure capability.

We have noticed that clients have benefitted immensely by aligning their cloud strategy to investing in the Microsoft cloud platforms across the 3 Microsoft clouds.

The solutions delivered have adhered to 4 tenets of platform based digital transformation of being open, scalable, connected and intelligent."

Srikar Reddy[98], CEO – Sonata Software

---

[98] https://www.linkedin.com/in/ratanjyoti/

LEGACY TO CLOUD IT TRANSFORMATION

In a traditional IT model, the IT unit owns the full stack and is responsible for end-to-end phases from evaluation to installation, configuration, management, and maintenance of all the resources in the stack. See **Figure 2-1** in the previous section. As the organizations move partially or completely into the public cloud the technology stack ownership will change depending on the cloud service model services (IaaS, PaaS, SaaS et. al) you acquire from the cloud provider.

Another key point to note here is that regardless of what model you use the underlying infrastructure (data centers, servers, routers etc.) is owned by the cloud provider and they are on point to manage and maintain it.

| Expert Opinion | "A successful cloud migration strategy is not just about technology; it's also about culture—people, processes, and tools. Every cloud migration conversation should center on setting realistic expectations with stakeholders, driving a cultural change, and enabling teams. One key element is to bring diversity to thought in this conversation and making sure that these conversations are inclusive."

Rashim Mogha[99], Business Executive \| Startup Advisor |

So, what does that mean for you as an organization planning to move to the cloud? It will result in faster deployment of services at a lower cost. This means that the consuming organization can focus on its core business functions and customers and not on its data center and infrastructure maintenance. But it also means that the IT unit will not have the full control over the technology stack for their cloud services, as they are used to in a traditional on-premises data center. If you have private cloud set up on-premises, you will still need to maintain the full technology stack for it including the infrastructure.

There are several approaches to consider when starting public cloud usage and adoption. You can start with signing up for and using some independent public cloud services, running some experiments, and/or moving non-production and dev/test workloads into the cloud. Once you are confident about utilizing the public cloud, you can start with moving some non-business critical

---

[99] https://www.linkedin.com/in/rashimmogha/

production workloads to the cloud. Most of the mid-sized to large organizations will take this phased approach before they decide to move their business-critical applications into the cloud utilizing a hybrid cloud.

If you are a small organization or a startup, you will probably just go straight to the public cloud instead of worrying about setting up an on-premises data center or private cloud. Public cloud has thus, spurred the movement of innovation and experimentation and has made it easy for tech. startups to get access to the resources and computer power in the public cloud that traditionally only larger enterprises had in their on-premises data centers.

A cultural change

Moving to the cloud will be a cultural change for an IT department. IT staff and personnel will need to think differently when working with the public cloud. Internal operational processes and procedures will also have to be reworked to adapt to the nature of the cloud.

With change and loss of control of the complete technology stack will come the fear and insecurity of losing jobs. Such culture challenges are much tougher and harder to handle that the technological challenges. To ensure that there is a personnel and team buy-in on cloud adoption, IT and senior leadership should have a clear cloud strategy defined and constantly communicate to the people being affected on what the change is, why it must be done, how to adapt to it and what is the long-term vision for the organization for public cloud usage.

While there will be lack of control of some of the resources in the technology stack, the IT unit and its staff will still have ample of management and maintenance control for the provisioned cloud resources. Cloud providers, in the last few years have gone out of their way to ensure that there are plenty of backend access, APIs, logs and tools provided to organizations to manage, maintain, and troubleshoot their cloud resources and infrastructure. We will explore some of these tools for the Azure cloud in the upcoming chapter.

Reskilling your IT department

Cloud adoption and usage does not necessarily equate to elimination of jobs. There may be some cuts that may be made in your IT unit, from some of the responsibility of the stack moving to the public cloud providers. In most cases, you will end up creating more jobs and roles to help manage the cloud environment. If you are going to set up a hybrid cloud, you will also create more roles to help you with managing the high complexity of hybrid environments.

Depending on the cloud adoption timelines, you may opt to bring in third-party consultants to help you onboard to the cloud initially, but your long-term strategy should be to train and reskill your IT personnel. This will help you effectively manage the public cloud resources. Traditionally, some of the roles that have existed in IT department have been:

- Help desk support
- Network administrators
- Network engineers
- Systems administrators
- Systems engineers
- Frontend developers

- Backend developers
- Full stack developers
- Database administrators

The cloud has created some unique requirements and you will need to map some of the traditional roles above to the new cloud roles:

- DevOps professional
- Cloud administrator
- Cloud engineer
- Cloud developer
- Cloud solution architect

As an example, a backend developer will have to morph into the DevOps cloud role. Help desk support can take on a cloud administrator role and your network and systems engineers will be a natural fit for the cloud architect role in the cloud world.

Also, depending on the public cloud you are using, you may want to consider getting your IT personnel certified in a particular public cloud. All top cloud providers (AWS[100], Azure[101], and Google Cloud Platform[102]) offer cloud certifications for their cloud.

Build a cloud Center of Excellence (CoE)

One of the key cloud strategy items to consider is to set up a center of excellence for your organization. Typically, IT unit will take a lead on this with CIO's

---

[100] https://aws.amazon.com/certification/
[101] https://www.microsoft.com/en-us/learning/azure-certification.aspx
[102] https://cloud.google.com/certification/

sponsorship and there will be representation from all other business units in the organization.

The goal behind this CoE is to have an entity that provides leadership, best practices, research, support and/or training for anything concerning with the organization's cloud computing strategy. CoE can be on point to set up a cloud and security governance framework which will be used across all the units in the organization which are planning to utilize the public or the hybrid cloud.

The world of public cloud is changing with public cloud providers adding features, functionality, and new services on almost daily basis. It should be the responsibility of the CoE to stay on top of the ever-changing public cloud to continue to refine the governance framework, best practices, and other guidelines.

The CoE will also play a key role in helping accelerate innovation and experimentation in the cloud with recommendations and best practices for all the units in the organization, which are interested in using the cloud for their proof-of-concept ideas and experimentation.

CLOUD CHALLENGES

There are several challenges that you face and should be aware of as your organization starts considering and utilizing cloud services. Key challenges include cloud costs waste, talent shortage, hybrid/multicloud complexity, security, and governance.

Cloud costs and waste

Lack of organization-wide governance framework around cloud utilization for both experimentation and production has resulted in cloud spend waste. Flexera State of the Cloud 2020 report estimated mid **30%** of the cloud spend as cloud waste. We will continue to see cloud waste metric in double digits in 2020 and beyond until the organizations get to point where they have a solid governance framework in place across all the units of the organization. According to Flexera's 2020 report, cloud costs optimization is a key priority now for enterprise IT and cloud CoE teams. Cloud costs optimization and governance are staying as the top two challenges for all companies regardless of what cloud maturity phase of adoption they are in (beginning, intermediate or advanced). A mix of a solid governance framework, best practices and several available tools will help you control and optimize cloud adoption and utilization costs.

Industry Statistics

30%

of cloud costs are wasted as part of the total cloud spend according to the Flexera 2020 State of the Cloud report[103].

Various tools and systems are available from top cloud providers and other vendors to help you along the way in managing cloud costs effectively. Azure's calculator is available[104] here, while AWS offers a TCO calculator[105] along with Google having their own pricing calculator[106]. Providers also offer API that can be used to build your own customized costs management system to keep track of your cloud spend. Along with these basic cost calculators, top cloud providers such as Microsoft and Amazon also offer extended cost management systems for customers and partners to help them manage their cloud spend for both Azure and AWS. Along with tools and utilities from top providers there are also third-party

---

[103] https://info.flexera.com/SLO-CM-REPORT-State-of-the-Cloud-2020
[104] https://azure.microsoft.com/en-us/pricing/calculator/
[105] https://aws.amazon.com/tco-calculator/
[106] https://cloud.google.com/products/calculator/

tools available that you can also use for cost optimization and management.

Complexity of hybrid and multicloud management

More and more medium to large enterprises are opting to adopt multiple public cloud providers and connecting their internal private clouds. With this trend multicloud is becoming a common scenario for these businesses. These companies are typically using multiple public clouds during their evaluation and experimental phases. While smaller businesses are typically using one public cloud provider, large enterprises may end up working with multiple public cloud providers. Typical reasons for multicloud adoption with multiple public cloud providers include availability of the needed cloud services in certain global regions, compliance, and costs. According to Flexera's 2020 State of the Cloud report **93%** of enterprises have a multicloud strategy now as they continue to use combination of multiple public and private cloud infrastructure.

As more and more enterprises have become comfortable with the public cloud adoption and usage, many will begin to connect their private cloud and data centers to the public cloud. Setting up a hybrid cloud optimizes their private cloud and on-premises data center investments while still utilizing the public cloud to realize key digital transformation scenarios.

Industry Statistics

87%

of the respondents have a hybrid cloud strategy according to the Flexera 2020 report[107].

We are going to see more and more organizations continuing to have multicloud and hybrid cloud configuration and they will all connect them together as one large, interconnected infrastructure. The use of these interconnected clouds is going to increase the complexity of managing and maintaining this infrastructure. Specialized IT personnel with expertise in private cloud, on-premises data center, and multiple public clouds will be required to manage this complex infrastructure.

Shortage of expertise

In the Pre-COVID-19 times, the low unemployment rate between **3-4%** in the US made it very hard to get good cloud talent. With organizations expanding their private cloud to multicloud and increased hybrid cloud configuration has led to the challenges of cloud expertise and resources shortage. In the long run, reskilling and retraining your current IT resources will solve this issue. In the short run, you may have to bring in outside cloud consultants, for your industry vertical. Lack of expertise in cloud computing is a challenge for all companies who may be in any stage of cloud usage and adoption. Multicloud and hybrid cloud configurations are also creating complex environments where you may need

---

[107] https://info.flexera.com/SLO-CM-REPORT-State-of-the-Cloud-2020

external deeper cloud expertise while you retrain your current IT staff. Use of multicloud will require you to train and certify your staff in multiple public cloud environments as you mature as a cloud organization. IDC's Worldwide CIO Agenda 2019 Predictions report predicted that **30%** of high-demand roles for emerging technologies will remain unfilled through 2022. According to the Challenges of Cloud Transformation report[108] published in early February 2020, **86%** of IT leaders think **shortage of cloud talent** will slow down cloud projects in 2020. While this was true when the research study was published, before the COVID-19 pandemic, things will look a bit different now. With many companies putting their IT projects on hold and in some cases laying off their technical personnel, it is going to make more technical talent available in the market. But still, at the end of the day there will be a shortage of talent and cloud expertise for managing and maintaining the complex multicloud and hybrid clouds.

Lack of governance

Without a proper governance framework, you run the risk of your organization having a huge cloud spend waste, non-compliance, and cybersecurity attacks.

Thus, an important part of cloud adoption and usage operations is to have proper governance in place to make sure that you take structured approach and have proper processes and procedures in place for experimenting and migrating production workloads into the cloud. Your internal controls will help you with making sure that not every team and unit starts using the cloud services

---

[108] https://go.logicworks.com/2020-cloud-transformation-challenges

without proper oversight and in alignment with the organization's goals. Even the units that try cloud services for proof-of-concept projects should require that someone reviews the requirements, approves, or rejects, provisions the services, and then shuts them down properly once the project is complete. Such controls will help you in reducing the cloud spend waste. Typically, your IT unit or the cloud CoE will play a key role in helping other business units with governance process, tasks, and enforcement.

Major part of your governance framework should revolve around proper security reviews and evaluation before moving any kind of production workloads into the cloud. You should consider the security measures already built into your workload along with what your cloud provider is going to offer. Depending on your industry type, you may also have certain regulatory compliance that you have to fulfill. In this case, you want to make sure that you sign up with a cloud provider that has been certified to have the regulatory compliance in place for their services in your geographic region of interest.

One caveat to consider, though, is to have that governance doesn't come in the way of innovation and experimentation but there is a good balance to make sure that experimentation can proceed in the cloud without too much procedural red tape in place.

Security

Security has and will stay as one of the top concerns for the cloud. When considering moving to the cloud, organizations should understand the fundamental differences between their on-premises data center and private cloud security vs. how the security looks like when you end up choosing one of the cloud providers. Moving into the cloud means that you are now dependent on the cloud provider for making sure that their data centers are secure and have proper identity management, physical security, personnel security, and privacy measures in place.

You, as an organization, still own the responsibility of making sure that your cloud resources including applications, data, databases etc. are properly configured for security. As you migrate on-premises assets to the cloud, you want to make sure that the security of these migrated assets stays intact or is reconfigured as needed. The onus of protecting your cloud assets is not only on the cloud provider but also on you, thus making it a shared responsibility between you and the provider.

As organizations initially adopt the cloud, the security scenarios maybe simple. But as we move into the future and large enterprises start implementing complex hybrid scenarios for splitting up their resources between their on-premises networks and the cloud, security scenarios are also going to get complex. It is critical that the current security best practices and policies which may already be in place for on-premises data centers and private cloud are tweaked and made suitable to be applied to the assets in the public, hybrid, or the multicloud.

Expert Opinion

"Some organization with high cloud adoption and with efficient security deployment has reported very high reduction in the number of incidents due to autonomous remediation in near real-time. The autonomous user behavior analytics can also help in the prevention or detection of malicious insider attacks as well as outside attacks. With these innovations whether self-securing clouds could replace security professionals? I do not think so, but this will certainly transform the security professional in a huge way, and they will have to change."

Ratan Jyoti[109], CISO - Ujjivan Small Finance Bank

◆ ◆ ◆ ◆ ◆ ◆ ◆ ◆ ◆ ◆ ◆ ◆

---

[109] https://www.linkedin.com/in/ratanjyoti/

CLOUD TRENDS & OUTLOOK

We are going to see some key trends emerge in the cloud computing world over the next two to three years. Some of these are being fueled by the COVID-19 pandemic while others are because of the organic growth and evolution of the cloud technology.

Key trends for the cloud because of the COVID-19 pandemic include increased adoption and usage of cloud SaaS services primarily because of remote workers using video conferencing and collaboration tools available via the cloud's SaaS offerings. Adoption of cloud PaaS and IaaS cloud services by organizations will also continue to rise as organizations continue to adopt and use these services to make sure that their business-critical applications continue to run in this remote, work from home scenario.

Larger, cloud mature organizations will shift their focus to integration of different clouds to enable multicloud and hybrid cloud. While small to large organizations will tap into the emerging technologies, available from the public cloud providers, such as ML, AI, IoT, blockchain etc. to realize of their key digital transformation scenarios.

Growth in SaaS spend

Overall, we saw a decrease in the IT budgets in 2020 due to COVID-19 pandemic because of the organizations becoming more cautious in their overall spend as a percent of their revenues but a few areas will continue to grow. Gartner estimated that overall IT spend globally went down by 8%[110].

IDC also lowered its 2020 IT spend forecast due to the COVID-19 situation but emphasized growth in the cloud adoption and usage.

Industry Statistics

5.1%

IT Spend forecast was lowered in 2020 according to the IDC report[111] but with strong cloud acceptance and utilization.

According to IDC, infrastructure cloud spend stayed up compared to the overall drop in IT budget spend. This is primarily due to the organizations sustaining remote work systems for their employees working from home.

---

[110] https://www.gartner.com/en/newsroom/press-releases/2020-05-13-gartner-says-global-it-spending-to-decline-8-percent-in-2020-due-to-impact-of-covid19

[111] https://www.idc.com/getdoc.jsp?containerId=prUS46268520

According to IDC, there was a **3.8%** increase in infrastructure and cloud spend compared to 2019.

Cloud computing is going to continue to flourish in these times interesting times as most of us work remotely. Without cloud computing in place and accessible to companies of all sizes, this massive remote work paradigm would not have been possible. Key cloud services such as Zoom Video conferencing, Microsoft Teams, and Google Meet *et al.* have saved us all from the huge layoffs that may otherwise would have happened in multiple industries. While some of the industries including leisure & hospitality, wholesale & retail, transportation, manufacturing, construction, and education & health have been really hit hard, other industries and specifically the IT sector has been saved the wrath of massive lay-offs and furloughs.

Cloud software services which have contributed to SaaS spend growth include email and video conferencing along with CRM (Customer Relationship Management) and ERP (Enterprise Resource Planning) applications required by the organizations to run their operations during the pandemic remote work and lockdown.

Email: Cloud SaaS services

Email is one of the basic communication tools of the modern society and we tend to use it without even thinking too much about it. Traditionally email for medium to large organization was hosted in their data center email servers back in the 1990s and early 2000s. Most of the companies have now migrated to using email services from the public cloud providers. Every company, no matter what their size, uses this basic cloud service to communicate with internal employees and external customers, partners, and other stakeholders.

Some of the largest email service providers include Microsoft with their Microsoft 365 cloud SaaS service and Google Workforce. All thanks to the cloud providers that we are continuing to use this very basic communication service because of the availability of cloud services during these times.

Video Conferencing: Cloud SaaS services

With most of the companies allowing majority of their employees to work remotely from home, we have heavily started depending on video conferencing software to conduct all our meetings. Two prominent video conferencing tools include Microsoft Teams and Zoom. Microsoft 365 service is part of Microsoft's cloud SaaS offering from within which Microsoft Teams is available. This is their audio/video conferencing software solution. Microsoft Team's utilization has exponentially gone up as the masses have started working remotely. Microsoft Teams collaboration platform reported more than 75 million daily users[112] back in April 2020.

Zoom is another popular audio/video conferencing service which has picked up in usage and now is the most used video conferencing software according to Prioridata and Statista. Most of schools and universities have started to use tools like Microsoft Teams, Zoom, Google Meet, and others to conduct online real-time sessions for their students. Zoom released data showing that their number of daily unique usage of around 300 million in April 2020, that was a **50%** increase from March.

---

[112] https://www.statista.com/chart/21191/daily-active-users-of-microsoft-teams/

Business operations and mission critical applications

During the COVID-19 pandemic we are also seeing that organizations are relying on the cloud to continue to smoothly run their business operations. Cloud-based CRM and ERP software is being utilized by organizations to manage their business operations remotely. SaaS software such as Dynamics 365 and Salesforce are just two of the examples of many popular business operations and customers relations management cloud software that exists in the market. While small to mid-sized business may not expand and customize their existing software, due to cost cutting and cautious budgetary approach, large corporations will continue to customize their software systems to make them more flexible to the current remote work situation.

If your business is more complex, then it may be using either PaaS or IaaS cloud services or a combination of those services from cloud providers such as Amazon, Microsoft, or Google. Most of the small to mid-sized businesses may have their business-critical applications and systems already in the cloud and it is easy for them to continue to conduct their operations normally regardless of the COVID-19 interruption. Large enterprises on the other hand may not be solely using the public cloud and may be in a hybrid cloud scenario where majority of their resources are in their private data centers and some resources exist in the public cloud. Their operations for sure have been significantly disrupted due to the workforce needed to run the data centers under the remote work and "social distancing" guidelines.

Hybrid & multicloud growth

Most of the large mid-sized businesses and enterprises are going to continue to adopt public cloud thus leading them to build a hybrid cloud which incorporates their on-premises data centers, private cloud and now the public cloud. According to the Flexera's report more that **80%**[113] of the organizations surveyed are in this scenario.

One of the primary reasons for hybrid cloud adoption for large enterprises is cost optimization. These organization have huge investments in their on-premises data centers but still want to use the flexible OpEx-based, pay as you use, public clouds to transform their business without any further CapEx investment in their on-premises data centers. This has led to many of these organizations to start utilizing one or more public clouds along with their current on-premises data centers and private clouds. Setting up a multicloud with on-premises infrastructure, private cloud, and multiple public clouds has contributed to increased complexity of such configurations. Such complex multicloud infrastructure is hard to monitor, manage, and maintain. Shortage of expertise and talent has also precipitated in organizations finding it harder to manage the multicloud and the hybrid cloud.

Expert Opinion	"The major challenge with Hybrid cloud is to ensure that all parties involved accept their responsibility in the complex Shared Responsibility Model, especially for cybersecurity."
	Johannes Drooghaag[114], CEO Spearhead Management

---

[113] https://info.flexera.com/SLO-CM-REPORT-State-of-the-Cloud-2020
[114] https://www.linkedin.com/in/johannesdrooghaag/

Majority of the public cloud providers, including Microsoft Azure, Amazon AWS, IBM Cloud, and Google Cloud Platform are now offering a full suite of hybrid cloud services for their customers. Azure Arc[115], AWS Outposts[116] and Google Anthos[117] are some of the examples of hybrid services and solutions available from Microsoft, Amazon, and Google respectively.

Integration of clouds

As many organizations take on to setting hybrid cloud and multicloud environments, integration and automation will become important for these different infrastructures including on-premises data centers, private cloud, and different public clouds. IDC FutureScale 2020 report[118] had predicted that by 2020, **70%** of the enterprises will have such integration and automation in place to help them get a holistic view of their environments. COVID-19 may have slowed down this integration but as mentioned before, the pandemic for sure has fueled the growth of public cloud. This integration, however, will continue in post pandemic years to come. Security, management, and maintenance of these environments will become key concerns for the enterprises.

Integration of these clouds will also lead to increased complexity and advanced security configurations. Tools and processes will have to be built to manage, monitor, and maintain these complex hybrid/multicloud environments. Hybrid and multicloud environments will also lead to a new breed of vendors and Managed Service

---

[115] https://azure.microsoft.com/en-us/services/azure-arc/
[116] https://aws.amazon.com/outposts/
[117] https://cloud.google.com/anthos
[118] https://www.idc.com/getdoc.jsp?containerId=US45599219

Providers (MSP) with the knowledge and expertise to help enterprises with their environments.

Rise of low code/no-code platforms

For organizations to build and deliver cloud-based digital services, with agility and utilizing the in-house talent, to their customers will lead to organizations looking to adopt and use low-code/no-code application platforms. Key advantages of these application platforms include shortened go-to-market timelines and ability to use existing power users within your organization to build applications on these platforms. These platforms are inadvertently trying to solve the talent shortage problem that exists in the IT industry almost all the time by avoiding hiring hard core developers to work on the traditional and legacy application development platforms. These platforms will also help organizations with building applications which can be used internally to improve and automate business processes and experiences.

Industry Statistics

75%

of large enterprises will be using multiple low-code development tools by 2024 according to Gartner magic quadrant report.

Expert Opinion

"As the ecosystems within cloud environments continue to expand and no-code/low-code become more common, organizations will be able to further optimize processes without the need for developers and the need to educate technicians in the business objectives. This also creates a new challenge: who owns the cyber security responsibility for no-code/lo-code solutions?"

Johannes Drooghaag[119], CEO Spearhead Management

Some of the key players offering such platforms include Microsoft, Salesforce, OutSystems, and Mendix. Amazon has also jumped into this domain with their Amazon Honeycode offering. According to a Gartner report, these low-code platforms are the next wave of digital transformation assets to help organizations gain competitive edge by reducing the time it takes to get your products and services to the customers.

Industry Statistics

65%

of overall application development will be using low-code/no-code in the organizations by 2024 according to Gartner magic quadrant report.

---

[119] https://www.linkedin.com/in/johannesdrooghaag/

Containers & serverless usage explosion

Containers and serverless are two key DevOps technologies which have seen huge growth in the 2019 and 2020. Cloud developers are swarming around these two technology offerings from the cloud providers for building and deploying native cloud apps. Serverless computing provides compute on-demand and removes the burden of server management away from the developers. It offers a scalable architecture, quick deployments, and removes latency by running the code closer to the user. Containers on the other hand are an abstraction at the application layer with logical container that has the application code, needed dependencies, files, and libraries. See **Figure 2-2**. Benefits of containers include lower overhead because of minimal required data in the logical container to run the app, portability across multiple public clouds and agility to build and deploy. Kubernetes, an open-source system, is used to manage and maintain multiple containers across multiple hosts.

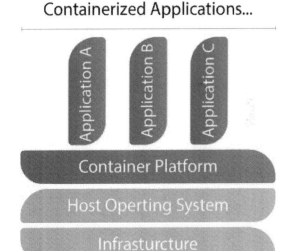

Figure 2-2

Containers have now become mainstream for developers and DevOps professionals. Docker adoption increased to **65%** whereas Kubernetes saw **58%** adoption in 2020. All the top tier cloud providers including Amazon's AWS, Microsoft's Azure and Google's GCP provide their own versions of container and serverless offerings. With the recent acquisition of Red Hat by IBM, we are going to see IBM aggressively try to penetrate the hybrid and multicloud market with their hybrid offerings and solutions. More about serverless computing, containers and related services will be discussed in the third chapter of the book when we review Azure Cloud Services.

Cloud's emerging technologies will play a key role

Cloud computing has become an enabler for many digital transformation initiatives and is key in helping organizations evolve their business model to compete in today's fierce tech environment. Some of the key emerging technologies available via the public cloud providers such as ML,
AI, IoT, blockchain et. al. will continue to be enhanced by the cloud providers to help organizations realize their digital transformation scenarios.

Cloud computing has put these key emerging technologies within the reach of small to mid-sized organizations whereas previously these were only in reach by the large enterprises with deep pockets and many available resources.

Customer Story

Bosch Building Technologies, Bosch Group's division, expanded is energy efficiency offerings to its customers by utilizing Azure IoT's Digital Twins. Using the capability from Digital Twins, its customers can build contextually aware solutions and create digital representation of assets, environments, and business.

Read the entire story[120]

Costs and resources required for acquiring and setting up the infrastructure or getting the needed compute power was a significant hindrance for small to mid-sized organizations to move forward on enabling many of their business transformation scenarios utilizing these key emerging technologies. Cloud computing has solved this problem now with the public cloud providers offering services, tools, infrastructure scale, and almost unlimited compute power to organizations of all sizes and shapes with the affordable pay-as-you use model.

Certain key technologies which have gained prominence and momentum in this cloud era include ML, AI, IoT, and blockchain. As an organization you may be interested in offering customer service via using a chatbot, or you may be interested in measuring the sentiment of customers across various social media channels, or you want to effectively monitor and manage an IoT network of geographically distributed devices. All these key scenarios and many others are now possible with cloud's emerging technologies offerings.

---

[120] https://customers.microsoft.com/en-us/story/790031-bosch-building-technologies-smart-spaces-azure

---

Customer Story | BBC utilizes Azure's Bot services from the Azure AI platform offerings to help them build a natural language branded virtual assistant for its multi-culture and international customers. The virtual assistant is going to be used by BBC's customers to access multiformat and multilingual content and services.

Read the entire story[121]

All major cloud providers are offering AI, ML, IoT, blockchain services to help companies move forward on their digital transformation. Public cloud providers have "commoditized" these technologies and have made them possible to be in reach for companies of all sizes. According to the IDC FutureScape 2020 report[122] prediction report cloud, AI and IoT/Edge computing are in the top ten areas of investments for many of the organizations.

---

[121] https://customers.microsoft.com/en-us/story/754836-bbc-media-entertainment-azure
[122] https://www.idc.com/getdoc.jsp?containerId=US44403818

SUMMARY

There are numerous benefits for using cloud computing, which we discussed in this chapter including:

- Global availability
- Cost savings
- Agile provisioning
- Hyper-scale
- Business continuity & disaster recovery
- Enhanced security services and tools from the cloud providers
- Availability of key emerging technologies to enable digital transformation.

We also reviewed the different cloud deployment and service models to understand the cloud infrastructure and class of services offered by various cloud providers. Cloud computing challenges were examined along with the future trends and the evolution of cloud computing.

In the next chapter, we will examine and learn about Microsoft Azure Cloud Services and the key services IaaS, PaaS, and DBaaS services they are offering. We will also review and explore the key technical trends in cloud computing including serverless, containers, and hybrid cloud computing.

CHAPTER 3:

AZURE CLOUD SERVICES

OVERVIEW OF AZURE CLOUD SERVICES

In this chapter, we will provide an overview of the Microsoft Azure Cloud Services. For a good understanding of Azure Cloud Services, it is important to understand the key building blocks of Azure. Microsoft Azure data centers are a key component of the cloud services. They are spread across the globe strategically to make sure that Azure Cloud Services are available in all key global markets. As of the writing of this book, Microsoft Azure Cloud has around **58 regions and is available in 140**[123] countries. Microsoft boosts it having the most cloud regional presence globally to any other cloud provider, along with having enterprise grade services available at hyper scale. Check out **Figure 3-1** to see all the Azure data centers across the globe.

To understand Azure Cloud, a good understanding of data center and networking terminology is important.

---

[123] https://azure.microsoft.com/en-us/global-infrastructure/geographies/

Azure Global Infrastructure

Azure global infrastructure is the actual physical infrastructure and connected network components. The physical infrastructure component consists of around 160+ physical datacenters, arranged into regions, and linked by the high bandwidth interconnected backbone.

Azure Data Center

Azure data centers are globally located in physical buildings that have a group of networked computer servers and other devices.

Azure Region

An Azure region is a set of datacenters connected through a dedicated regional low-latency and high bandwidth network.

Azure Zone

Azure zone is made up of one or more datacenters outfitted with independent power, networking, and cooling systems.

Figure 3-1

This global presence in multiple regions gives the users the advantage to provision cloud services in their preferred physical location so they are close to a particular data center for faster access to their data, along with data redundancy and data backup in different global data centers. The global spread of Azure data centers makes it a good choice for organizations looking for disaster recovery options. In case of a natural or any other disaster in a particular part of the globe, Azure Cloud can fail over to another global data center for majority of its core services.

Azure has hundreds of cloud services[124] available and this numbers keeps going up on regular basis. One caveat, however, to consider is that not all cloud services are available in all Azure regions. This is one of the key reasons that many of the organizations are now in multicloud environment where they may be using multiple public cloud providers. Along with its own cloud services, Azure also offers various third party and open-source solutions to its customer via the Azure Marketplace[125].

From public cloud adoption perspective Amazon Web Services (AWS), Azure and Google Cloud Platform (GCP) are the top three cloud providers respectively among others including VMWare on AWS, Oracle Cloud, IBM Cloud and Alibaba Cloud according to the Flexera State of the Cloud 2021 report. AWS leads the pack with 50% respondents running significant workloads in the AWS cloud.

---

[124] https://azure.microsoft.com/en-us/services/
[125] https://azure.microsoft.com/en-us/marketplace/

Industry Statistics

41%

of the respondents are running significant workloads in the Azure behind AWS according to the Flexera State of the Cloud 2021 report[126].

From security perspective, Azure offers physical data center security, various security tools and utilities available to its customers making it one of the favorite choices for many of its current and potential customers. Depending on your industry, you may also be interested in knowing that Azure is compliant with many of the required standards and regulations for many industries. Azure offers more than **90 compliance offerings**[127] as of this writing.

Microsoft traditionally has had the biggest share of the enterprise customer market along with large mid-sized organizations. This gives them the additional advantage of being the top choice cloud provider for hybrid cloud that most of these organizations are now looking to setup. Microsoft Azure covers a wide array of hybrid scenarios and services[128]. Azure hybrid cloud services and offerings will be covered in detail later in this chapter.

---

[126] https://info.flexera.com/CM-REPORT-State-of-the-Cloud
[127] https://azure.microsoft.com/en-us/overview/trusted-cloud/compliance/
[128] https://azure.microsoft.com/en-us/solutions/hybrid-cloud-app/

| Expert Opinion | "We have noticed that clients have benefitted immensely by aligning their cloud strategy to investing in the Microsoft cloud platforms across the 3 Microsoft clouds.

The solutions delivered have adhered to 4 tenets of platform based digital transformation of being open, scalable, connected and intelligent."

Srikar Reddy[129], CEO – Sonata Software |

Azure also comes with many customer service and support options which include both free and paid offerings[130]. Free options include Microsoft Learn, videos, documentation, and community support whereas paid support is available for developers, production, and business critical workloads. Microsoft Learn is a great place to get started with learning about using Microsoft Azure.

◆ ◆ ◆ ◆ ◆ ◆ ◆ ◆ ◆ ◆ ◆

---

[129] https://www.linkedin.com/in/srikar-reddy-676986/
[130] https://azure.microsoft.com/en-us/support/plans/

TOOLS AND UTILITIES

Graphical User Interface (GUI) portals and Command Line Interface (CLI) tools are available to Azure Cloud customers to help them provision, deploy, configure, manage, maintain, and troubleshoot their cloud services. GUI portals are available for cloud customers with minimal IT experience whereas CLI tools are available for experienced IT users, who may already be using the CLI tools in their on-premises data centers and private clouds. Azure provides the Microsoft Azure portal[131] as the GUI portal which can be used to find information about your cloud subscription along with provisioning, deploying, and maintaining cloud services.

CLI tools such as Azure CLI, PowerShell and Linux Bash shell are provided for experienced IT network engineers,

---

[131] https://docs.microsoft.com/en-us/learn/azure/

systems administrators, and developers who may already have experience in managing their on-premises systems using these tools. Along with these primary tools there are other essential tools available within the Azure portal which help you optimize your cloud services configuration, security, and utilization. Three of these key tools are:

Azure Advisor

Azure Advisor tool analyzes your cloud services configurations and usage data and then offers personalized recommendations to assist you optimize your Azure resources.

Azure Cost Management

This tool helps you analyze cloud costs, monitors your budget, and optimizes cloud cost with customized recommendations.

Azure Security Center

Azure Security Center[132] is a security management tool that oversees the security of all your public cloud, private cloud, and on-premises data center resources thus spanning across your entire digital estate in a hybrid cloud environment. It constantly assesses your environment, provides a bird's eye view of your cloud resources along with making recommendations to secure your resources against any threats.

---

[132] https://docs.microsoft.com/en-us/azure/security-center/security-center-introduction

Developer tools

Developers make up the primary and majority of Azure Cloud users. Developer Integrated Developer Environment (IDE) tools such as Visual Studio and open-source Visual Studio Code are also fully supported, integrated, and optimized for Microsoft Azure. Visual Studio Code is an open-source version of Visual Studio and is freely available for Windows, Linux, and MacOS systems. This is yet another example of Microsoft fully embracing, creating, and supporting open-source technologies and tools working with their Azure Cloud.

Many tools at one time that were available as standalone tools for working with Azure now are getting integrated into the Azure portal so that the cloud administrators, network engineers, and developers can fully manage their environments from within the portal rather than separately using those standalone tools.

STORAGE OVERVIEW

Storage is a basic component of any cloud service. Azure Cloud providers offer various storage options to organizations for fulfilling all their requirements. Key characteristics of Azure Storage include security, low latency, and redundancy. Several different storage types are available to Azure customers including Azure File, Azure Disk, Azure Blob, Azure Data Lake, Azure Archive, and Azure High Performance Computing Cache storage.

Storage types

In this section, we review the different storage types that are available via Azure Storage options. Once a storage account is created within the cloud service, it can be configured for various storage options.

File

Azure File Storage is available for setting up file shares using Server Message Block (SMB) protocol. This storage allows you to setup file shares which are accessible to Windows, MacOS, and Linux machines in both the cloud and from the on-premises networks. There are options available to you to provision premium file shares for performance sensitive requirements.

Disk

Disk storage, with its high performance and durability options, is available for Azure virtual machines. It is all ready to use for your mission-critical workloads. Four options that you can choose from include: Standard HDD (Hard Disk Drive), Standard SSD (Solid State Disk), Premium SSD and Ultra Disk Storage.

Blob

Blob storage is perfect for you to save unstructured data, typically used with your applications. Typical examples of unstructured data include videos, images, and social media posts. Options are available for high performance needs.

Queue

Queue storage is primarily used by developers and DevOps professionals who develop applications which may generate many messages which need to be temporarily stored, tracked, and then processed. One example of such an application can be an ecommerce application where the customer orders from the shopping cart are queued into this kind of storage for processing.

Table

Table storage is utilized for storing semi-structured and non-relational data. It is used by developers for storing and retrieving this type data for their applications. One example of this data can be social media tweets, which are semi-structured yet non-relational in nature.

Data lake storage

Data lake storage is perfect for data analytics workloads and works with leading data analytics frameworks including Apache Spark and Hadoop. Built to scale, with high performance and high security, it is one of the most cost-effective data analytics storage options available in the market.

Archive

Archive storage is perfect for cost effective storage where data is infrequently used. Security options include data encryption at rest. Typical scenarios for using archive storage include:

- Backups
- Magnetic tape replacement
- Public security & safety data
- Healthcare data retention
- Legal and compliance data requirements

High Performance Computing (HPC) Cache

HPC Cache storage provides file caching for high-performance computing thus enhancing access speeds for your HPC activities. It can be utilized to access Azure Blob Storage or Network Attached Storage (NAS) across WAN (Wide Area Network) links. Once the data is in the HPC cache it can be used with a high-performance compute cluster.

Storage tools

Microsoft Azure provides a tool called Azure Storage Explorer to work with storage in the cloud. This tool is now also integrated in the Azure portal. Using this tool, you can work with storage accounts, blobs, files, queues, tables, Azure Cosmos DB and Azure Data Lake.

CLOUD SERVICE MODEL SERVICES

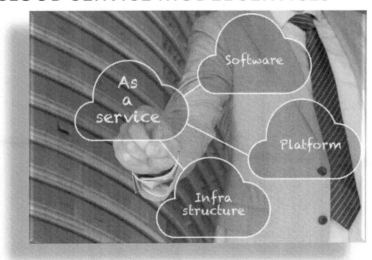

In the next three sections, we will discuss core cloud services provided by Azure for the IaaS, PaaS and the DBaaS cloud service models. While each service model has multiple services, which are offered for it, we will touch on some of the key services for each of these models.

AZURE IAAS CLOUD SERVICES

IaaS services are the most consumed services in the cloud and were among the very first offerings that the cloud providers had when cloud computing became commercial. Azure offers various IaaS services to its customers. The three key ones being virtual networks, virtual machines, and high bandwidth dedicated fast connections. IaaS services are most used by systems and network administrators along with developers who may be working on highly customized applications which requires virtual machine(s).

Azure Virtual Networks

Azure offers basic infrastructure services including setting up virtual networks. Network administrators and engineers are the ones who will use this service to setup and configure these virtual cloud network(s). This would be a starting point if you are interested in testing out the cloud environment, run experimentation, setting up virtual machines, or are planning to extend your on-premises infrastructure to the Azure Cloud. Virtual networks in Azure come with standard features of setting subnets along with optional security options that you can enable in your network including Bastion host, DDoS (Distributed Denial of Service) protection and a firewall. Azure Virtual Networks can also be connected to other virtual networks that you may have in the same or different Azure regions through the peering feature. Once the virtual network is setup you can monitor the network connections along with access to detailed logs.

Azure Virtual Machines

Along with setting up virtual networks and subnets in Azure, you can also provision virtual machines. Systems administrators, developers and DevOps professionals are the key users of this service.

There may be several reasons for you setting virtual machines:

- Innovating and experimenting in the cloud
- Using virtual machines as the frontend web servers for an application
- Setting up database and identity systems in the cloud for extending your on-premises network
- Requirements for a highly customized application which requires dedicated virtual machine compared to just using Azure PaaS App Service
- Migrating current virtual machines from the on-premises environment to the cloud. This is typically referred to as "lift and shift".

Depending on the size of a virtual machine selected, it takes a couple of minutes or less to provision it. Machine size option allows you to pick a virtual machine with your desired memory, storage, and number of virtual CPUs. For virtual machine disks, Azure offers both HDD and SDD options. Virtual machines come with configurable standard network security groups to manage inbound and outbound traffic. Azure offers both Linux and Windows highly available virtual machines with its availability set feature. The virtual machines can also be scaled out as needed and work with an Azure Load Balancer. This scenario applies to applications which have unpredictable levels of ingress network traffic. A typical example will be an ecommerce application which may have burst of traffic coming to it during the holiday season.

Depending on how your virtual machine(s) are configured Microsoft Azure boosts an uptime SLA of **95% – 99.99%**. Single virtual machine with HDD managed disks for operating system and data disks are guaranteed at **95%** SLA whereas virtual machines setup across multiple Azure zones will be warranted at **99.99%** uptime. For business-critical usage of virtual machines, you want to settle for the higher SLA with machines configured for high availability across multiple Azure zones.

Once a virtual machine on Azure is deployed, you have the option to connect to it remotely either directly or via a secure Azure Bastion host. If you decide to scale up the machine to satisfy your higher compute needs, you can change the size of the virtual machine and pick another VM size with higher number of virtual CPUs, memory, and storage.

Operationally, there are various options available to manage and maintain your virtual machines including auto-shutdown, managing updates to the host and guest operating systems, backing up your virtual machine using a schedule, or enabling disaster recovery using Azure Site Recovery services.

There are also a wide range of options available to you for monitoring, diagnosing, and fixing issues that you may encounter with your virtual machines. Over time, Microsoft has added capabilities to make sure that networks administrators, systems administrators, developers, and DevOps professionals can self-help and fix the issues themselves rather than calling and engaging with Microsoft to fix any issues that come up with the machines.

Monitoring and maintaining your virtual machines are a big part of a systems administrator or DevOps professional's job and it is important to understand that Microsoft Azure provides various tools and utilities for them to properly monitor and troubleshoot any issues that may arise. Monitoring utilities include performance monitoring using machine metrics (CPU utilization, memory usage, input/outbound traffic, etc.), network traffic monitoring, and access to virtual machine console and logs. For troubleshooting one can perform connection troubleshooting, resetting the administrator's password, and in case of irreparable issues redeploy the machine.

Azure ExpressRoute

If you are an organization interested in getting a private and a high bandwidth connection directly to Microsoft Azure network, then Azure ExpressRoute is the service for you to use. Using this service, you connect from your physical network to an intermediary network provider, which connects you directly to the Microsoft Azure network. This direct connection will give you the privacy where only your traffic flows on this private network instead of sharing your network traffic on a public network. Along with the security and privacy of this dedicated connection, you also get the added benefit of high bandwidth up to 100Gbps or more. Such private and high width bandwidth connections can be perfect for mission critical applications and systems where you need high speed access to resources in your on-premises infrastructure.

AZURE PAAS CLOUD SERVICES

Platform as a Service services are primarily used by developers and DevOps professional who want to create apps and then host them in the cloud. Traditionally, developers are not interested in installing or configuring the virtual machine, operating system, or even the required application platform for their application. They are more interested in understanding the business requirements and then coding the requirements and the logic into their applications. That is exactly what Azure PaaS services offer. It provides them with ready to go application platform, so they spend more time on understanding and coding the business requirements rather than worrying about setting up the virtual machine, the underlying operating system, or installing and configuring the application platform on top of it.

Azure offers this capability via its App Service offering. Quick setup, within a minute to a couple of minutes along with easy configuration of the application platform, Azure App Service is a big favorite among the developers.

Using Azure App Service, you can build and deploy web, mobile and API-based applications on wide range of application platforms including .NET, .NET Core, Java, Ruby, Node.js, PHP, or Python. The underlying operating system for these application platforms can be Windows or Linux. Developers also don't have to worry about the updates to the underlying operating system and application platform since that is all managed by Microsoft Azure. With Azure App Service you have the option to work with traditional code or use the cloud native way of utilizing containers for your application. Containers will be covered later in this chapter. Azure App Service also provides an added benefit of seamless integration with Azure DevOps, GitHub, BitBucket, Docker Hub, or Azure Container Registry for continuous integration and deployment (CI/CD). Along with that, developers can use their IDE tools such as Visual Studio or open source based Visual Studio Code to work with the service.

Using Azure App Service is the recommended way for developers if they are building a web application, mobile app, or an API. The service enables these scenarios for the developers along with offering the options to the developers to build modern cloud native apps using serverless services, Containers and DBaaS services. Serverless services, containers and DBaaS services will be covered later in this chapter.

When provisioning Azure App Service, you have the option to pick an App Service plan to decide if you are going to use the service for dev/test workloads, production workloads or highly secure isolated workloads. These Azure App Service plans[133] are as categorized Free, Shared, Basic, Standard, Premium, and Isolated offerings. Other than the free and shared plans all other plans offer a dedicated virtual machine to host

---

[133] https://azure.microsoft.com/en-us/pricing/details/app-service/windows/

your application. Isolated plan goes one step further by offering a secure virtual machine in a private network in the cloud. Isolated service plan will be ideal if you are interested in creating a hybrid environment and connecting your on-premises network and resources to the applications in the isolated environment.

Once the web application platform has been setup you have the options to configure your application and application platform in the Azure portal regardless of what programming stack you want to use (.NET, .NET Core, Java, Ruby, Node.js, PHP, or Python)

Azure web application offers various options to fully configure and optimize your application and environment. Some key options include:

Authentication and Authorization

Once you setup an application platform you get the option to enable authentication and authorization for your application instead of having it be open to everyone to access. Out of the box, Azure provides various authentication providers you can use for your application including Azure Active Directory, Microsoft Account, Facebook, Google, and Twitter.

Application Insights

Application insights can be utilized by developers and DevOps professional for monitoring the applications. It can help with understanding the usage of the application along with detecting issues within your application.

Networking

Various networking options are available to your application including using Azure Virtual Networks, setting up hybrid connections between your application and the on-premises network, installing a CDN (Content Delivery Network), along with an application firewall and access restrictions to further secure you application.

Custom domains & TLS/SSL Settings

You get the options to create a vanity domain for your web application along with securing it with a digital certificate to allow for secure HTTPS traffic to and from your application.

Backups

For guarding against accidental or intentional data deletion or corruption, you can setup scheduled backups of your application along with the backup of any database you may be using for your application. As of this writing, a new feature called snapshot backup was available as preview for creating snapshot backups along with options to restore previous snapshot backups.

Scaling Up

As the demand for your application goes up you do have the option to scale up the compute, memory, and storage of your web application environment along with moving it to an isolated environment within Azure for extra security and scale. Scaling up is performed by changing your App Service plan.

Scaling Out

Scaling out option is available to increase the number of virtual instances of your web application to meet the increase in demand. You can manually scale your environment or custom scale your application. Custom scale is very flexible and allows you to scale your instances on some metric (such as the CPU utilization going above a certain set threshold) or scaling out automatically during certain months, weeks, or time of the day. An example is an e-commerce website that gets heavy traffic during the holiday season.

Monitoring

Azure provides various tools and option to help you monitor and troubleshoot your application appropriately. You can setup alerts when certain conditions in your applications trigger such as CPU usage, network traffic ingress and egress, memory usage etc. Access your application logs and analyze them using Azure Analytics. Get access to all your web application service logs (application tracing logs, web server logs, detailed error message log, and failed tracing log). You also have the option to view a real-time stream of your logs along with monitoring application processes using the Process Explorer. As of the writing of this book a new tool called, Health Check, has been added to the monitoring option which allows unhealthy instance to be removed from the load balancer or restart them if you have a load balancer setup for your application.

AZURE DBAAS CLOUD SERVICES

Database as a Service cloud services are complimentary to PaaS services and are primarily used by developers and DevOps professionals as they work on creating applications with database needs. Traditionally, developers have relied on Database Administrators (DBA), who would setup a virtual server and then install an on-premises based database server software such as Microsoft SQL Server on top of that server. Through this database server, the developers would create databases and use them for their web and mobile applications.

With the cloud, this model of relying on a dedicated database server has changed. A developer can now has options to use various cloud databases such as Azure SQL[134] or many other Azure managed database services including Azure Cosmos DB, Azure Database for PostgreSQL, Azure Database for MySQL, Azure Database for MariaDB and Azure Cache for Redis. There

---

[134] https://azure.microsoft.com/en-us/services/azure-sql/

may, however, be instances where developers may have to use the Microsoft SQL server for their database needs instead of using the popular Azure SQL database service. This underline[135] provides a reference to features comparison between Azure SQL and Microsoft SQL server. It should be noted that every feature available in Microsoft SQL server is not available in Azure SQL.

Azure managed databases have some inherent benefits which make them a perfect candidate to use them for cloud native, enterprise scale applications. With Azure SQL, the developers don't have to worry about managing database servers but rather can concentrate on building applications using the latest version of the database servers provided to them through the Azure managed database services.

Customer Story	**TeamSystem**, an Italian organization specializing in ERP systems reduced costs and gained efficiencies by choosing to run Microsoft SQL Server on Linux-based Azure Virtual Machines for their data workloads. This helped them with improving their speed of deployment without any performance issues.
	Read the entire story[136]

Key features for Azure SQL Databases include:

---

[135] https://docs.microsoft.com/en-us/azure/azure-sql/database/features-comparison
[136] https://customers.microsoft.com/en-us/story/809018-teamsystem-partner-professional-services-sql-server-azure-virtual-machines

Fully managed databases

Microsoft Azure takes care of the management of these databases with automatic feature and patch updates along with guarantees of up to **99.999%** uptime SLA.

Scalability

Azure managed databases offer scalability to hundreds of database server nodes and 100s of TB storage data.

Customer Story	**AllScripts**, a software manufacturer specializing in the healthcare industry lifted and shifted around 600 of their on-premises based virtual machines to Azure Virtual Machines utilizing their existing Windows Server and Microsoft SQL Server licenses. This migration led to substantial cost savings for them. Read the entire story[137]

Advanced Security

Security features of databases include data masking, encryption, threat detection, and alerts with recommendations on potential security threats.

Open-source support

Azure provides a wide range of support for open-source databases including MySQL, MariaDB and PostgreSQL for developers who are developing their application using open-source technologies.

---

[137] https://customers.microsoft.com/en-us/story/allscripts-partner-professional-services-azure

Azure has three different high-level offerings for developers requiring SQL databases and servers:
- SQL Server on Azure VM
- Azure SQL Managed Instance
- Azure SQL Database

SQL Server on Azure VM

SQL Server on Azure VM is best for applications which require operating system level access and control, which is provided to them through the Azure VM. This option is good for a typical legacy application which may already exist in your on-premises environment and is using a dedicated Microsoft SQL Server installed on a virtual machine. You can setup a similar virtual machine in Azure with a Microsoft SQL Server installed on top of it. Alternatively, you can lift and shift the on-premises virtual machine to the cloud.

Customer Story	**dv01,** a Fintech organization decided to migrate from PostgreSQL and RedShift to Microsoft SQL Server on Azure Virtual Machines to improve query times for their financial and analytics platform. This migration helped them reduce the query times from 30 seconds to one or two seconds.
	Read the entire story[138]

---

[138] https://customers.microsoft.com/en-us/story/dv01

Azure SQL Managed Instance

Azure SQL Managed Instance is a good option if you want to modernize your existing applications. This option offers high compatibility with Microsoft SQL Server. If you are using on-premises Microsoft SQL Server databases for your current applications and would rather not lift and shift these databases onto an Azure VM into the cloud, then this is a perfect option for you. It will however, mean extra effort for you to retrofit your applications and migrate your data to use the Azure SQL Managed Instance. If you are planning to build new cloud applications and require all the functionality of a Microsoft SQL Server, then this will be a good option for you to consider.

Customer Story	**Komatsu,** a heavy equipment manufacturer was looking to migrate from mainframe applications to the cloud and settled on Azure SQL Managed Instance to get the benefits of cost, scalability, and performance. They boosted of **49%** cost savings and **25-30%** net gains in performance after moving to Azure SQL Managed Instance. Read the entire story[139]

---

[139] https://customers.microsoft.com/en-us/story/komatsu-australia-manufacturing-azure

Customer Story	**Legacy Health,** a US-based healthcare provider was looking for a disaster recovery solution for their Electronic Medical Record (EMR) application and turned to Microsoft to provide a solution using Azure Virtual Machines, Azure Storage (Azure SQL Managed Instance) and Azure Backup. This has led to **65%** cost savings for the organization.

Read the entire story[140]

Azure SQL Database

The third and the most common option that developers often use is Azure SQL Database. While this may not provide all the features and functionality of a dedicated Microsoft SQL Server, it is perfect for majority of applications and is the choice of many developers who are building new cloud applications requiring SQL databases. With extremely simple setup and configuration, it makes it easy for developers to provision this service within minutes than to worry about installing and configuring a SQL server on an Azure VM.

---

[140] https://customers.microsoft.com/en-us/story/724167-legacy-health-health-provider-azure

---

Customer Story	**Icertis,** an organization specializing in contract management, was looking for a cost-effective database solution to help them scale on demand during peak times. They decided to go with Azure SQL Database to help them with almost instant scaling leading to **70%** cost savings. Read the entire story[141]

Customer Story	**Benesse,** a Japanese digital education provider wanted to cut down its database costs with minimal impact to its customers. They decided to migrate away from Oracle database to Azure SQL Database with almost zero downtime and cut down on their operational expenses by **70%**. Read the entire story[142]

When provisioning Azure SQL Database, Azure offers various database transaction unit (DTU) service tiers to choose from depending on your needs of storage, performance, and business continuity. DTU is a performance metric for Azure SQL Database. It is a blended mix of three metrics including CPU, memory, and data input/output. These DTU tiers[143] are referred to as **Basic**, **Standard** and **Premium**. It should be noted that Azure SQL Managed Instance doesn't support DTU

---

[141] https://customers.microsoft.com/en-us/story/781602-icertis-partner-professional-services-azure
[142] https://customers.microsoft.com/en-us/story/732188-benesse-education-azure-sql-database
[143] https://docs.microsoft.com/en-us/azure/azure-sql/database/service-tiers-dtu

service tiers. Azure SQL Database also offers high end virtual core (vCore) service tiers[144]. vCore service tiers are usually utilized for general purpose, hyperscale or business critical databases. Azure SQL Managed Instance supports vCore-based service tiers.

Regardless of which tier you use, there are a rich set of features you get with utilizing Azure Cloud databases including:

- Backups
- Failover and replication
- Active Directory Administration
- Restoring deleted databases
- Virtual networks
- Firewalls
- Automatic database tuning
- Database recommendations
- Security Center

◆ ◆ ◆ ◆ ◆ ◆ ◆ ◆ ◆ ◆ ◆

---

[144] https://docs.microsoft.com/en-us/azure/azure-sql/database/purchasing-models

DATABASE MIGRATION

Database migration is important for many organizations, especially for the mid-sized to large enterprises which are interested in moving their on-premises databases to the cloud so that they can use these databases for their cloud native and cloud-based applications and systems.

Database migration is not easy and requires extensive analysis, planning, coordination, and tooling before an organization can successfully move their database to the cloud.

There are two options to migration that organizations may consider when dealing with databases:

1. Migrating the databases from on-premises infrastructure to the cloud
2. Migrating from other database vendors to Microsoft SQL Server

---

For **option 1**, organizations have a choice of using Microsoft SQL Server on Azure VM in the cloud. They can lift and shift their databases from their on-premises Microsoft SQL Server to this Azure VM. The second choice for this option is to not setup a Microsoft SQL Server on Azure VM but rather use the secure, high performance-based and fully managed database services via their Azure SQL Managed Instance offering. This choice provides the organizations to get the same capability and functionality as their would if they were hosting their databases on their on-premises Microsoft SQL Servers.

Option 2 is primarily for organizations which may be interested in migrating away from other non-Microsoft database providers such as Oracle, MySQL, PostgreSQL, MongoDB, AWS, and Google Cloud to Microsoft SQL databases. This migration option may be part of your consolidation strategy to use a single database and cloud provider to optimize costs, operational management, security, and performance of the database workloads.

There are various best practices documentation, tools, and utilities available to help you with either of the options mentioned above. Your IT department or one of the many Microsoft partners out there can help you perform the migration.

A typical migration strategy can be broken into three phases:
1. Assessment
2. Migration
3. Optimization

We review each of these phases in the next three sections.

Assessment

During the assessment phase you will generally look at how many applications you have, application dependencies, databases sizes, which databases to be migrated and how many of them can be migrated together. You will also have to understand if there are schema changes needed for the selected databases to make sure that they are compatible with the target Azure database platform.

Migration

This the phase in which you are moving your database to the selected Azure database platform. Migration includes moving the schema, data, and other database artifacts such as credentials and ETL (extract, transform, load) jobs etc. Depending on the size of the databases you are migrating you should consider the bandwidth of your network connection to the Azure Cloud along with planning around how much time it may take to migrate the databases from your on-premises network to the cloud.

Optimization

The last phase of the database migration journey is the optimization of the migrated databases. You can use the native Azure database tooling and features to optimize operational cost and performance. Azure has built-in automated database tuning and security recommendations that can be used to keep your databases secure and running efficiently.

Migration tools

There are several tools available to assist with migration of databases. Migration is supported for both older versions of Microsoft SQL Servers along with other non-Microsoft databases. **Azure Database Migration Service** can be used to migrate Microsoft SQL Server 2005 through 2017, Oracle, MySQL, PostgreSQL, and MongoDB databases. This list of supported databases which can be migrated is current as of the writing of this book but will grow over a period, so check the latest documentation and guidance from Microsoft for your database when you are ready to migrate it to Azure.

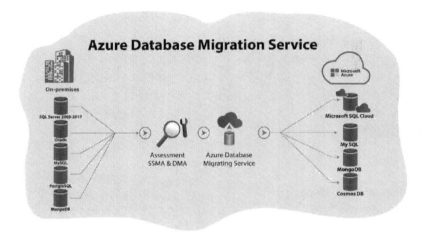

Figure 3-2

There are two tools which can be used for the migration of databases to the Azure Cloud.

Database Migration Assistant (DMA)

This tool helps with the assessment of on-premises Microsoft SQL databases. It assists with choosing the right target Azure database tier along with identifying any migration breaking changes and the required remediations before the actual migration to one of the Azure database platforms.

SQL Server Migration Assistant (SSMA)

This tool is used for assessing the heterogeneous database platforms (Oracle, MySQL, PostgreSQL, and MongoDB etc.) for migration to Azure. It does the schema conversion to make sure that it is compatible with the chosen target Azure database platform.

Customer Story	**Willis Towers Watson** is a global organization providing advisory, brokering, and solutions primarily to the insurance companies. It migrated its on-premises Microsoft SQL Servers to Azure Cloud in minimal amount of time and avoided days or weeks of downtime. Read the entire story[145]

After the assessment is done, Azure Database Migration Service can be used to migrate the database. Azure Database Migration Service is a fully managed service in Azure. It can migrate extremely large databases, can scale to migrate thousands of databases, reducing downtime for databases, along with providing a resilient migration experience in case of network or other issues. It can also gracefully recover from any intermittent issues which can happen when migrating large databases over an extended period.

---

[145] https://customers.microsoft.com/en-us/story/willis-towers-watson-partner-professional-services-azure

Detailed migration guide[146] is also available to understand best practices and how to migrate from different source databases to a specific target database. It is a step-by-step guide on how to migrate and then optimize your migrations.

Customer Story	**Capita Reading Cloud,** a UK-based organization, which works with school libraries to track resources and help student learning, was looking for cost savings and meeting UK and international library customer demands. It decided to migrate 10,000 databases from third-party hosted on-premises SQL servers to Azure SQL Database with minimal effort and only one dedicated IT resource to help them with this move. Read the entire story[147]

---

[146] https://aka.ms/datamigration
[147] https://customers.microsoft.com/en-us/story/724217-capita-uk-professional-services-azure-sql-database

SQL VS NOSQL DATABASES

Along with using the SQL databases, many of the cloud native and modern applications are using NoSQL databases to store, manage, and visualize data. NoSQL databases stores non-structured/semi-structured and non-relational data that many of the current modern systems generate. A little deeper understanding of NoSQL and differences with SQL will help you decide on which database to use for your workloads.

SQL databases are the traditional relational databases where data is stored in SQL tables. Some examples of relational databases include Oracle, MySQL, Microsoft SQL, and PostgreSQL. NoSQL databases refer to any non-relational database and store data in format other than relational SQL tables. Just like SQL, NoSQL databases store relationship data but unlike SQL it allows for related data to be stored within a single data structure. NoSQL database supports dynamic schema compared to SQL databases and store data in multiple ways **documents, key-value pairs, column-oriented** and **graph-based** databases.

Document databases

Document databases store data just like JSON objects. Which means that each document contains pairs of fields and values. The values for these can include numbers, strings, arrays, Boolean, and objects. Thus, it is very easy for developers to work with these values since these values align with the objects the developers are working with in their code. MongoDB and Azure Cosmos DB are two examples of document databases.

Key-value databases

Key-value databases is where each item is stored as a key-value pairs. Querying such databases is done by referencing the value of any item. Such key-value databases are great for scenarios where large amounts of data is stored but you don't need to perform complex queries to retrieve it. Common scenario includes storing user preferences for an application or caching. DynamoDB and Redis and are two examples of key-value databases.

Column-oriented databases

Column-oriented databases store data in tables, rows, and dynamic columns. This structure provides flexibility over relational databases because each row is not required to have the same columns. Column-oriented databases are good for storing large amounts of data and when you can predict what your query patterns will be. Wide-column stores are commonly used for storing IoT data and user profile data. HBase and Cassandra are two of the most popular column-oriented databases.

Graph databases

Graph databases store data in nodes and edges. As an example, nodes can store information about people, places, and things while edges store information about the relationships between the nodes. Graph databases great for scenarios where you need to navigate relationships to look for patterns such as social networks, fraud detection, and recommendation engines. Janus Graph and Neo4j and are two examples of graph databases.

SQL databases are typically capable of being scaled up by adding additional CPU, memory and disk space to the same physical machine or virtual server. NoSQL databases can be scaled out by adding additional servers and distributing the data on these additional servers (this process is referred to as "sharding").

Azure supports NoSQL databases with its premium NoSQL database offering of Azure Cosmos DB. Azure Cosmos DB is a fully managed NoSQL database service for modern app development. It boosts extremely fast access and response times, **99.999%** availability, automated scalability, ability to run real-time analytics, and open-source APIs for MongoDB and Cassandra. Considering all these factors, Azure Cosmos DB is perfect for your mission critical applications for a wide range of industries. You can use Azure Cosmos DB in IoT scenarios to stream and analyze data from hundreds of thousands of devices to obtain real-time insights to take operations actions. For e-commerce and retail scenarios, you can provide real-time shopping carts, product recommendations, dynamic pricing, inventory updates, and more. Cassandra and MongoDB API and compatibility support will help migrate MongoDB and

Cassandra applications to Azure Cosmos DB with minimal changes to your application logic.

Along with support for Azure managed databases, there are several options available in the Azure Marketplace[148] for other third-party cloud databases which are available for use with your custom application. Visit the Azure Marketplace or talk to a database provider to see if they have an Azure Cloud version of their database.

◆ ◆ ◆ ◆ ◆ ◆ ◆ ◆ ◆ ◆ ◆

---

[148] https://azure.microsoft.com/en-us/marketplace/

AZURE SERVERLESS SERVICES

Serverless computing is about helping the developers focus on coding along with building and implementing business logic rather than worrying about the servers and infrastructure to provide the compute and data storage. The time saved from this gives the developers more time to innovate and building applications faster. Server infrastructure is still needed to run the code and to manage the data, but the cloud providers have taken that burden on and will automatically provision, scale and manage the infrastructure as needed. All these mentioned operations are invisible to the developers and are managed by the providers. All major cloud providers including Amazon AWS, Microsoft Azure, and Google Cloud Platform offer their own version of serverless computing.

Serverless computing architecture provides a clear separation between the code and its infrastructure. Developers implement code in a function that is invoked by a trigger. The trigger can be manual, a timed process, an HTTP request, or a file upload. When the trigger occurs, serverless computing allows for running and managing the code in the function on the required infrastructure. Once the code in the function has executed, all its needed infrastructure resources are freed up.

Serverless is most often discussed in the context of compute but can also apply to data. For example, Azure SQL and Cosmos DB both provide cloud databases that don't require you to configure host machines or clusters.

Key benefits serverless computing include:

Support for multiple coding languages
Serverless computing doesn't put any restrictions on the development language you need to use for serverless computing. Developers can use the language of their choice to access and use serverless computing. Thus, making it ideal for developers with different development expertise and skills.

No infrastructure provisioning and management
Developers focus on coding the business logic and innovating rather than worrying about the servers and infrastructure required to run and manage the data. Cloud providers are offering fully managed high availability serverless services to help developers avoid server and infrastructure administrative tasks.

Scalability
As with many cloud services, serverless services also offer the scalability features. The required infrastructure needed to run the developer's code is dynamically scaled up and down to match the requirements of any workload.

High availability
Serverless computing has built-in high availability and fault tolerance capability, which is guaranteed by the cloud providers. Since Azure is responsible for the provisioning and configuration of the underlying infrastructure for the developers to run their code, they are also on point to make sure that there is redundancy and fault tolerance for this infrastructure.

Faster delivery to market
Without the operational management of the underlying infrastructure required to run the code or to manage the data, organizations can cut down considerably on their development cycles. This leads to developers innovating, experimenting, and bringing agility to the creation of products and services and getting them to the market much faster than the traditional product release cycles. Moving to serverless computing is helping organizations in reducing the total cost of ownership and efficiently reallocating human resources to key initiatives and projects.

Azure serverless compute

Azure offers serverless computing services for both compute and databases. Let's examine Azure serverless compute first.

Serverless Azure Functions

For this scenario, the developer creates the code within a function and the function gets invoked when a particular event happens in the system. Azure will take care of running the code in the function on their infrastructure without the developer worrying about the server-side requirements for executing their code. The developers are charged only for the time the function runs. Such scenarios, where the developers don't have to know or worry about the server-side infrastructure, accelerate development, and helps them concentrate on building and integrating business logic into their code rather than additionally worrying about what they will need to setup and configure to run their code.

Example 1: Mobile backend

The event-driven model of serverless computing makes it ideal for mobile apps and the backed ends required for such applications. In a typical mobile application, a mobile device triggers an event that invokes the function to execute the code in it. Serverless computing basically is abstracting away the server- side complexities and helping the developers concentrate on building the required business logic for their apps.

Example 2: IoT backend

Another major scenario for event-triggered model is for Internet of Things (IoT) where hundreds to thousands of devices may be connected on a network to the cloud. Devices such as cars, vending machines, smoke detectors, motion detectors, to weather monitoring devices are some of the examples of IoT devices. These devices are sending data back to the cloud for analysis. The sheer volume of devices and data dictates an event-driven model where the data can be processed and analyzed as events coming back to the cloud. Azure IoT hub is an example of an Azure service which is based on event driven model and processes all the data coming back from the IoT devices. In such scenarios, serverless computing can be used to automate common IoT device tasks such as device registration, policy enforcement, tracking, and deployment of code to devices.

Serverless Kubernetes

Kubernetes is an open- source project, initiated by Google, where a developer can have her application run in a container (containers will be covered later in this chapter) with all the application code and required dependencies (libraries, extra binary files, and configuration files) and host it on one or multiple server nodes. These nodes are referred to as a Kubernetes cluster. Kubernetes provides all the required capability such as replication, scaling, and state management for the applications.

Azure offers Azure Kubernetes Service as their version of Kubernetes for helping developers host and manage their container-based applications across various Kubernetes nodes in a cluster. On top of that, Azure provides the concept of 'virtual nodes' where a developer can scale their application as needed by using virtual serverless containers rather than adding another virtual machine node to the Kubernetes cluster. Azure accomplishes this by Azure Container Instance (ACI) service where new containers are provisioned on-demand in a serverless environment, thus providing almost unlimited scale as needed by the application.

Along with scaling Kubernetes clusters as needed with serverless containers, Azure is now also supporting Kubernetes-based Event-Driven Autoscaling (KEDA). KEDA provides support for Azure functions running in your containers in a Kubernetes cluster, where it actively monitors your functions and looks for events defined in the functions. As events are triggered, it will scale your containers to handle the load. This autoscaling thus helps the developers in not worrying about the infrastructure since Azure functions and KEDA will work together to help in spinning up or down the required Kubernetes infrastructure.

Serverless web applications

Typically, a single page application (SPA) is a good candidate for serverless applications. A Web page like this will typically have HTML, CSS and JavaScript which resides in storage. As an example, in **Figure 3-3**, an HTTP request made through an API management interface will trigger an Azure Function, which in turn can work with Cosmos DB to get data or save data to the database.

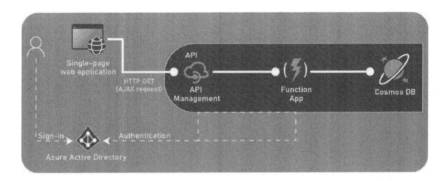

Figure 3-3

Azure serverless databases

Along with serverless compute Azure also offers serverless databases for both Azure SQL and Cosmos DB. Both database cloud services offer serverless options where the developers don't have to setup or configure database servers to use Azure SQL or Cosmos DB databases.

For Azure SQL Databases, you can opt for serverless databases by choosing the **general-purpose** tier when provisioning an Azure SQL Database. There are certain scenarios which lend themselves to using serverless databases vs. dedicated databases. Single databases with unpredictable and intermittent usage are a perfect candidate for serverless database. Another scenario is when you are deploying a database and are unsure about the size and usage of the of the database after it is set up.

Along the same lines as the Azure SQL Databases, Cosmos DB now also offers serverless database option for situations where you require databases where you are unsure of the load and usage of the database over a period or have a workload which might have interspersed spikes in your database usage such as shown in **Figure 3-4**.

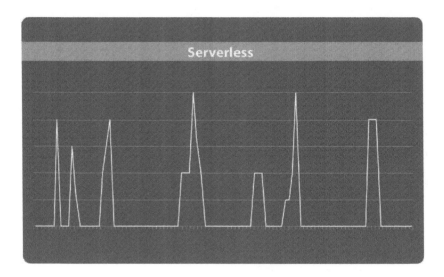

Figure 3-4

Along with the above scenario, there are certain other practical use cases where serverless databases are a great candidate rather than a dedicated provisioned Cosmos

DB database. These include when working with development or testing workloads, building prototypes, and doing proof of concepts.

AZURE CONTAINERS SERVICES

One of the key phenomena which has swept public cloud computing, in the last couple of years and has evolved the application development domain, is the concept of containers. Developers now can use containers for hosting their applications rather than using dedicated virtual machines from the cloud providers.

Key advantages of using containers compared to virtual machines include shorter deployment times, portability of containers across different cloud providers, and the scalability that cloud providers are offering for containers.

Container basics

Developers use containers over virtual machines due to its primary advantages of agility, portability, and scalability. Using the containers, the developers or DevOps professionals can just concentrate on coding their applications and getting it ready and packaged, including only the necessary libraries, and required configuration files, into a deployment package called a container image. They no longer require a full virtual machine to deploy their application. Containers are portable between different operating systems and are scalable depending on your applications needs. Most of the cloud providers offer container services. Container services are offered to the developers in Azure via the Azure App Services and Azure Kubernetes Services (AKS).

According to a survey report, which included **263** senior IT leaders across US, by Forrester Consulting, **86%**[149] of the organizations are using containers for applications. This highlights the popularity of the containers in application development, deployment, and management.

Containers use the concept of packaging the application code and the required dependencies, including libraries, additional binaries, and configuration files required to run the application. Thus, using containers abstracts away the underlying operating system and infrastructure for the developers. The developers can just concentrate on building the applications using the business logic, packaging it with the required dependencies in a container, and then uploading it to the container services provided by the cloud vendor.

It is also important to clarify the container terminology here. A **container image** is a lightweight, standalone, package of software that includes everything (code, libraries, and configuration files) needed to run an application. Container images become **containers** at runtime.

---

[149] https://www.capitalone.com/tech/cloud/container-adoption-statistics/

It is important to understand the differences between containers and virtual machines running the applications. In virtualization, a single host machine can run the Hypervisor virtualization layer and run multiple virtual machines on it with separate guest operating system and an instance of the application on top of it. If the application is required to run on each virtual machine, the developer must configure the application three different times on these three different virtual machines with three different guest operating systems. See **Figure 3-5**.

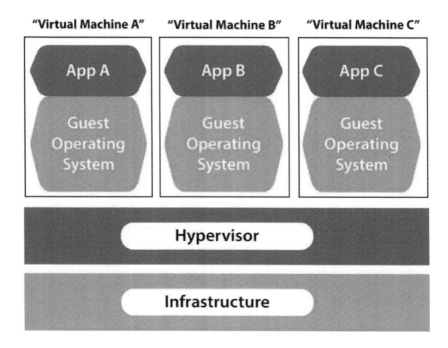

Figure 3-5

Containers on the other hand run on top of a host machine with an operating system and a Docker or any

<u>Open Container Initiative (OCP)</u>[150] container layer platform software, which supports containers. See **Figure 3-6**. The containers can run the same or different applications in them. Docker has been the most popular container platform software compared to others, with over **80%**[151] of the share as of this writing, there are other container formats out there which are also popular including **CoreOS Rkt, Mesos Containerizer, LXC Linux Containers, OpenVZ, Hyper-V Containers, Podman** and **runC**.

Containerized Applications...

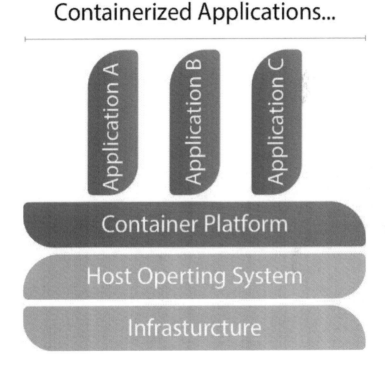

Figure 3-6

---

[150] https://opencontainers.org/
[151] https://containerjournal.com/topics/container-ecosystems/5-container-alternatives-to-docker/

Three key advantages of running containers are:

Development and deployment agility

Developers can focus on coding the business logic into the applications and then quickly packaging the application code and the required dependencies into a container. They don't have to worry about the underlying infrastructure needed to deploy and run their container applications.

Portability

Standardized format of a container backed by the Open Container Initiative (OCP)[152], one of the Linux Foundation projects makes it easy for organizations to port their container-based applications between different operating systems and different cloud providers.

Customer Story	Hafslund is a Norwegian power grid operator and was looking to develop its own meter reading software and decided to use Azure platform utilizing containers and Azure Kubernetes Service to manage them. This helped them with improvements in speed of development without sacrificing the security and performance at the same time. Read the entire story[153]

---

[152] https://opencontainers.org/
[153] https://customers.microsoft.com/en-us/story/hafslund-nett-power-and-utilities-azure

Scalability

The small footprint of a container compared to a virtual machine makes it easy and quick to scale containers up or down as needed. Such fast scalability helps in rapid deployment of application containers across the infrastructure. The small size of the container also allows for running many more containers than virtual machines on the same infrastructure.

Understanding Kubernetes

While it is easy to manage a single container running on a container-supported infrastructure, things become very complex very quickly once the app gets deployed across multiple containers and they are being scaled up and down as needed. This is where Kubernetes comes into play helping to manage multiple containers. *Kubernetes*, also known as K8s, is an open-source system initiated by Google Inc. for automating deployment, scaling, and management of containerized applications.

Customer Story	**Maersk,** a shipping and a logistics organization wanted to streamline their IT operations, maximize productivity for their developers along with building and maintaining open-source solutions. They decided to go with Azure Kubernetes Service for managing and maintaining their containers. Using Azure and its container services gave more time to their developers on innovating and working on key business projects. Read the entire story[154]

---

[154] https://customers.microsoft.com/en-us/story/maersk-travel-transportation-azure

Kubernetes manages clusters of virtual machines and schedules containers to run on these virtual machines based on their available compute resources and the container resource requirements. Containers are grouped into pods, and they scale to your desired state as required. Pod is a group of one or more containers, with shared storage/network resources.

Kubernetes offers various advanced deployment and management operations including service discovery, load balancing, resource allocation, and scaling based on compute utilization. It is also responsible for checking the health of individual resources and enables apps to self-heal by automatically restarting or replicating containers. Kubernetes system is also accessible via a Kubernetes API set.

Azure container offerings

Azure supports Kubernetes through its Azure Kubernetes Service (AKS)[155]. Azure Kubernetes Service (AKS) is a managed container management and orchestration service based on Kubernetes. An organization can use AKS to deploy, scale, and manage Docker containers and container-based applications across a cluster of container hosts.

---

[155] https://azure.microsoft.com/en-us/services/kubernetes-service/

Customer Story	**Finastra,** a Fintech software and cloud solutions provider, decided to use Azure Kubernetes Service with Docker containers so that they minimize the container management burden on their developers. This strategy freed up their resources to be used to speed up their customers' deployments projects.

Read the entire story[156]

Azure offers various container services including Azure Container Instances (ACI)[157]. ACI can be used to create containers when you don't need any orchestration between these containers. Key advantage of ACI is to not worry about the underlying infrastructure of an Azure container instance. It enables container deployment with simplicity and agility. It is a fully managed service and Azure will take care of any infrastructure management and maintenance. It is good for use cases such as dev and test environments, tasks automation, simple web apps, creating prototypes, doing quick proof of concept experiments and small-scale batch processing.

Azure also has the Azure Container Registry (ACR)[158] offering. ACR is a managed service allows developers to build, store and manage container images and artifacts in a private registry for container deployments. It is based on Docker 2.0 open-source registry specification.

Azure App Services has container option available when you are setting up a web app from Azure App Services.

---

[156] https://customers.microsoft.com/en-us/story/finastra-fusion-fabric-cloud-azure
[157] https://azure.microsoft.com/en-us/services/container-instances/
[158] https://azure.microsoft.com/en-us/services/container-registry/

You have the option to publish your application as code or as a container. Azure supports both Windows and Linux containers as shown in **Figure 3-7**.

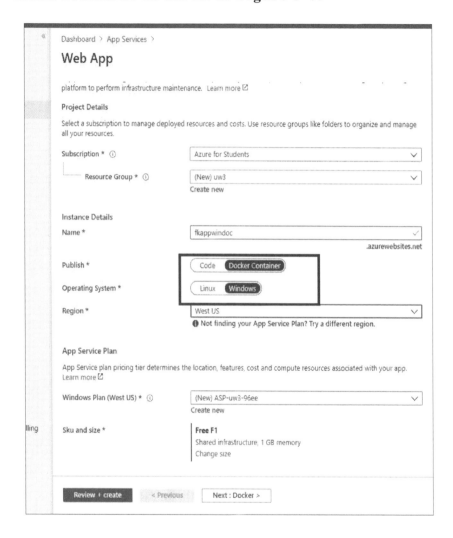

Figure 3-7: Publishing an app as code or a container.

Azure container tools

Azure provides and support various tools used by cloud administrators and developers for managing and maintaining the various container services provided by Azure. Key tools supported include Azure portal, Azure CLI, Visual Studio, Visual Studio Code and Kubectl. Azure portal and Azure CLI are standard tools provided by Microsoft Azure to create and manage various Azure Cloud services including Azure container services. They can be used to create and manage Azure Kubernetes Service, Azure Container Registry, and Azure Container Instances. IDE tools such as Visual Studio and Visual Studio Code are used by developers to create applications and manage them in containers both locally and in the cloud. Kubectl is a CLI tool used to manage and maintain the Kubernetes service which is accessible via the Kubernetes API. See **Figure 3-8**

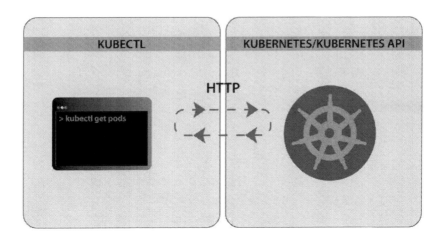

Figure 3-8

AZURE HYBRID CLOUD SERVICES

The concept of hybrid cloud was introduced in chapter 2 of this book and refers to connecting on-premises networks, private cloud, and public cloud together. This scenario usually applies to mid to large enterprises which already have a large data center and infrastructure footprint and are interested in connecting these on-premises data centers to the public cloud to reap the benefits of both their local and public cloud infrastructure and services.

Azure is tied in first place with AWS in public cloud adoption by the large organizations with these enterprise customers running signification workloads, running some workloads, experimenting, or planning to use the public cloud.

Industry Statistics

92%

of the enterprise respondents are using Microsoft Azure according to the Flexera State of the Cloud 2021 report[159].

Hybrid solutions from Azure are available across six different domains of IT, thus providing a complete portfolio of services and solutions to build, manage, and maintain your hybrid environment. In the following sections we will review these domains (Apps, Management, Data, Networking, Identity, and Security) and the set of services provided by Microsoft Azure to help you with enabling hybrid cloud scenarios.

Apps

Azure Stack, Visual Studio, Visual Studio Code and Azure DevOps are examples of services and solutions which will help you in this IT domain. Using these solutions and tools, you can maintain a consistent environment of creating and deploying applications across the on-premises infrastructure, private cloud, or the public cloud.

Azure Stack[160] offers **Azure Stack Hub**, **Azure Stack HCI** (Hyper Converged Infrastructure) and **Azure Stack Edge**. **Azure Stack Hub** is a hardware-based solution via Original Equipment Manufacturers (OEM) – Dell, HPE,

---

[159] https://info.flexera.com/CM-REPORT-State-of-the-Cloud
[160] https://azure.microsoft.com/en-us/overview/azure-stack/

Lenovo, Cisco, and Fujitsu to name a few key ones. This converts the on-premises infrastructure into a private cloud where you get access to the core services, that you have access to in the public cloud, such as VM, app services and databases using the same consistent experience as the public cloud. Using Azure Stack, you can provision virtual machines and create an application platform using the Azure App Services on your private cloud to build a customized application running in your on-premises environment.

Azure Stack HCI
Azure Stack HCI utilized the on-premises infrastructure and resources to provide a virtualization host for your mobile or field personnel who would like to access the corporate network resources and virtualized applications through their devices.

Azure Stack Edge
Azure Stack Edge is a cloud appliance supplied and managed by Microsoft and is connected to the edge of an organization close to their IoT devices. It supports both connected and disconnected to the cloud scenarios. It allows you to process your IoT data on your network rather than sending it back to the cloud, run machine learning and AI models locally and gain insights with minimal latency, thus leading you to make quick decisions.

Visual studio
Visual Studio provides you with the integrated development environment (IDE) to build, deploy, and manage your applications across your private, on-premises infrastructure and the public cloud. **Azure DevOps** on the other hand provides you with development planning, collaboration, and agility in

---

shipping your development solutions. Azure DevOps includes:

- Agile planning tools
- Continuous integration/continuous deliver (CI/CD) support for any language for deployment to any environment such as the on-premises environment, private cloud, or the public cloud
- Container deployment support to Kubernetes hosts
- Free and unlimited private code repositories

Customer Story	**Haivision** is a real-time video streaming and networking solutions provider catering to certain sectors such as disaster relief, public safety, and professional sports. They use AI for to process and provide analytics and visualizations for their customers to make critical and timely decisions. They were looking for a provider to help them with their edge and remote location scenarios with limited or low bandwidth connections to the cloud. They decided to go with Azure Stack Edge to enable all their restricted bandwidth and disconnected scenarios.
	Read the entire story[161]

Management

As your infrastructure grows and you connect your on-premises data centers, private cloud, and the public cloud, it becomes important for you to manage all your spread-out resources in these different environments. It

---

[161] https://customers.microsoft.com/en-us/story/841426-haivision-azure-stack-edge

is important for an organization to have tooling and dashboards to help you to manage all these resources across your IT estate. With Azure you can manage one-premises data centers, multicloud, and edge environments.

Azure Arc

Microsoft offers Azure Arc[162] which will help your organization to manage all your resources in your IT estate across the on-premises network, private cloud, multicloud environment and the edge environment. Azure Arc will seamlessly monitor and manage resources across the hybrid cloud. Arc offers standard monitoring and management features such as logs, health events, service events, alerting for thresholds, and detecting anomalies. Azure Arc can be used along with Azure Defender and Azure Sentinel to strengthen your security for all your resources in different environments.

Customer Story	**Siemens Healthineers** is part for Siemens and offers healthcare solutions. They use Azure for their teamplay health platform to healthcare providers using devices. Utilizing Azure Arc, their teamplay platform can set governance for the healthcare devices remotely and perform near real time software updates. Thus, Azure and Azure Arc is enabling remote edge and management scenarios. Read the entire story[163]

[162] https://azure.microsoft.com/en-us/services/azure-arc/
[163] https://customers.microsoft.com/en-us/story/844606-siemens-healthineers-health-providers-azure-arc

Customer Story	Ferguson, the largest plumbing equipment wholesaler in the United States is utilizing Azure Arc to manage both its on-premises and cloud resources. They can perform automated updates, backups/restores, and remote monitoring for both their cloud and on-premises resources by using Azure Arc, thus saving IT staff valuable time, by utilizing one tool for all their distributed resources. Read the entire story[164]

Azure VMware solution

Microsoft Azure now also offers hybrid solutions for organizations who already may have a huge investment in VMWare workloads in their on-premises data centers. Microsoft Azure is fully verified by VMWare and offers services for you to move your VMware workloads from the on-premises data centers to Azure. Such migrations can also be automated via API calls and CLI.

Once migrated, you can continue to use the existing VMware tools and utilities to manage your workloads in Azure. Typical scenarios for such migration maybe lack of additional physical space in the on-premises data center to expand, additional compute power needed without a huge upfront financial investment or thinking about using the public cloud as you consider additional IT investments.

Key advantage of moving your VMware workloads to Azure is the ability for your organization to continue

[164] https://customers.microsoft.com/en-us/story/844232-ferguson-enterprises-retailers-azure-arc

your investment in VMware but reap the benefits of Microsoft Azure's hyperscale, holistic infrastructure management and enhanced security services.

Data

There are several Azure hybrid solutions available to help you with your data management and migration across the hybrid cloud. Typically, on-premises applications have had complex SQL requirements which could not be realized initially with the cloud databases such as Azure SQL Database service and required a dedicated Microsoft SQL Server. Alternatively, you could setup a SQL server on a virtual machine in the cloud to get all the SQL functionality you needed for your applications. Now with the availability of Azure SQL Managed Instance, you don't need to setup a dedicated VM to host your Microsoft SQL Servers.

Azure SQL Managed Instance is a fully managed cloud database service which provides almost **100%** parity with a fully dedicated Microsoft SQL Server. The availability of Azure SQL Managed Instance has made it easy for developers to build complex applications which may require advanced SQL capability. Azure SQL Managed Instance is a fully managed database service, so you don't have to worry about patching and keeping it up to date with the latest software and security updates. Microsoft Azure will take care of that. It also has intelligence built into it, via machine learning, to monitor and manage the databases. Machine learning constantly monitors all the database queries activity and makes recommendations on fine tuning your databases for optimal performance. Along with performance monitoring and management, it also offers rigorous security features of auditing, threat detection and vulnerability assessment.

For migration, Microsoft Azure provide various tools and utilities to help you with moving your SQL databases to the cloud. Using these tools, you can move Microsoft SQL Server databases from on-premises infrastructure to the public cloud along with migrating databases from other vendors (such as Oracle, MySQL, MongoDB *et. al*) to the Azure Cloud. Refer to the previous sections in this chapter to learn more about database migration.

For business continuity and disaster recovery plans for your data, Microsoft Azure also offers data backup and recovery services to make sure that your business and operations are not halted in case of a disaster occurring. Microsoft offers Azure Site Recovery and Azure Backup services for this scenario. These services will help you backup data both from your on-premises infrastructure to the public cloud and also back up your existing cloud data from primary region to other cloud national or international regions in case of a disaster in your primary cloud region.

As mentioned in the management section above, Azure Arc offers management capabilities for you to manage resources and infrastructure across on-premises networks, edge, and the multicloud. Along with that it now also offers a new feature called Azure Arc-enabled data services[165], under preview as of the writing of this book, which allows for data services to be setup in your on-premises data centers, Currently, Azure is supporting Azure SQL Managed Instance and Azure PostgreSQL Hyperscale.

---

[165] https://azure.microsoft.com/en-us/services/azure-arc/hybrid-data-services/

Networking

Several options are available to an organization wanting to extend their on-premises infrastructure to the public cloud. You can start from the simplest option of setting up an Azure virtual network in the cloud and then utilizing a VPN (Virtual Private Network) gateway to connect your on-premises infrastructure to create a hybrid cloud. Azure VPN gateways offer industry standard site to site security, high availability, and SLA of **99.9%**. See **Figure 3-9.**

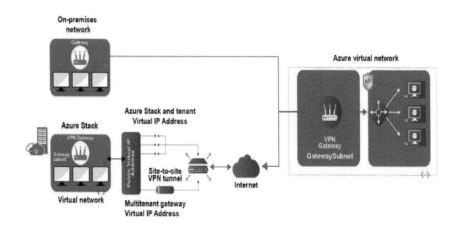

Figure 3-9

As described in the Azure IaaS cloud services section previously in this chapter, Microsoft Azure also offers Azure ExpressRoute[166] to offer a private connection from your on-premises network directly to the Azure Cloud. These private connections offer increased reliability and speed and bandwidth up to 100Gps. See **Figure 3-10.** Such connections may be required if you have business

---

[166] https://azure.microsoft.com/en-us/services/expressroute/

critical IT resources which are split between the on-premises infrastructure and the public cloud.

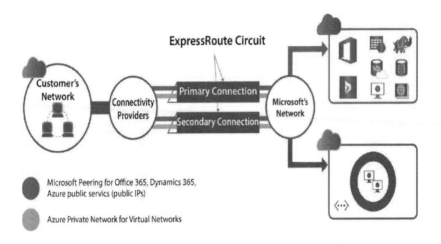

Figure 3-10

Customer Story	**Smithfield Foods** uses Microsoft technologies and Azure Cloud services for its internal operations and for its hybrid cloud. They are using Azure ExpressRoute and Equinix to connect their major global office locations privately to the cloud gaining high performance network connection speeds while maintaining a secure connection to the cloud. Read the entire story[167]

---

[167] https://customers.microsoft.com/en-us/story/smithfield-azure-us-en

Customer Story	**City of Hope** is a research and medical treatment organization looking to find the cure and treatment for cancer, diabetes, and other serious illnesses. The researchers and scientists need high speed access to resources both from the on-premises network and the Azure Cloud. City of Hope decided to use Azure ExpressRoute to connect their on-premises data centers to the cloud to meet their requirements for private, secure and a high bandwidth connection to the cloud.
	Read the entire story[168]

Another hybrid networking option to consider is Azure Virtual WAN [169]. By utilizing this option, you can connect your global branch offices to the Azure Cloud at scale. See **Figure 3-11.** This service provides the standard network security, monitoring, and policy management features.

---

[168] https://customers.microsoft.com/en-us/story/cityofhope
[169] https://azure.microsoft.com/en-us/services/virtual-wan/

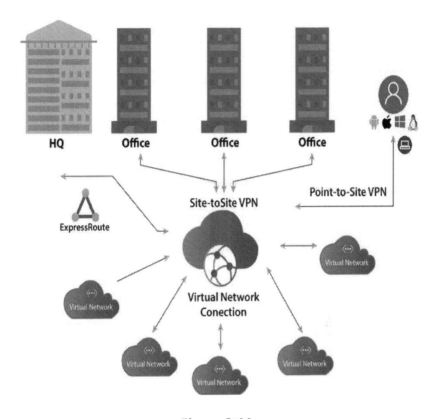

Figure 3-11

Customer Story	Sword Technologies, Switzerland has deployed Azure Virtual WAN to deploy remote locations easily in minutes with proper access controls in place. They have been able to cut down cost and complexity by using Azure Virtual WAN service.

Read the entire story[170]

---

[170] https://www.sword-technologies.ch/en/drive-customers-in-their-digital-and-technology-transformation/

Identity

Identity management is core part of any IT infrastructure and is a major consideration when connecting your on-premises infrastructure to the public cloud. Azure Active Directory (AD) is the primary identity service available from Azure and is the primary identity system for securing access to all Azure Cloud resources. It allows you to connect and keep in sync your on-premises Active Directory identity system to the cloud's Azure AD identity system to provide a single sign on experience for its users accessing resources from either the on-premises network or the Azure Cloud. Azure AD is also available to developers building on-premises and cloud applications to use it as their primary identity system. Just like any identity system, Azure AD comes bundled with robust security features including deep monitoring, threat detection, risk analysis, best practices recommendations, auditing, and reporting.

Security

Azure offers two key security solutions for your hybrid cloud environment: Azure Defender and Azure Sentinel. Azure Defender[171] can be accessed via the Azure Security Center dashboard. Azure Defender protects your multicloud, on-premises, and Edge environments. See **Figure 3-12.** It monitors and protects both Windows and Linux virtual machines against any security threats for blocking them. Virtual machines are not the only digital assets it monitors and protects. Azure Defender also examines, detects, and protects users, devices, applications, Azure storage accounts, on-premises or cloud SQL databases and servers, App services,

---

[171] https://azure.microsoft.com/en-us/services/azure-defender/

---

container images in your Azure Container Repository, and Azure Kubernetes Service instances. Defender uses Microsoft's threat intelligence along with Machine learning and AI capabilities to detect and deter any security threats along with making security recommendations. Defender brings all the security analytics into a uniform view into Azure Sentinel.

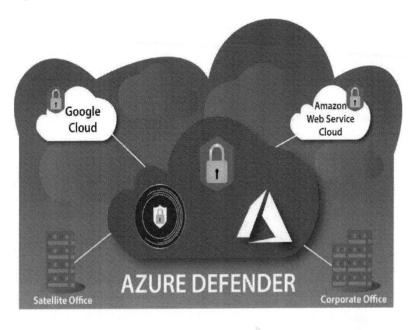

Figure 3-12

Digital and IT estate landscape is growing with organizations now in a multicloud environment with on-premises infrastructure, private cloud and connecting to multiple public clouds to create a hybrid multicloud. Security operations teams are challenged and overwhelmed to monitor, analyze, and protect digital assets across the various connected infrastructures. With the growing number of threats across the digital estate, the traditional security information and event management (**SIEM**) solution cannot be used to efficiently manage and respond to threats across your security landscape. A typical SIEM solution aggregates and analyzes activity from many different resources across your entire IT infrastructure. They are costly, slow to scale and generate too many alerts to be effectively used by your IT security operations teams. This is where Azure Sentinel[172] comes into play and is a premium and a modern security information and event management (SIEM) solution collecting and analyzing data from various public clouds (AWS and Google Cloud), on-premises infrastructure, edge network, and remote branch offices. See **Figure 3-13.** Sentinel is powered by Microsoft's threat intelligence and AI and analyzes trillions of signals to provide immediate detection, security insights and recommendations for your security teams to respond.

Figure 3-13

---

[172] https://azure.microsoft.com/en-us/services/azure-sentinel/

| Customer Story | **First West Credit Union,** based out of Langley, British Columbia Canada has around 50 branches in British Columbia. Before the merger in 2010 they were using a different SIEM solution. After the merger they settled on Microsoft 365 internally and decided to shut down a few of their data centers in favor of using the cloud. They were looking for a SIEM solution that would help them consolidate and manage both their on-premises and cloud security activity into one view. They decided on Azure Sentinel and were able to feed **80%** of their logs into it versus taking 18 months to do the same for their previous SIEM system.

Read the entire story[173] |

---

[173] https://customers.microsoft.com/en-us/story/790006-first-west-credit-union-banking-and-capital-markets-azure-sentinel

SUMMARY

This chapter reviewed and discussed the key cloud services provided by Microsoft Azure from the IaaS, PaaS and DBaaS service models. Along with that we also reviewed the key technologies in the cloud which are evolving cloud computing landscape including serverless computing and containers.

We explored the common scenarios, benefits and challenges of hybrid cloud computing and what Microsoft Azure has to offer for hybrid services for the core IT domains:

- Apps
- Data
- Management
- Security
- Identity
- Networking

In the next chapter, we will start exploring the emerging technologies starting with machine learning (ML). We will learn the basics of machine learning and related technologies including artificial intelligence (AI) and deep learning. Common business use cases will be reviewed along with services and tools offered by Microsoft Azure. ML and AI is at the core of majority of business uses cases and is a key technology being utilized by many organizations now to help them successfully achieve their digital transformation goals.

CHAPTER 4:

MACHINE LEARNING

MACHINE LEARNING OVERVIEW

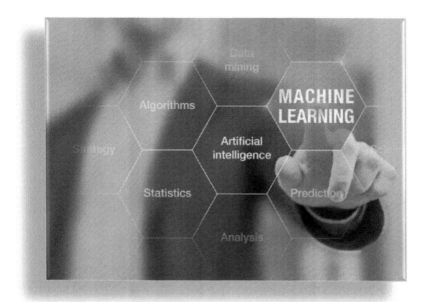

Machine learning is a field where computer systems or machines predict, forecast, suggest, or provide an answer to a question or an input you have about a particular topic. All this, without being explicitly programmed to answer in a certain way.

So how do computer systems do this? Simplistically speaking, these machines have already been trained and tested on some data by the person or organization who created them. They continuously learn and become more "intelligent" and accurate in predicting, forecasting, or giving an answer.

At the core of each machine learning system is an algorithm that decides how to respond to any input received. These algorithms are based on complex formulas from the specialized fields of mathematics and statistics. That is why many data scientists who typically work with machine learning algorithms have experience with calculus, linear algebra, probability, and statistical inference. The function of the algorithm is to work on the data provided to it, using mathematical and statistical formulas, and output an answer within an acceptable range of accuracy.

When building a machine learning system, the algorithm is provided with clean and prepared data to train it. In turn, this allows it to understand similar kinds of input data once it is fully ready to be implemented into production. Once a machine learning system, with an algorithm in it, has been trained and ready to answer, predict, or forecast, it is referred to as a machine learning model. Most AI systems and applications have these machine learning models as a core component of the overall AI functionality.

Industry Statistics

42%

Projected Compound Annual Growth Rate (CAGR) of global Machine learning market from 2018 to 2024. It will be worth $30.7B by 2024 according to a research report[174].

If you have used LinkedIn's built-in chat application to connect with others in your professional network, you have already used a machine learning model. The chat application in LinkedIn provides suggestions to you on possible responses you can give back to the person

---

[174] https://www.marketresearchfuture.com/reports/machine-learning-market-2494

chatting with you. The chat application uses a machine learning model in the background, which has been trained on typical responses to common questions, comments, and statements people make when chatting. It makes predictive text suggestions as you chat with others within your network.

Why is it important?

Machine learning technology is becoming increasingly essential for organizations and for good reason. One of the most significant benefits that businesses can reap from machine learning is automating many typical manual labor tasks. An organization's customer expectations, operational efficiency gains, and cost savings are the primary reasons for machine learning-based automation. Along with the business reasons to move to digital automation, COVID-19 has also accelerated the need for efficient automated tasks. During the pandemic, we have moved away from face-to-face customer interactions to online solutions to the customers due to social distancing restrictions. The business use cases section later in this chapter will discuss other business scenarios where machine learning has proven effective.

Expert Opinion	"I hate the word automation as it sets a high bar on people's expectations that results can be fully automated and human less. While that's more possible when we use technology to script manual business processes with tools like RPAs, CI/CD, and Infrastructure as Code, the real promise for machine learning and artificial intelligence is when it's used to augment and enhance customer and employee experiences."

Isaac Sacolick[175], President of StarCIO[176], and author of Driving Digital[177]

Many automated projects in an organization end up using some AI system with a machine learning model in the backend. For example, you may decide to use a chatbot on your company's website instead of having a live person answer current and prospective customers' questions. These chatbots have machine learning models trained on typical questions that customers ask about your products and services. Such automated experiences are now part of customer expectations and can be part of your digital transformation for all your online channels.

---

[175] https://www.starcio.com/isaac-sacolick
[176] https://www.starcio.com/
[177] http://driving-digital.com/purchase

Industry Statistics

$28.5B

Investment in machine learning applications in the first calendar quarter of 2019, leading all other AI investment categories according to a Statista report[178]. Such large spending will continue beyond 2020 for the next couple of years.

Who plays a role?

Most machine learning projects within an organization are initiated because of digital transformation strategy from the top senior leadership. Typical reasons for machine learning-based projects are customer experience improvements, costs savings, operational efficiency, and potential revenue growth. An IT unit in an organization may take the lead in experimenting with various machine learning technologies, tools, and services. At a senior leadership level, a Chief Information Officer (CIO) or a Chief Data Officer (CDO) will be overseeing and managing the teams with machine learning expertise.

When it comes to building, deploying, and maintaining machine learning systems, there can be several roles that can exist within an organization. The three key ones are a data scientist, a machine learning engineer, and a business intelligence (BI) analyst. In larger organizations, these are typically distinct roles, whereas in a small or a mid-sized organization, the same person may take on all the responsibilities that come with each of the three roles.

---

[178] https://www.statista.com/chart/17966/worldwide-artificial-intelligence-funding/

As mentioned before, machine learning requires mathematics and statistics knowledge for working with and tweaking machine learning algorithms that can accurately predict, forecast, or suggest an answer to any input. People with such knowledge and who work with machine learning algorithms and models are referred to as the data scientists. Typically, they have a master's or a Ph.D. degree in a quantitative and technical discipline. Along with a mathematics and statistics background, they tend to have refined coding skills in machine learning development languages such as Python or R. Data scientists are responsible for understanding the organization's products and services through data lens. They work closely with the business stakeholders to understand the business requirements for automation or forecasting for the machine learning model they will build. Their responsibilities include data analysis, data cleaning, algorithm selection, algorithm fine-tuning, building a training model, and testing the training model against different data sets.

Once the machine learning model is trained, the data scientist will typically work with a machine learning engineer. A machine learning engineer has a firm grasp of machine learning algorithms and models and is highly skilled in software engineering with knowledge of languages such as Python, R, C++, Java, or Scala. They assist the data scientist with the deployment, configuration, management, and maintenance of the model in the AI applications and products within the organization. They utilize their DevOps process knowledge to manage the machine learning lifecycle from implementation to maintenance.

The BI analyst role is responsible for identifying business trends, visualizing them, and communicating to all the stakeholders involved. This role will typically build dashboards and reports to communicate the business results before or after any ML or AI system is used by an organization or by its customers. Thus, a BI analyst is critical in helping with highlighting the Return on Investment (ROI) that any machine learning system will bring into an organization.

As far as the consumers of machine learning systems is concerned, such systems will either be used internally by employees or the organization's external customers, depending on where the system is deployed and its targeted users.

How to go about it?

Before you dive into the details of the tools and technologies needed for machine learning, you should carefully evaluate the business impact of using machine learning. It is recommended that larger organizations work across the different units in the company to form a steering committee. This committee can then be on point for each unit to identify the business requirements that are potential candidates for automation and prediction systems via machine learning. This steering committee will have a set of business vision driven criteria which will be used to assess all the requests from various units in the organization. Typical criteria factors are highest impact on revenue and profit growth, improvement in customer or employee experiences, providing a competitive edge, or enhancing operational efficiencies.

Industry Statistics

69%

of IT leaders saying that ML and AI is transforming their business according to the Enterprise Technology Trends, Salesforce Research report[179].

It is always wise to start small and go through an experimentation and innovation phase before deciding to build and deploy a machine learning system at scale. The IT unit with technical skills can help with this phase by providing technical assistance in identifying tools and services, technical implementation, and maintaining the experimental systems. A crucial part of this experimentation exercise is to show the possible ROI if your experimentation were to be converted into a full-fledge production system. You can also, at this time, extrapolate the potential ROI from a production system. With this ROI intelligence in hand, you can be ready to move forward with a machine learning system at scale. Next steps would be securing a budget, hiring the right talent, and deciding on the proper set of tools and technologies.

As you start your machine learning journey within your organization, it is imperative to have your machine learning lifecycle management framework defined. Machine learning lifecycle management is referred to as Machine Learning Operations (MLOps). MLOps is analogous to a DevOps framework and what the traditional developers use for their Application Lifecycle Management (ALM). As mentioned previously, data

---

[179] https://www.salesforce.com/research/market/

scientists focus on business analysis, data preparation, and training a machine learning model with complex under-the-hood mathematics and statistics algorithms. Compared to this, a machine learning engineer concentrates on MLOps, which concerns the deployment, optimization, maintenance, and management of machine learning models.

Several machine learning tools, and services vendors are available to help you with machine learning development, implementation, and lifecycle management.

All top cloud providers, including Microsoft, Amazon, and Google, provide practical tools and services to build a holistic machine learning system. Amazon offers AWS SageMaker[180] while Google has its Google Cloud AI Platform[181]. If you decide not to go with the cloud provider's ML tools, there are many other vendors who offer ML tools, including Algorithmia, Domino Data Lab, HPE Ezmeral ML Ops, Metaflow, MLflow, Paperspace, and Seldon. Later in this chapter, in the Azure Machine Learning section, we discuss various tools and services available[182] from the Microsoft Azure Cloud, which help build, manage, and maintain machine learning models.

Understanding the differences: ML, AI, deep learning, and data science

Before we get deeper into understanding machine learning, we need to understand various other interrelated topics. This section will explore machine

---

[180] https://aws.amazon.com/sagemaker/
[181] https://cloud.google.com/ai-platform/
[182] https://azure.microsoft.com/en-us/services/machine-learning/

learning, artificial intelligence, deep learning, neural networks, and data science and how they are related to each other, discussing their similarities and differences.

Artificial intelligence (AI) is a science that studies how to build intelligent systems and machines that can simulate human behavior and creatively solve problems as humans do. Amazon's Echo, Apple's Siri, or Google Assistant are all examples of AI-based systems.

Machine learning (ML) is a subset of AI and provides systems the ability to learn and then forecast or predict without being explicitly programmed to do so. Machine learning systems use various mathematical and statistical algorithms to help them forecast and predict. Examples include Amazon's product recommendation system, Google's search algorithms, and LinkedIn's suggested replies in their in-app messaging system.

Deep learning is a subset of machine learning, which uses artificial neural networks, inspired by the human brain's neural system, to analyze information and make decisions. Deep learning systems use a set of algorithms referred to as neural networks. Computer vision systems that recognize images, speech recognition systems, natural language processing, robots, and autonomous self-driving cars are examples of deep learning.

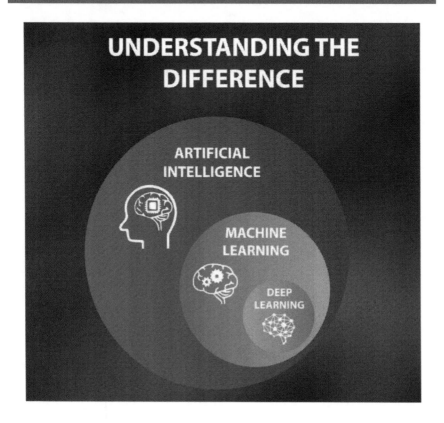

Figure 4-1

Algorithms

An algorithm is a core part of a machine learning model based on mathematical and statistical formulas. Its function is to work on the data provided to it, using the mathematical and statistical formulas, and output an answer or prediction within an acceptable range. The data scientist's job is to fine-tune and tweak these algorithms to provide the expected output when data is inputted into a machine learning model.

Customer Story	**TalentCloud,** a startup in China used Azure Machine Learning and Internet of Things (IoT) to help farm owners to setup sustainable practices that could scale to thousands of hectares of land. Using Azure Machine Learning the company's data scientists cut down the model debugging time by almost **65%**. Read the entire story[183]

The whole premise of a machine learning system is that it learns and becomes "intelligent" as more data is fed into it. There are four major types of learning styles used by machine learning algorithms: supervised learning, semi-supervised learning, unsupervised learning, and reinforcement learning.

Under each of these learning styles, the algorithms perform specific tasks such as **classification**, **regression**, **clustering**, **anomaly detection**, and **association**. For each of these tasks, various algorithms are used in a machine learning model. See **Figure 4-2**. Once you have identified the task you want to perform on your data, you will need to decide on the relevant algorithm for the learning style.

---

[183] https://customers.microsoft.com/en-us/story/811327-talentcloud-partner-professional-services-azure

---

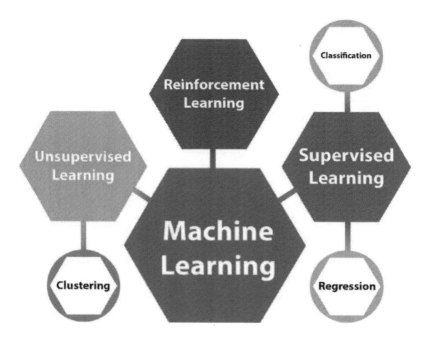

Figure 4-2

Algorithm selection considerations

A few key factors need to be considered when selecting an algorithm for your task and the machine learning model. These include **accuracy**, **training time**, **linearity**, number of **parameters**, and number of **features**.

Accuracy is how closely a model can predict the outcome compared to the actual outcome. Accurate models require large training data sets and more time to train to ensure that the final model produces very accurate results when deployed in production.

Training time is the time required to train a model to predict the outcome accurately. The model's training time

depends on the infrastructure you are using to train the model, the algorithm selected to be used in the model, how much you refine the algorithm, and how many features you want to consider for the model.

Linear models are essentially an equation that describes the relationship between two entities with a constant rate of change. In mathematics, this is a straight line. Models represented by a linear equation are usually faster to train but do not have high predictive accuracy.

Parameters or **hyperparameters** are the knobs and dials that a data scientist can turn for an algorithm, or in other words, fine-tune the algorithm to build the best model. Such tweaking of the algorithm in the model will affect the training time and the model's accuracy.

Features are the variables in the data set that you want to consider for the model to predict the output. Imagine a machine learning-based hotel reservation system where the customer can decide what factors are important to them to see the best hotels based on their criteria. Typical factors for such a system typically include the hotel's location, room size, number of beds per room, view from the room, room service, restaurant service in the hotel, etc. All these factors are referred to as the "features" that a machine learning model can use to predict the output, or in this case, recommended hotels that a customer will choose. Too many features in a model will slow down the model's training time.

Supervised learning

In this machine learning style, the model learns by example. It is a learning process in which a machine learning model is trained using a data set where some of the data is well labeled – meaning some data is already tagged with the correct answer. This helps the machine learning algorithm learn from this type of data and gives it the ability to analyze any new similar data sets. For instance, you train the model with a set of dog pictures with their types and breed. Once the model has learned, we can deploy it and provide it a new dataset with unlabeled dog pictures. The model then makes predictions by correctly labeling the breed type. Thus, supervised learning is used for **classification** tasks. There are two types of classification tasks: two-class classification or multiclass classification. Two-class classification is when you categorize data for two entities (e.g., whether a tumor is benign or malignant). Multiclass classification is when you are trying to categorize more than two entities (e.g., classifying multiple breeds of dogs).

Table 4-1 shows some examples of algorithms and their key properties used for classification tasks in supervised learning.

Task	Machine Learning Type	Algorithm	Algorithm Properties
Classification	Supervised Learning	Two-class Support Vector Machine (SVM)	Under 100 features, linear model
		Two-class averaged perceptron	Fast training, linear model
		Two-class Bayes point machine	Fast training, linear model
		Two-class decision forest	Accurate, fast training
		Two-class logistic regression	Fast training, linear model
		Two-class boosted decision tree	Accurate, fast training, large memory footprint
		Two-class decision jungle	Accurate, small memory footprint
		Two-class locally deep SVM	Under 100 features
		Two-class neural network	Accurate, long training times
		Multiclass logistic regression	Fast training times, linear model
		Multiclass neural network	Accurate, long training times
		Multiclass decision forest	Accurate, fast training times
		Multiclass decision jungle	Accurate, small memory footprint
		One-vs-all multiclass	Depends on the two-class classifier

Table 4-1

Regression tasks are another commonly used form of supervised learning. Regression in machine learning refers to predicting an output value considering one or more input variables in the data set. The input variables are the features that a machine learning model considers in predicting the output value. For example, a machine learning-based system that predicts the monthly rent for an apartment considering features such as the location, the size of the apartment, number of bedrooms, essential appliances included, availability of swimming pool and gym, etc.

Table 4-2 shows some examples of algorithms and their key properties used for regression tasks in supervised learning.

Task	Machine Learning Type	Algorithm	Algorithm Properties
Regression	Supervised Learning	Ordinal regression	Data in rank ordered categories
		Poisson regression	Predicts event counts
		Fast forest quantile regression	Predicts a distribution
		Linear regression	Fast training, linear model
		Bayesian linear regression	Linear model, small data sets
		Neural network regression	Accurate, long training times
		Decision forest regression	Accurate, fast training times
		Boosted decision tree regression	Accurate, fast training times, large memory footprint

Table 4-2

Unsupervised learning

In this learning process, the machine learning model is trained using a data set where data is neither classified nor labeled and allows the algorithm to act on that information without guidance. Here, the algorithm's task is to group unsorted information according to similarities, patterns, and differences without any prior training on data. An example can be a group of customers who are from the same geographic region of the world. **Clustering** of data is a typical task performed by the unsupervised learning algorithms. K-means is an example of an unsupervised learning algorithm used in models for clustering together similar data. For example, you provide a data set of customer purchase history to the model to create clusters (groups) of customers considering their purchasing behaviors.

Semi-supervised learning

This type of machine learning process uses the combination of unsupervised learning and supervised learning methods. The data set used for this learning process consists of a small set of labeled data and a large amount of unlabeled data to train the model. The labeled data is first used to train the model, and then the model uses that knowledge to label the unlabeled data. This process is referred to as pseudo-labeling.

Anomaly detection

Anomaly detection tasks are performed by algorithms that are used in either supervised or unsupervised learning models. Anomaly detection is useful when you want to detect unusual behavior in your data. From a business use case perspective, this is when you want your machine learning model to find unusual occurrences in your data so you can take some further actions after such detection. Identifying credit card fraud, forecasting credit risk, or pinpointing faulty manufacturing equipment are all business examples that use anomaly detection. These scenarios are discussed further in the Business Use Cases section in this chapter. **Table 4-3** shows some examples of algorithms and their key properties, which may be used for anomaly detection tasks using supervised or unsupervised learning.

Task	Machine Learning Type	Algorithm	Algorithm Properties
Anomaly Detection	Supervised OR Unsupervised Learning	One class SVM	Used for datasets with less than 100 features, slow training time
		Principal Component Analysis (PCA)-based anomaly detection	Fast training times
		K-Means	Reasonably fast training times

Table 4-3

Reinforcement learning

This machine learning method is like how humans learn, where constant supervision is not required. This type of learning considers deep learning systems. Reinforcement learning does not need labeled data for training. It learns by trial and error, just like humans do in certain situations when they have no guidance. If the model makes a correct decision, it is rewarded and if it makes an incorrect decision, it is penalized. Thus, the model learns from previous outcomes where it may have been rewarded or penalized and then uses that information to decide on its next set of actions. Computer game systems, robot navigation, and making real-time decisions are a few examples of reinforcement learning.

This kind of learning is appropriate for AI systems that must make many small decisions without any human guidance.

Business use cases

All the hype for new emerging technologies aside, all these technologies are of no use until we can fully understand them and use them for our solving our business problems or evolving the business models. That to me is when the rubber hits the road, and we can fully reap the benefits of using the emerging technologies. They can help us create new revenue streams, stay ahead of the competitors, create a new products or services, or improve customer experiences.

Customer Story	TransLink, Vancouver. Canada's transportation system authority utilized Azure Machine Learning to improve their customer experience in accurately estimating the bus departures times. Azure machine learning services helped them improve the bus departure estimates by **74%**. Read the entire story[184]

There are several business use cases where machine learning is beneficial. In the following sections, we will review some of those to see how machine learning leverages data to provide helpful business insights. For instance, machine learning models can be used to

---

[184] https://customers.microsoft.com/en-us/story/768972-translink-travel-and-transportation-azure

forecast product and sales demand. Using algorithms from the regression family, you can predict your products and services' sales numbers or estimate your products and services' demand.

Industry Statistics	38% - Reducing company costs 37% - Generating customer insights & intelligence 34% - Improving customer experiences Three most popular ML use cases according to the Algorithmia report[185].

Anomaly detection

You can apply the anomaly detection family of machine learning algorithms to multiple business scenarios. Anomaly detection refers to unusual occurrences in the data you are collecting from various aspects of your business. In financial sector, anomaly detection algorithms from machine learning can help you predict credit risk if you are processing and providing personal and business loans. For organizations providing credit cards and related services to consumers, you can utilize machine learning to detect fraud and stop any credit card transactions before they become a liability for your organization. Many banks and financial institutions already use machine learning to harness this scenario of preventing fraudulent credit card transactions.

---

[185] https://info.algorithmia.com/hubfs/2019/Whitepapers/The-State-of-Enterprise-ML-2020/Algorithmia_2020_State_of_Enterprise_ML.pdf?hsLang=en-us

In the manufacturing and industrial sector, anomaly detection via machine learning can help you find any abnormal readings from your monitored equipment or devices. Any unusual data from these devices can be an indication of some potential issue with the equipment. You can proactively service this equipment before it becomes a bigger problem, leading to cost savings from this equipment permanently going bad. On the other hand, it also improves customer service since you proactively fixed the issue without any downtime for your customers. This is one of the key business scenarios when using Internet of Things (IoT) technology in the manufacturing and industrial sectors. A detailed discussion on IoT will follow in chapter 6.

Grouping data

Using machine learning, you can analyze collected business data by grouping. Grouping of data can help you understand your customers, products, and services at a deeper level. Using the clustering algorithm, you can segment your customers, predict their preferences for your products and services, or figure out which one of your product offerings lacks in demand and potential profitability. Many e-commerce sites use customer preference predictions via machine learning to offer their customers recommendations on additional products they can buy, considering the products they currently are about to purchase or have previously purchased. Amazon is a prime example of this scenario where it makes recommendations on other related products that you can buy along with the current products in your shopping cart. Such simple use of machine learning has the potential for revenue growth for your organization.

Classifying data

When you must choose between two categories, such as answering a yes/no question or a true/false question, this is where machine learning can help by using the two-class classification family of algorithms. As an example, if you use social media channels to promote your products and services, you may be interested in understanding your customers' positive sentiments across relevant social media posts. You can use machine learning with two-class classification algorithms to see if relevant social media posts have a positive sentiment or not (sentiment analysis). Another scenario where the two-class classification machine learning model will be useful is if you are about to offer a new product to your current customers and are interested in knowing whether the customers will like the product. Similarly, you can use this model when you are offering two promotions for your product and want to know which one will be more successful with your current customers.

What if your business scenario has more than two categories to consider? Can machine learning still help you? Yes, of course, it can. You would need to use the multiclass classification family of algorithms to help you find the answer to your business question. It is not much different from two-classification, as you have more categories (classes) to predict. Consider the examples mentioned earlier. You can predict customer sentiment on social media to see if it was positive, negative, or neutral. For product promotion scenarios, you can offer more than just two promotions and figure out which one will be more successful with your customers. Another scenario where you may find the multiclass classification machine learning model useful is when you offer your product through various channels such as via retail outlet, online store, or a partner and wanted to understand which had the highest potential for revenue growth. As you can imagine, the opportunities here are countless when answering the many business questions that you previously either had to guess or took too long to figure out the answer.

Customer Story	**Carhartt** is a manufacturer of rugged workwear. They were looking to open new retail locations in 2019. They turned to Azure Machine Learning to help them make that decision. Using models built and trained by Azure ML, they decided on opening three locations. These new stores outperformed all other stores and have exceeded expected revenue by almost **200%** along with being ranked the best sores in their respective districts. Read the entire story[186]

Machine learning development languages

Several languages can be used for machine learning development, including Python, R, Java, C++, JavaScript, and Scala. Python and R are the two most popular languages in the machine learning domain. Both are open-source languages with a vast developer community following. Python is more of a general data science language, whereas R is mostly for deep statistical computation needs. For developers starting in machine learning, Python is the obvious choice with a strong community, plenty of books, resources, and online

---

[186] https://customers.microsoft.com/en-us/story/816179-carhartt-retailers-azure

courses available through many commercial and non-commercial channels, including Udemy, Coursera, and LinkedIn. Many colleges and universities are also offering these Python courses through their regular undergraduate curriculum or via continuing education programs.

Microsoft offers free Python learning modules[187] for a beginner, intermediate and advanced users through its Microsoft Learn portal. Tiobe, a company that measures the popularity of different development languages in the industry through its TIOBE index[188], currently ranks Python as the third most popular language above C++ and behind C and Java. Tiobe also ranked Python as their choice for the programming language of 2020. In the academic sector, Python is the language of choice for students, learners, and educators learning or working with machine learning. GitHub Education, which works with educators and students, published their latest Classroom Report 2020[189] and ranked Python as the most used language.

The availability of many libraries and frameworks and an ever-growing community has made Python the language of choice for machine learning engineers and data scientists. Data scientists who spend a lot more time working with machine learning algorithms may prefer R because of its statistical computation and visualization capabilities. Later in this chapter, we will discuss the Azure Machine Learning service and how it supports both Python and R when utilizing Azure Machine Learning Studio. See **Table 4-4** for comparison between Python and R programming languages.

---

[187] https://docs.microsoft.com/en-us/learn/browse/?terms=python
[188] https://www.tiobe.com/tiobe-index/
[189] https://education.github.com/classroom-report/2020

Criteria	Python	R
Who uses it?	Data Scientists, Machine Learning Engineers, General Developers	Primarily Data Scientists and Machine Learning Researchers, with a few machine learning Engineers
Primary Use	Used for general Data Science and is a general-purpose language	Utilized for statistical computations, analysis, and visualization
Learning curve	Easy to learn and start using with a very simple and intuitive syntax	Difficult with a sharp learning curve
Availability of resources	Many online resources available to get started and learn	Limited resources available to get started and learn
Popularity	Highly popular with Machine Learning Engineers and enthusiasts	Popular with Data Scientists
Community	Large community to get help and engage in deep discussions	Comparatively smaller community
Availability of Libraries and Frameworks	Large collection of libraries to develop many common applications	Large collection of libraries for statistical analysis and visualizations
Popular IDE available	Jupyter Notebooks,	Jupyter Notebooks and RStudio

	Spyder, and PyCharm	
Performance	Fast and rapidly performs many data science tasks	Relatively slow compared to Python
Availability of expertise	Many more developers available in the market	Fewer developers available

Table 4-4

Machine learning frameworks and standards

Machine learning frameworks are a set of libraries, tools, and an interface that a developer can use to build and deploy machine learning models quickly and easily without the need to understand the underlying algorithms' low-level details. Some of these frameworks' key features include ease of use, transparency, optimized performance, and parallelization for distributed computational processes. Hence, these frameworks help in the democratization of machine learning for developers. Some of the popular frameworks are TensorFlow, PyTorch, Scikit-Learn, Gluon, Caffe2, ML.NET, and Microsoft Cognitive Toolkit. Several technical organizations have also partnered to release an open-source standard called Open Neural Network Exchange (ONNX), to bring all the frameworks together for building and training deep learning and traditional machine learning models.

Machine learning frameworks are very popular with developers, and it is worthwhile looking at some of these a bit closer to understand what they offer.

TensorFlow is an open-source framework and library, initially developed by Google, for numerical computation and to build production neural network models and algorithms. It provides Python front-end API access for building production machine learning models with enhanced performance.

PyTorch is an open-source library created by Facebook's AI lab. It is a framework used in building and training extensive and complicated deep learning models utilizing Python. PyTorch boosts GPU usage to enhance the performance of deep learning and regular machine learning models. It is competing with TensorFlow for the framework of choice for building complex deep neural network machine learning models.

Scikit-Learn is a ubiquitous framework used by many developers and students starting to learn about and build their preliminary machine learning models. It is easy to understand, use and helps the learner grasp the basic concepts of machine learning including building, training, and deploying models. This framework is an open-source library for Python, and it is built on other libraries such as NumPy, SciPy, and Matplotlib. The Scikit-Learn framework supports both supervised and unsupervised machine learning algorithms.

ML.NET
Microsoft created this open-source, cross-platform machine learning framework for the .NET developer platform. It runs on Linux, MacOS, and Windows. Using #C and #F, developers with no prior machine learning experience can train, build, and deploy customized

machine learning models. It also offers AutoML, which automatically selects machine learning algorithms and their respective hyperparameters to create highly accurate models for a given business scenario. ML.NET can also use and work with other popular and standard machine learning libraries and frameworks such as TensorFlow, Infer.NET, and ONNX.

To bring all these popular machine learning frameworks together, we have **ONNX** as mentioned earlier. ONNX is an open-source open format standard that allows for framework interoperability. It was developed as a collaboration between Microsoft, Facebook, and AWS. ONNX allows for various machine learning models to be built using existing machine learning frameworks (such as TensorFlow, PyTorch, Scikit-Learn, Caffe, etc.).

These models are then deployed to various hardware targets, including CPU, GPU, Field Programmable Gate Array (FPGA), and Neural Processing Unit (NPU). See **Figure 4-3**. An FPGA is a customizable hardware device controlled by a hardware description language (HDL), such as Verilog or VHDL. An NPU is a specialized microprocessor that specializes in the acceleration of machine learning algorithms. ONNX is used to deploy machine learning models to IoT and edge devices to reduce the latency from running the same models in the cloud.

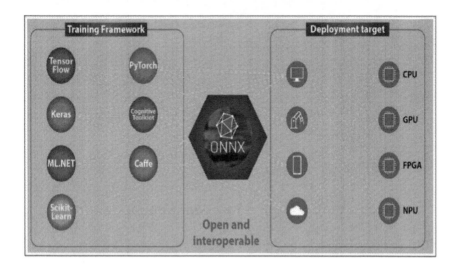

Figure 4-3

As an example, machine learning models can first be built utilizing any open-source frameworks, then ingested into a model registry, and finally packaged into a container. The containers are hardware-specific, and ONNX runtime from Azure then deploys them to different kinds of edge devices where each device can either be using a CPU, GPU, FPGA, or NPU for the needed ML model compute.

Machine learning tools

Large tech companies, such as Microsoft, Amazon, Google, and IBM, provide a low barrier to entry into the machine learning field with a whole set of tools and services to commoditize machine learning and AI.

Industry Statistics

5,538

Active machine learning and artificial intelligence patent families owned worldwide by IBM to be ranked #1 as of November, 2020 with Samsung and Microsoft following at number two and three respectively according to a Statista report[190].

For beginners with zero development experience interested in learning the basics of machine learning technology and wanting to build basic machine models without a more profound knowledge of the algorithms, Azure offers the designer authoring tool in the Azure Machine Learning portal[191]. The designer authoring tool is discussed later in this chapter.

For an experienced developer, you can use any of your integrated development environments (IDEs), like Visual Studio or Visual Studio Code with R and Python support, locally on your device to build and run your machine learning models and experiments. Then, deploy them to the cloud as services to be used by any AI applications you might be building.

Alternatively, advanced developers can use Azure Notebooks as an alternative to using locally installed IDE tools to write code to build, train, and deploy their production machine learning models. Azure Notebooks gives you the ability to use your browser to develop your

---

[190] https://www.statista.com/statistics/1032627/worldwide-machine-learning-and-ai-patent-owners-trend/
[191] https://ml.azure.com/

models — more about Azure Notebooks later in this chapter.

All cloud providers offer various machine learning tools and services for their users. Amazon has <u>AWS SageMaker</u>[192], and Google Cloud provides machine learning and AI services and tools through its <u>Google Cloud AI platform</u>[193]. This book will explore and discuss machine learning tools and services offered through Microsoft's Azure cloud later in this chapter.

---

[192] https://aws.amazon.com/sagemaker/
[193] https://cloud.google.com/ai-platform/

AZURE MACHINE LEARNING

In this section, we review Microsoft Azure's machine learning services and tools to understand how to build, train, and deploy machine learning models. We will discover the no-code tool - designer, learn about Azure AutoML for automatic selection and configuration of the algorithms in our models, and Azure Notebooks for creating, training, and deploying models by coding inside the browser. We also review Azure's machine learning compute infrastructure options to build, train, and deploy machine learning models. Azure Machine Learning provides a separate machine learning portal[194], other than the Azure portal, for you to create, build, train, deploy and manage your models with options to scale the models as needed.

Figure 4-4 shows a process of building, training, assessing it and then deploying a machine learning mode. Azure machine learning services has tools and services to help you end to end through all these phases.

---

[194] https://ml.azure.com/

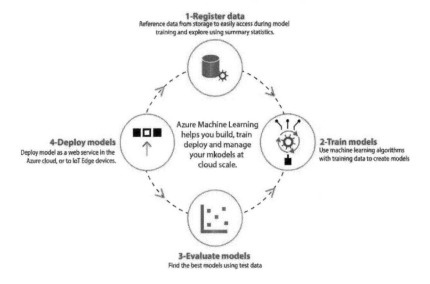

Figure 4-4

Using the Azure Machine Learning portal, you can access a machine learning studio for building and deploying your models. This portal gives you access to three different authoring tools: **Designer**, **Automated ML(AutoML)**, and **Azure Notebooks**. Using the **Assets** section of the portal, you can prepare your data, run, and monitor jobs, access your experiments, view, and deploy models, and manage the API endpoints. The **Manage** section can be used to view and manage your compute and datastore within your workspace. See **Figure 4-5**.

Figure 4-5: Azure Machine Learning portal

Azure Machine Learning portal tools

Regardless of which machine learning authoring tool you decide to use, you must first create an Azure Machine Learning workspace within the Azure portal. Other services such as Application Insights and Key Vault are made available when the workspace is created. These additional services are used as you build, train, and deploy your machine learning models.

Azure Machine Learning designer

One of the benefits of using Azure Machine Learning is that you do not need a data scientist or a developer to help you build and train a machine learning model for many of your business use cases. A power user within your organization with some experience in Azure can build, train, and deploy a model as a web API service.

Azure Machine Learning's designer authoring tool is an interactive canvas-based tool where you can drag and drop modules to build a model. Once the model is built, you can train and evaluate it and eventually deploy it as a web service endpoint as an API. Training a model can be performed on an Azure Machine Learning compute (a managed cloud-based workstation for data scientists) or an Azure Machine Learning compute instance (a managed-compute infrastructure that allows you to create a single or multi-node compute easily). Once you have evaluated a model and are ready to deploy it for production use, you would use Azure Kubernetes service as the compute target.

The designer tool has built into it all the functionality to help you build, test, and deploy your machine learning model from the ground up. Key functionalities include data splitting, data cleaning, selecting an algorithm, scoring, evaluating, or choosing the compute target for either testing or deployment production. To build a model, you simply drag and drop these specific modules onto the canvas and connect them together to create a pipeline for your model. See **Figure 4-6**. Common modules include datasets, data transformation (cleaning, splitting), algorithm, training, and scoring and evaluation.

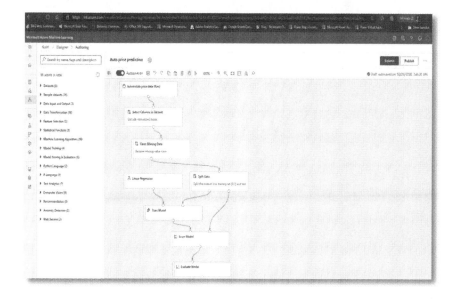

Figure 4-6: Azure Machine Learning designer tool showing a complete pipeline.

The steps required to build and deploy a machine learning model in the designer authoring tool can be summarized as follows:

- Start by using the <u>Machine Learning portal</u>[195] using the designer authoring tool.
- Create a new pipeline.
- Import data.
- Clean and prepare data.
- Select an algorithm.
- Split the data for training and production model.
- Train a machine learning model.
- Score the model.
- Evaluate a machine learning model.

---

[195] <u>https://ml.azure.com/</u>

- Deploy the model as a service with a real-time endpoint.
- Test the real-time endpoint.

Once you have deployed your model as a web service with an API endpoint, you can build a customized AI application to use the endpoint.

Automated ML in Azure Machine Learning

Automated machine learning, also known as AutoML or automated ML, is where you have the system do the work on creating the best model using the best algorithm that gives the desired results. It is different from using the Azure designer authoring tool and helps with the situation where you do not know which algorithm is the best one to use for your data set and model. As mentioned previously, when you use a designer to build and train a model, you must manually decide on the algorithm you want to use for your model. In AutoML, you do not have to determine the algorithm upfront. Still, you must decide on the overall task you wish to perform, such as classification, regression, or time series forecasting. Then, let the AutoML system do the hard job on trying various algorithms to see which one is the best to use with the given data set.

Along with deciding on which algorithm to use for your machine learning model, AutoML also has built-in algorithm hyperparameter optimization and feature engineering capabilities. Recall that machine learning algorithms can be fine-tuned by tweaking various parameters to increase, potentially, the model's predictive power. Hyperparameter tuning is typically in the data scientist's domain that requires mathematics and statistics knowledge and is somewhat hard for developers to grasp. Fortunately, AutoML performs hyperparameters tuning under the covers as it works with your supplied data set to come up with the best predictive machine learning model for you. Analogously, you can think of hyperparameters as ingredients for a recipe (algorithm) that you are trying to use to cook a dish (model). Feature engineering involves working with various features from your dataset to see which one will work the best with the model. In machine learning, features are individual measurable properties of something you're interested in predicting. Alternatively, a feature is one column in your data set. Imagine you have a dataset with data about cars, including make, model, gas mileage, color, cost, engine type, etc. Each one of these is considered a feature for your dataset. AutoML uses various combinations of algorithm hyperparameters and features to develop the best model, with the highest score, based on your success metric.

Automated ML in Azure Machine Learning supports various open-source machine learning frameworks and standards, including ONNX, TensorFlow, PyTorch, and Scikit-Learn. A developer can use Visual Studio or Visual Studio Code (with Python SDK installed), or the Automated ML authoring tool, or Azure Notebooks from the machine learning portal to build and deploy AutoML models. The easiest way to start with automated ML is to use the automated ML authoring tool with the Azure Machine Learning portal. However, you also have a choice to use Azure Notebooks or IDEs like Visual Studio Code. **Figure 4-7** shows how you can use the automated ML authoring tool to start and create a new experiment.

The following summarizes the steps required to build and deploy a machine learning model using the automated ML authoring tool:

- Start by using the Machine Learning portal[196] , and use the automated ML authoring tool.
- Import data set.
- Select and preview the data set.
- Select features and configure schema of the dataset.
- Select data set.
- Configure the AutoML run:
  o Create an experiment.
  o Select the target column/feature (This is the column you want AutoML to predict)
  o Select or create a compute cluster.
- Select task type for this experiment (Classification, Regression, or Time series forecasting)
  o Configure a few additional key settings:
    ▪ Primary metric: is the evaluation metric that the machine learning algorithm will be measured against
    ▪ Explain best model: Can be enabled or disabled. When enabled shows details and explains the model created.
    ▪ Blocked algorithms: Algorithms that should be excluded when creating the model.
    ▪ Exit Criterion: Specifies the criteria that AutoML should use to stop training the model.
- Deploy the best model identified by AutoML.

Once the model is deployed as a web API service, any AI application or system can use this API endpoint and use the model to predict the relevant values if the required data (features) are provided to the API.

---

[196] https://ml.azure.com/

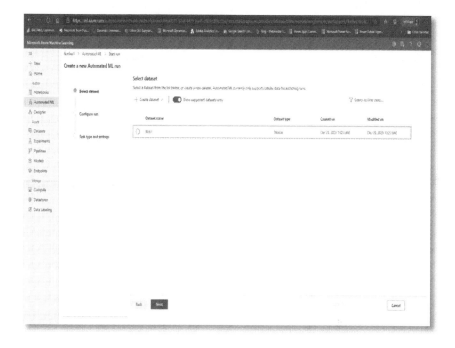

Figure 4-7: Automated ML authoring tool

There are currently three types of major tasks that an automated ML in Azure Machine Learning can perform on your dataset including classification, regression, and time series forecasting. Let's review some of the business use cases that fall under each of these task categories.

For the classification task, let's review three business use cases around fraud detection, content classification and fare prediction by using AutoML in Azure Machine Learning.

Fraud detection
An AutoML model can be built and used to detect fraudulent transactions in a data set. This use case is

typical in the financial and banking sector. It can help these organizations with substantial cost savings by catching these fraudulent credit card transactions in real-time as they occur. Many banks already use machine learning models to detect these transactions. The dataset, code, and instructions for building and testing this type of model are available on GitHub[197].

Marketing prediction

Another example of how AutoML can be used is where a marketer can use a data set to build a model to predict if a customer will sign up for new products or services from your organization. For this example, the data set is from a bank and has data on the customer's preference on setting up a term deposit with the bank. The model built from this data set can help you predict if other new customers will sign up for the term deposit. The dataset, code, and instructions for building and testing this model is available on GitHub[198].

Content classification

If you are in the business of content curation, you can use machine learning models to help you classify data from various content sources. Content sources can include web pages, blogs, social media, news, e-books, industry journals, and learning content. These sources include content for various fields and interests such as science, education, technology, engineering, etc. You can build a machine learning model to help you classify

---

[197] https://github.com/Azure/MachineLearningNotebooks/blob/master/how-to-use-azureml/automated-machine-learning/classification-credit-card-fraud/auto-ml-classification-credit-card-fraud.ipynb
[198] https://github.com/Azure/MachineLearningNotebooks/blob/master/how-to-use-azureml/automated-machine-learning/classification-bank-marketing-all-features/auto-ml-classification-bank-marketing-all-features.ipynb

and categorize all this content from various sources. Learn more about this use case from this blog[199].

For regression tasks:

Fare prediction
AutoML can be used to predict taxi fares by using a data set that already has historical information about the previous trips by customers. Historical data available includes different taxi vendors ID and specific customer information such as pickup date/time, drop-off date/time, trip distance, the amount paid, etc. Automated ML can build a machine learning model to predict taxi fares. Tutorials on building such a model with AutoML are available[200]. The dataset used for this example is from the New York City (NYC) taxis. Similar machine learning models are used in popular web services such as Uber and Lyft to calculate taxi fares.

AutoML in Azure Machine Learning can also be utilized for time-series forecasting tasks and business use cases such as sales and demand forecasting.

Sales forecasting
Sales forecasting is a big part of any organization with historical data sets interested in forecasting the sales of their products and services to its current and prospective customers. Automated ML in Azure Machine Learning can be utilized in this scenario using the times-series forecasting task to predict future forecasts. An example of this is the University of Chicago's Dominick's Finer Foods dataset used to forecast orange juice sales.

---

[199] https://towardsdatascience.com/automated-text-classification-using-machine-learning-3df4f4f9570b
[200] https://docs.microsoft.com/en-us/azure/machine-learning/tutorial-auto-train-models

---

Dominick's Finer Foods was a grocery store chain in the Chicago metropolitan area but is no longer operating. The data set, code, and instructions for building and testing this model is available on GitHub[201].

Demand forecast - 1
Demand forecasting is another significant business need of many organizations. Sometimes businesses are interested in understanding the demand for their products and services. Again, via Automated ML in Azure Machine Learning, you can carry out time-series forecasting to build a model that can forecast product demand. For example, the NYC energy demand dataset is available and can be shown to forecast the energy demand by NYC consumers in the next 48 hours. The dataset, code, and instructions for building and testing this model is available on GitHub[202].

Demand forecast - 2
Another example that highlights understanding demand forecasting using AutoML in Azure Machine Learning is the dataset for a bike-sharing service. The data set, code, and instructions for building and testing this model is available on GitHub[203].

---

[201] https://github.com/Azure/MachineLearningNotebooks/blob/master/how-to-use-azureml/automated-machine-learning/forecasting-orange-juice-sales/auto-ml-forecasting-orange-juice-sales.ipynb
[202] https://github.com/Azure/MachineLearningNotebooks/blob/master/how-to-use-azureml/automated-machine-learning/forecasting-energy-demand/auto-ml-forecasting-energy-demand.ipynb
[203] https://github.com/Azure/MachineLearningNotebooks/blob/master/how-to-use-azureml/automated-machine-learning/forecasting-bike-share/auto-ml-forecasting-bike-share.ipynb

---

Azure Notebooks

Azure Notebooks is the third tool available to you in the Azure Machine Learning Studio within the Azure Machine Learning portal. See **Figure 4-8**. It allows developers to write and run code within the browser without the need for an IDE such as Visual Studio or Visual Studio Code installed on a developer's workstation. Azure Notebooks is based on Jupyter, an open-source project that allows for both code and comments to be written in "cells" within a browser. Azure Notebooks support both Python and R for building, training, and deploying machine learning models. You can run the code created in Azure Notebooks interactively, one code snippet at a time or as an entire batch of all code lines.

Azure Notebooks is primarily for data scientists or machine learning developers who want to create custom machine learning models in Python or R, use different frameworks, and then interactively run their code to build, train and deploy their models.

There are sample notebooks available to developers and data scientists to clone from GitHub and immediately start using them to create, train, and deploy customized models. The sample notebooks contain several tutorials, AutoML samples, and various examples for different frameworks, including TensorFlow, PyTorch, Scikit-Learn, Keras, and Fast.AI. These are provided to get developers to hit the ground running in working with machine learning. There are also examples available to help developers understand the various critical phases of model development, including data handling, training, deployment, and managing the Azure Machine Learning service. These cloned notebooks are indeed a treasure for

---

any developer wanting to get started with machine learning development.

Instead of using the sample notebooks developers and data scientists can also start from scratch and create Python scripts or R programs. Currently, Azure Notebooks supports Python 3, Python 3, and R.

Azure Notebooks also give you the ability to provide the required compute infrastructure, referred to as compute instance, using virtual machines with an option to use the CPU or the GPU. These virtual machines host and run the code you create using Python or R. This compute is also available for use if you prefer to work in JupyterLab, Jupyter, or RStudio.

Azure Notebooks offer the following essential features to developers as they use Python or R to create, train and deploy their models:

- Move to focus mode for focused coding environment.
- Add code and markdown content in the cells.
- Use built-in IntelliSense support to do auto-complete of code as you write the code.
- Convert cells from code to markdown and vice versa.
- Move cells up and down as needed.
- If required, edit and work with your notebooks in Jupyter or JupyterLab.
- Run the code in the cells one at a time or all at once.
- Clear output from the code execution as needed.
- Interrupt kernel during the run to terminate the program.

Figure 4-8: Azure Notebooks

Azure machine learning compute infrastructure

Azure Machine Learning offers several options for the compute infrastructure needed by data scientists and developers to do custom development by building, training, and deploying their models.

An Azure Machine Learning **compute instance** is a managed cloud-based workstation for developers, machine learning engineers, or data scientists. Compute instances make it easy to get started with Azure Machine Learning development and are the default option when working with Azure Notebooks. They are a fully configured and managed development environment in the cloud for machine learning. They can also be used as a compute target for training and inferencing for development and testing purposes.

Customer Story	**Walgreens Boots Alliance (WBA),** a retail pharmacy chain both across the United States and Europe was looking to understand all the data it was collecting from customers as part of their two-decade old Advantage Card loyalty program. They wanted to use all the collected data to understand customer behavior and preferences. They decided that Azure Machine Learning was the best solution to accomplish this. With Azure ML's huge compute scalability offering, WBA was able to create and train models in minutes instead of days.

Read the entire story[204]

For production-grade model training, use an Azure Machine Learning **compute cluster** with multi-node scaling capabilities. It is a fully managed infrastructure that scales up as needed and can be placed in an Azure virtual network.

For production-grade machine learning model deployment, Microsoft recommends using the Azure Kubernetes Service cluster.

See **Figure 4-9** to view and access all the compute infrastructure options.

---

[204] https://customers.microsoft.com/en-us/story/733091-walgreens-boots-alliance-pharmaceuticals-azure

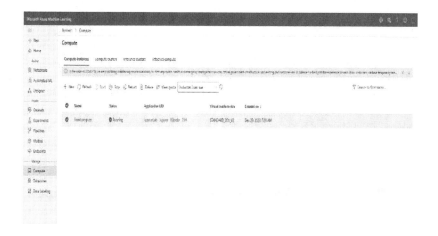

Figure 4-9: Computer Infrastructure in Azure Machine Learning portal

◆ ◆ ◆ ◆ ◆ ◆ ◆ ◆ ◆ ◆ ◆ ◆

ML CHALLENGES

There are several challenges that organizations face in using and adopting machine learning. In this section, we will review some of the common challenges for using and adopting this technology. Challenges facing organizations range from the availability of relevant and clean data sets, scalable compute infrastructure needs, lack of ML professionals, complexity of machine learning-based systems, long ML training times, ML bias and ethical issues, and lack of Machine Learning Operations(MLOps).These key factors are hindering organizations from using and adopting machine learning systems. In the following sections, we review these factors in detail.

Availability of data

The whole premise behind machine learning is about providing historical data about the entity you are trying to find answers on or predict. The entity can be anything related to your organization, such as your product, service, or customer experience, as examples. One of the most significant issues with adopting and using machine learning is that such historical data may not exist in an organization or might be in a format that cannot be directly ingested into a machine learning model. Suppose your organization falls in the latter category where the data exists but is not in a format to be consumed by the machine learning model. In that case, you will first have to spend time preparing and processing the data to get it ready for consumption by a machine learning system.

While several public data sets are available for various business scenarios and industry verticals and can be used to get a machine learning proof of concept going, they should not be used for enabling your specific scenarios in your production machine learning systems. Kaggle[205] and UCI[206] are two very popular sites for you to get started with machine learning with publicly data sets on these sites. Your business scenario should use its own business-generated data, with all its own nuances, so that you can build a machine learning model specifically for your organization with representative data powering its backend.

Compute infrastructure requirements

Building and training a machine learning model requires dedicated infrastructure and compute resources. If you are interested in training multiple models, it will require compute-intensive and dedicated infrastructure for a longer time. If you a startup or a small organization, just starting to experiment with machine learning, you may

---

[205] https://www.kaggle.com/datasets
[206] https://archive.ics.uci.edu/ml/datasets.php

---

not have the luxury of having this dedicated infrastructure available for your team to create or train the models. Larger enterprises can temporarily dedicate part of their infrastructure for initial machine learning innovation and experimentation. However, they will eventually have to carve out a dedicated budget to set up and sustain such infrastructure for the long run for their production machine learning system.

Another consideration for the long-term adoption and use of machine learning systems is its ability to scale, as your compute requirements fluctuate for your machine learning model. Imagine a machine learning model behind your e-commerce site, making product recommendations to the customers considering the current items they have in their shopping cart. The load and usage of your e-commerce site during the holiday season will be high. Correspondingly you would like to make sure that the machine learning model powering this site can also keep up with the site's load and make recommendations to the customers in real-time during their purchase process.

Shortage of talent

Data scientists with machine learning expertise, as expected, are in high demand. Data scientists are also required to have some software development experience in Python, R, or any other machine learning language of choice. A data scientist with balanced experience in machine learning algorithms and software development would be a catch for any organization.

Along with a data scientist, a machine learning software developer is also required for an ML team. A machine learning developer is knowledgeable in multiple machine learning languages, experienced in DevOps processes to manage and maintain machine learning code along with knowledge of computational infrastructure and operations.

As with any nascent and emerging technology, machine learning also suffers from talent shortage. However, we have come a long way from the days where machine learning practitioners were being offered salaries ranging from $300K to $1M or more. Key AI and ML leadership roles have even heftier compensations that can go past the seven-figure mark. A case in point is Anthony Levandowski, who started with Google in 2007 and quit Google to join Uber and took home $120M in compensation. A rigorous understanding of machine learning algorithms requires in-depth knowledge of mathematics and statistics, a domain for the Ph.D. and graduate-level students concentrating in these specific areas. Most of the larger enterprises working on building machine learning tools, models, and systems will go out of their way to hire these fresh, out-of-college students to work in their research and development teams to build the next generation of machine learning servicers and tools.

Companies like Google, Microsoft, Amazon, and Facebook are some of the big names that have snatched these fresh graduate students from college campuses to build machine learning systems. High demand and lack of supply for these Ph.D. holding experts have led to higher-than-expected salaries. Most of the skills for understanding and managing simple algorithms can be self-learned via online courses or college programs. Expert knowledge to fully understand and tweak algorithms in the machine learning models still requires concentrated mathematics and statistics expertise.

Smaller organizations can start with experimenting and using machine learning with a machine learning developer with some knowledge of data science. Most of the ML developers in the current market have this is skillset and can help small companies get started into the ML field. Mid-sized organizations may consider hiring a data scientist along with a machine learning developer to form a ML team and not hiring additional operational staff.

Larger organizations may, however, hire for multiple roles for their machine learning or AI teams. Their machine learning teams include a dedicated data scientist(s) with deep experience in algorithms, machine learning software developer(s) with expertise in machine learning languages and DevOps processes along with IT operations personnel to help with the machine learning infrastructure and operations.

Complexity

As evidenced from the shortage of talent machine learning is a very specialized field requiring deep mathematics and statistics knowledge. Many large tech companies such as Microsoft are trying to unravel and simplify this field with easy-to-use tools and services such Azure Machine Learning designer and automated ML. It, however, still stays a very complex field requiring expert knowledge. Large technical organizations are working hard to democratize machine learning and building tools and services to simplify this technology for developers and business power users to utilize their current skills, with a minimal learning curve, to build and deploy machine learning models. The nascent nature of the technology is also one of the hindrances for its accelerated advancement and adoption.

While web application development and corresponding popular frameworks have existed for almost 15 to 20 years, most of the vital machine learning frameworks and standards such as TensorFlow, PyTorch, and ONNX have come into existence in the last couple of years. It will for sure take a few more years before the technology matures and becomes easier to use and understand for all in an organization.

Time consuming

Unlike a typical software development project, machine learning modeling is very time-consuming because of the multiple phases and activities required to build, train, and deploy the model for production use. An organization's first challenge is the availability of historical data relevant to the business scenario you are trying to resolve via machine learning.

Industry Statistics 45%

Time spent by data scientists on data preparation tasks, including loading and cleaning data according to the Anaconda report[207].

Once data is found, data scientists must prepare and clean it before it can be fed into a data model for training and evaluation. After data cleaning and prep, a

---

[207] https://www.anaconda.com/state-of-data-science-2020?utm_medium=press&utm_source=anaconda&utm_campaign=sods-2020&utm_content=report

fair amount of time can be spent on building the model with a suitable machine learning algorithm to handle different relevant data sets. After algorithm selection, data scientists must train the model to make sure that it will accurately predict on any contextually relevant data set. Model training is followed by model deployment. Most tech cloud organizations such as Microsoft, AWS, Google, and IBM are now offering tools and services to help you with all these phases end to end. Azure Machine Learning Studio with its designer and automated ML tools are just two examples of Microsoft's tools. Microsoft is continuing to evolve and improve these tools and services to assist developers and business power users in starting to realize their business scenarios through machine learning.

Regardless of the complexity, cost, and time requirements associated with this technology, the business gains to be achieved from this technology are immense, and companies are moving ahead with using the technology to help them with common business goals of revenue and profit growth, cost savings, operational efficiencies gains, and building personalized customer experiences.

Bias and ethical issues

Introduction of bias through the models is one of the key challenges of using and building machine learning systems. These challenges can be introduced advertently and inadvertently into a machine learning model by the data scientist or a machine learning developer.

A few essential topics recently have become the centerpiece of discussion on machine learning. They are the questions of ethics and bias that may exist in the machine learning models. Unfortunately, societal biases exist that may creep into our AI systems that use machine learning models.

Expert Opinion

"Ethical considerations and liability for AI/ML will continue to be the biggest challenge for organizations."

Johannes Drooghaag[208], CEO Spearhead Management

One example of bias driven system was Amazon's recruiting system, which was using ML in the backend, in 2018 Amazon suddenly decided to scrap this AI recruiting tool that was supposedly showing bias against women. It turned out that the machine learning model behind the recruiting tool was trained on a dataset from the last ten years, which was representative of mostly males.

Let's try to understand how biases may creep into the machine learning systems before we investigate some ways to avoid them. There are two key factors to look at when working with machine learning models to consider ethics and potential biases embedded in your machine learning model.

Dataset

The first one is the dataset used to train the model. Suppose the training data set already had data that was biased. Then, your production model will inherit and make decisions and predictions biased in nature since it was trained on biased data. Consider a credit risk

---

[208] https://www.linkedin.com/in/johannesdrooghaag/

prediction system that a financial institution uses to assess the risk of offering loans to consumers. Suppose the model was trained on a data set that included features such as gender, race, and ethnicity. The model may start making predictions based on race and ethnicity and deny loans to the already-marginalized consumers because of their race and ethnicity.

Algorithms

Another area where you need to consider bias is the algorithm itself within the model. There are instances where the algorithm fails to account for the context in which it is used. A data scientist or machine learning expert is responsible for understanding the context in which the model will be implemented and used. They need to fully understand how and where your machine learning model will be used and how the algorithm will react to it.

An example to show this issue is when Microsoft deployed an experimental chatbot called Tay. Tay was implemented to interact with Twitter users and then continue to learn to evolve. This was an experiment to highlight machine learning-based language understanding. In their naivety, Tay's creators did not consider the context in how the Twitter users can use this chatbot. The Twitter users who interacted with it turned Tay into a racist chatbot, within a matter of hours, because of how they interacted with it.

There are various open-source tools available in the market to assess bias and help data scientists and Machine learning experts with ethical engineering.

FairML[209], LIME[210], IBM AI Fairness 360[211], SHAP[212], Google What-If Tool[213], and Deon[214] are some of such tools that you can look into for ethical and bias evaluation. As a data scientist, you may be more interested in working on the overall development of a machine learning model rather than considering all the repercussions of your model through the lens of ethics and bias. However, evaluating a machine learning system's fairness and ethical bias has become an essential part of creating machine learning models and an integral part of a data scientist's or machine learning practitioner's role.

Lack of Machine Learning Operations (MLOps)

Machine Learning Operations (MLOps) is the practice where data scientists and machine learning operations personnel in an organization collaborate and communicate to manage and maintain the machine learning lifecycle successfully.

Operations professionals include the machine learning operations developer and/or additional DevOps developers. The machine learning lifecycle consists of building, training, deploying, and maintaining machine learning models.

---

[209] https://github.com/adebayoj/fairml
[210] https://github.com/marcotcr/lime
[211] https://github.com/Trusted-AI/AIF360
[212] https://github.com/slundberg/shap
[213]
https://github.com/tensorflow/tensorboard/tree/master/tensorboard/plugins/interactive_inference
[214] https://deon.drivendata.org/

In a typical MLOps environment, a data scientist would concentrate on understanding the business requirements and data, building, and training a model with the best algorithm to provide accurate and timely answers and predictions. On the other hand, operations personnel have business operations knowledge. They will partner with the data scientist to deploy the model on the machine learning infrastructure, manage the infrastructure, and maintain the model with any changes required over the model's lifespan. Operations professionals, which may include DevOps developers, will help maintain the models with Continuous Integration/Continuous Delivery CI/CD processes utilizing various standard developer tools. Depending on the organization's size, machine learning operations developers and DevOps developers may be two separate roles, or one person may be handling the responsibilities of both roles.

Azure offers a set of tools and services to help you have a seamless MLOps lifecycle. Data scientists and operations professionals work in tandem to utilize these tools and services to manage and maintain a machine learning modeling lifecycle successfully.

Key components and features of Azure MLOps include:

- Training and building reproducible machine learning models via Azure's Machine Learning service.
- Deploy machine learning models at scale with industry-standard Kubernetes service clusters.
- Create CI/CD DevOps workflows utilizing GitHub, Azure DevOps, Azure Applications Insights for continuous improvements and changes to the model and subsequent deployment into production.

- Governance of machine learning models using the Azure Machine Learning portal. Each model considered and utilized by Azure Machine Learning can be evaluated for fairness and audited for any bias that may exist in the model.

One of machine learning's key challenges is that organizations don't know or think through the end-to-end machine learning operations and workflows or basically the lack of MLOps. A successful machine learning practice in an organization will require data scientists working closely with operations professionals with the right set of processes and tools. Breaking into the machine learning domain to utilize it in your AI applications does not mean that you can hire a data scientist and let them do all the required work to manage the machine learning lifespan. Instead, it requires you to define processes and get the proper tools to make the data scientist and operations professional successful in delivering and maintaining machine learning models.

When it comes to selecting the right tools and services, there are many tools available in the market to help you with machine learning operations. Suppose you choose to use one of the cloud providers, such as Microsoft, Amazon, or Google, for your machine learning needs. In that case, you may want to consider exploring the tools available from these providers to keep things simple and integrated while working with only one vendor for all your requirements. As mentioned above, Azure offers a whole set of tools and services to help you successfully manage your end-to-end machine learning lifespan.

ML FUTURE

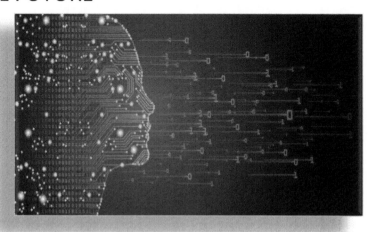

In this section, we will review the future trends for machine learning and where this technology is progressing. We will review the role large technical companies are playing in advancing this technology its awareness, usage, and education. We will review the the importance of following responsible machine learning practices, and the need for machine learning governance in organizations which are or planning to use and adopt machine learning systems.

Tech giants leading the way

Companies like Google, Microsoft, Amazon, and Facebook will continue to lead the way in democratizing and simplifying machine learning. All these big-name companies have already released their version of open-source machine learning frameworks and standards. Examples include TensorFlow, PyTorch, Caffe2, Gluon, Fast.AI, and ML.NET. They have collaborated on an open-source standard called ONNX. ONNX brings together all machine learning frameworks so that models can be trained and deployed on any computer target regardless of what framework the data scientist or developer may have used to custom-build their model.

Along with frameworks, these tech companies are also working on building tools to simplify the models' creation, training, and deployment. Azure Machine Learning designer authoring tool is an example of that. This tool doesn't require any coding experience at all for anyone to use it to create a machine learning model. To further streamline and assist users in creating and deploying customized and high-quality production models, they continue to improve the AutoML offerings. Automated ML in Azure Machine Learning is an example of such a service.

These efforts aim to get away from the traditional thinking of machine learning technology as a black box and to help everyone by unraveling this technology's inner details. It is a journey and will take time before we get to the point where machine learning is not considered a mystery.

Majority of the above-mentioned technical companies are also cloud services providers. They stand to win in the long run as they will continue to offer these machine learning tools and services through their cloud offerings. These cloud providers are also leading the way in providing the required compute infrastructure and on-demand scalability for training and deploying the models.

Building awareness and education

Realizing the importance and use of machine learning and AI in the business world, many large organizations now offer free training and resources to educate developers, IT professionals, and power users about machine learning and AI. Google is offering Machine Learning and AI courses[215] through the AI education portal. On the other hand, Microsoft has its ML and AI course offerings via its learning portal[216]. It also has a video series[217] for people interested in learning Python, the preferred programming language of machine learning experts. AWS offers around 30 online training courses[218] on machine learning, including labs, videos, and documentation.

Along with providing training and educational resources externally, many of these same large organizations and others have embarked on a journey to upskill their internal workforce about machine learning and AI. Amazon is an example where it plans[219] to spend $700 million to retrain 100,000 members of its U.S. workforce over the next six years. Upskilling will entail training people with some technical skills to learn about machine learning and AI. One of the objectives behind this upskilling is to make up for the talent shortage that Amazon is seeing now and, in the future, using these emerging technologies. Another example of a large corporation upskilling its **non-development staff** is JPMorgan, which understands both the development and business usage sides of machine learning and AI technologies.

---

215 https://ai.google/education/
216 https://docs.microsoft.com/en-us/learn/
217

https://www.youtube.com/playlist?list=PLlrxD0HtieHhS8VzuMCfQD4uJ9yne1m
E6
218 https://aws.amazon.com/training/learn-about/machine-learning/
219 https://www.aboutamazon.com/news/workplace/upskilling-2025

Along with training within the corporate environments, many different online companies such as Udemy, Coursera, and LinkedIn are also offering a plethora of courses on machine learning and AI systems development. Many universities and colleges not only have certificate programs in machine learning but also offer Bachelor of Science degrees in data science, where students are taught machine learning and its application, in multiple courses within such programs.

Responsible machine Learning

Any machine learning system built, used, and managed in your organization should follow the responsible machine learning principles. Three fundamental principles of responsible machine learning include:

- Understanding the models
- Protecting the models
- Controlling the models

Figure 4-10

Understanding the models

It is important to understand why a machine learning model made a particular decision or a prediction it did. This is important to know since we don't want ML systems making unfair or unethical decisions and, we also want to have the ability to inform the people getting affected by the decisions made by a ML system. All systems using a machine learning model should have explainability built into it so the final model that is going to utilized in an AI system is fully explainable. Decision may also have to made on choosing between a highly accurate models, a highly explainable models or a balanced model which provide a good mix of both accuracy and explainability. A data scientist can review the explainability of the final model to make sure that if has not inadvertently introduced bias into the model to make unfair decisions or predictions based on age, ethnicity, gender, economic status, education level, or religion.

Protecting the models

Machine learning models should protect the privacy of an individual's data in the model. Differential privacy technique, which interjects statistical noise into the dataset, is used to protecting the privacy of individual's data. The ML systems should also provide encryption and security of the data both in transit and in rest.

Industry Statistics

71%

Organizations which spent more on machine learning for cybersecurity than they did two years ago according to a report[220].

Controlling the models

Your machine learning model should be traceable and reproducible, and it should provide an end-to-end audit trail of the machine learning lifecycle from data set, training, code, and environment to model deployment. Audit trails should include activity logs which can be used by data scientists and ML developers to diagnose and troubleshoot issues around data sets, training models, compute targets and deployments. Training environments can be reproduced to create a reproducible ML model. Audit trails also help meet any regulatory compliance requirements. Model data sheets can be used to document the model by using model metadata.

Customer Story

EY, Ernest Young utilizes Microsoft Azure Machine Learning in their AI platform and that has led to increased adoption of their platform by their customers, and it is trusted by the regulators to satisfy all regulatory and compliance requirements.

Read the entire story[221]

---

[220] https://www-cdn.webroot.com/6015/4999/4566/Webroot_AI_ML_Survey_US-2019.pdf
[221] https://customers.microsoft.com/en-us/story/809460-ey-partner-professional-services-azure-machine-learning-fairlearn

---

Azure Machine Learning services offer tools and services to make sure that you can build ML systems utilizing the fundamental principles of Responsible machine learning.

Machine learning governance

As your organizations starts to experiment with ML systems, consider creating a ML governance framework which adheres to the responsible ML principles and considers other key factors including bias evaluation, model explainability, human-based model assessment, reproducible operations, privacy, security, and regulatory compliance.

Expert Opinion	"Regulated industries will face growing challenges with auditing of AI/ML, especially in regards of the complexity of algorithms, data, purpose, and utilization." Johannes Drooghaag[222], CEO Spearhead Management

The Institute for Ethical AI and Machine Learning[223], a UK-based research center, offers a great eight principles framework that can be adopted as is or used with adjustments relevant to your organization. These principles are built considering all the phases of the machine learning systems including development, deployment, and operations of. Any organization can

---

[222] https://www.linkedin.com/in/johannesdrooghaag/
[223] https://ethical.institute/

take these principles and create their own version of machine learning governance framework.

Figure 4-11 highlights the eight principles that data scientists and machine learning experts can follow as they build, implement, and maintain their models.

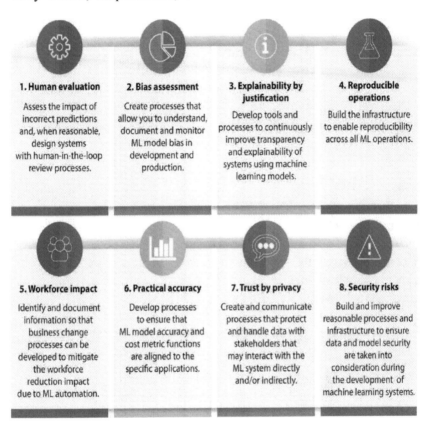

Figure 4-11

A typical machine learning governance framework within an organization should include the following core elements along with any other relevant components pertaining to your organization.

Human evaluation

Humans should review all machine learning processes and models to assess the accuracy of the results and predictions that a model may be making. This stems from the fact that models are not perfect, and we want to make sure that humans review them for the correctness of the results. This is where a data scientist or business analyst can double-check the results produced by machine learning models rather than putting their blind trust in the machine learning model results. Complementing human validation with explainability output from the machine learning tools being utilized will help in making sure that models are producing results and making predictions which are fair, ethical and can be explained.

Bias assessment

As discussed previously in the challenges section of this chapter, bias and ethical issues are one of the key issues that you may face when working with ML models. These biases can enter the system primarily due to the data set or the algorithms utilized in training or building the model. You should have processes in place to evaluate the models and how they are going to be used to make sure that it will not make unfair or unethical decisions.

Model interpretability and explainability

Transparency should be a key consideration when using machine learning models. You should have complete insights into any final model used in any of your systems and have the know-how to explain the entire model's behavior or why it is making certain predictions. Such explainability and interpretability of ML models ensures that the model is not making biased or unethical decisions and predictions. As an example, when utilizing AutoML in Azure Machine Learning and it comes up with a model recommendation, it also has corresponding information that explains model behavior. Azure machine learning offers tools and services for building models with explainability output.

Reproducible operations

Reproducibility is when you can run your model with different datasets and get the same or similar results. Reproducibility of machine learning models helps with smooth operations as you deploy the model in your AI systems and continue to improve it. Reproducible models help reduce errors and improve operational efficiencies as you move your models from development to production. Reproducible models also lend themselves to be easily scaled as business needs grow.

Privacy and security

There should be processes to handle, protect, and store the data generated from users of the machine learning systems. All these measures must consider the privacy of the users' data as they interact with the machine learning systems. Security should be part of the entire end-to-end journey of a machine learning system, from access to processing to data storage. Azure Machine Learning provides the responsible ML framework, as discussed previously, to warrant the privacy and security of ML models.

Expert Opinion

"Most organizations still underestimate their responsibilities towards managing, filtering, and securing the data to feed AL/ML based systems and applications."

Johannes Drooghaag[224], CEO Spearhead Management

Regulatory compliance

Depending on your industry, you may have to maintain specific compliance standards for your ML systems. Make sure that the machine learning systems are compliant with all the regulations of your industry. Create and document how the machine learning system is compliant with any of your industry's required regulations.

Customer Story

SAS, Scandinavian Airlines is utilizing Azure Machine Learning to detect fraud for their EuroBonus loyalty program with almost 99% accuracy. Along with that they are also utilizing Azure ML to improve their operation including ticket sales forecasting, full flight prediction, and reduction of fresh food wastage.

Read the entire story[225]

---

[224] https://www.linkedin.com/in/johannesdrooghaag/
[225] https://customers.microsoft.com/en-us/story/781802-sas-travel-transportation-azure-machine-learning

SUMMARY

This chapter reviewed machine learning basics and its several components, including algorithms, models, and training. We understood some of the business use cases where machine learning helps you in achieving your business objectives. We looked at various machine learning tools and frameworks to help you get started with machine learning development. We explored Azure Machine Learning services and tools to build no-code machine learning models, AutoML to help with automatic algorithm selection and tweaking, and Azure Notebooks to do customized machine learning model creation, training, deployment, and management. Business challenges were discussed, and the future of the technology was explored. In the next chapter, we will review artificial intelligence and available cognitive services to build AI systems.

CHAPTER 5:

ARTIFICIAL INTELLIGENCE

AI INTRODUCTION

Modern artificial intelligence (AI) was first introduced in 1956 in a conference at Dartmouth College. Building practical business use case products and services and the adoption of AI has been slow. This was primarily because of the need for massive compute infrastructure, special tools, services, and specialized expertise needed to build and maintain AI-based systems.

With the current IT systems now spewing data out from every crevice and corner, availability of inexpensive storage, and the massive compute power from the cloud service providers, it has now become possible to create intelligent AI-based products and services. Thus, leading to organizations, small and large to realize their AI business use cases.

Industry Statistics

$126B

d The global artificial intelligence (AI) software market is forecasted to grow rapidly in the coming years, reaching around 126 billion U.S. dollars by 2025 according to a Statista report[226].

There are two types of AI that should be differentiated and understood: **Narrow** or **weak AI** and **general** or **strong AI**. Narrow AI is defined as AI which is performing a single or multiple interrelated tasks. Typical examples include digital assistants, chatbots, and customer sentiment analysis systems. These systems have narrow scope and are helping us again efficiencies and improve user experiences. When done right and strategically, these narrow AI systems are the basis for gaining competitive edge and evolving business models.

General or strong AI is what you we may see in the science fiction movies where AI systems can think on their own like humans, making decisions, and performing complex tasks, without human interaction or intervention. This kind of AI is far from realization for practical business use cases and is something we may see in the future.

---

[226] https://www.statista.com/statistics/607716/worldwide-artificial-intelligence-market-revenues/

Benefits of AI

There are several benefits of AI which has made it a prime candidate technology to be used in the business world. Improved efficiency, intelligent decisioning, additional business model opportunities, automation, and enhanced customer services are some of the reasons why this technology is sweeping many organizations, from small to large. To reap maximum benefits from AI, your AI strategy should be aligned with your business strategy.

Industry Statistics 66%

Executives who believe that AI is extremely or very important to their company's success according to a Cognizant report[227].

Some fundamental benefits of AI include:

Agility

One of the key advantages of AI is its ability to improve efficiency. It brings agility to data processing, analysis and storage without human errors thus reducing business costs.

Data-driven decisions

AI's ability to process massive amounts of data in minimal time compared to humans along with recognizing data patterns and providing intelligent

---

[227] https://www.cognizant.com/artificial-intelligence-adoption-for-business

insights from it can help business decision makers with data-driven decisions to stay competitive and efficient.

Business model evolution

Customer data analysis and predictions from AI offer an opportunity for you to assess your current business model and realize if this technology can be used to create products, services, and experiences for your customers to unlock additional revenue streams.

Expert Opinion	"Early adopters report an improvement of almost 25 percent in customer experience, accelerated rates of innovation, higher competitiveness, higher margins, and better employee experience with the roll out of AI solutions. Organizations worldwide are adopting AI in their business transformation journey, not just because they can but because they must, to be agile, resilient, innovative, and able to scale."
	Ritu Jyoti[228], IDC Program VP, Artificial Intelligence Strategies

Automation

AI is a prime candidate technology for automating mundane tasks, which traditionally have been performed by humans. While this can lead to some job losses, your existing workforce performing these tasks can now be utilized to perform other higher value tasks which can improve your customer experiences.

---

[228] https://www.idc.com/getdoc.jsp?containerId=PRF004814

Industry Statistics

50%

of the businesses report that they have adopted AI in at least one business functional area. Top areas of AI adoption are for **product/service development**, **services operations**, and **marketing & sales** according to a McKinsey report[229].

Improved customer service

Machine learning models and conversational AI is being utilized to create chatbots which can help your customers with their common questions and needs through the websites and other customer digital channels. This 24x7 customer service is leading to higher level of customer satisfaction and retention.

Customer Story

Kotak Mahindra AMC, a financial services organization based in India was overburdened by the daily customer inquiry emails. They decided to use Azure Bot services to supplement their traditional human-based customer service with an email bot system to accurately tackle **85%** of customer email inquiries.

Read the entire story[230]

---

[229] https://www.mckinsey.com/Business-Functions/McKinsey-Analytics/Our-Insights/Global-survey-The-state-of-AI-in-2020
[230] https://customers.microsoft.com/en-us/story/736716-kotak-artificial-intelligence-cognitive-services-india-en-banking-ccentric

---

Competitive advantage

AI is also helping companies compete aggressively with each other via new products, services, and enhanced experiences. Democratization of AI by the cloud providers via their tools, services, and infrastructure is enabling companies big and small to tap into the world of AI. AI is no longer a realm of the large enterprises, with their deep pockets, and could afford of have their own compute infrastructure, customized AI tools, and services. Organizations from startups to mid-sized to large organizations can now start creating AI systems working with cloud providers, thus gaining competitive edge.

AI BUSINESS USE CASES

While technologies are great, we can't realize the potential and benefits of these new emerging technologies until we utilize them to solve business issues or create new business opportunities. AI is already being utilized in many common scenarios in various industries. In the following sections, we explore some of the common scenarios where you will see AI in action in the background.

Email spam and security filtering

Email spamming is one of those issues that every IT department and specifically the email administrators must deal with for managing their organization's email. Smart AI-enabled systems are now available to help organizations detect spam and security threats and then take appropriate action on it including deleting or moving it to the junk/spam folder. Various organizations deploy email gateway appliances with built-in AI systems to help detect spam and security threats. These AI-systems have built-in machine learning models that have been trained on spam email dataset and can detect spam email from valid emails. They also are continuously learning and improving their detection capability of identifying spam vs. valid emails.

Expert Opinion	"Contrary to conventional technology, AI/ML is living technology which evolves based on the information it processes."

Johannes Drooghaag[231], CEO Spearhead Management

Autocomplete

Almost all popular search engines, including Google and Bing, organizations' internal sites, and mobile devices use this feature to help the user with completing their search phrases. This feature helps with having the user to avoid typing the complete phrase but shows the most popular phrases that the search system already knows or what the user previously may have typed. Autocomplete system uses AI which is constantly learning as more people use the system and it uses this gained knowledge to make recommendations to a user on possible ways to create a search phrase for the search engine.

Auto-correction

AI-based auto-correction systems are very common in text editors where they help correct the grammar and

---

[231] https://www.linkedin.com/in/johannesdrooghaag/

spelling as you are typing the text. Auto correct is one of my favorite features in Microsoft Word. We have created this book using Microsoft Word and auto correct saved us from correcting the spelling and grammar mistakes which occur when you are typing fast. Search engines, such as Google, offer this feature by showing you the correct word in a phrase after you have typed a misspelled phrase to search in the search engine. As you type out the misspelled search phrase in the search box, it shows the corrected phrase and other related phrases for you to pick from the drop-down selection. If you don't select the correctly spelled phrase form the drop-down selection, it will still show you the results for the corrected phrase and tell you that it has done so by displaying that on top of the search results page.

Autosuggestions

Another key example of where AI is being used to make our lives simple is with autosuggestions. If you have used LinkedIn's messaging feature, then you will know what we are talking about here. When you communicate with other LinkedIn's network members, the AI system automatically suggests responses for each message that you get from the members as you communicate with them. The AI system behind the messaging feature, first takes the message that the member has typed, understand it using an AI-based Natural Language Processing (NLP) system, and then suggests typical responses you can give back to the member. This helps you with quick replies rather than typing out the response.

Personalization

We are seeing more and more examples of personalization in the Web and mobile applications we use. AI is being used in the background to show us what we are interested in seeing rather than showing what may not be of interest to us. Companies are tracking and collecting data on our usage of their products, services, and digital experiences. Many companies are using this data for their   AI models. These AI models are analyzing the customer data, predicting customer's future behavior, and then making recommendations to the customer. Typically, these recommendations are fed back onto the customer digital experiences to personalize their overall experience when they are interacting with you company. One example of this is the product recommendation system you see behind Amazon.com. When you are purchasing something from there, it shows other products and services you may be interested in purchasing.

Another key thing to consider here is that the customer behavior predictions from the AI systems can also be used to build new products and services to evolve your business model.

Expert Opinion	"Hyper-personalization of Customer Experience needs capabilities that bring data from all relevant touch points, then make this data actionable so that organizations can create a personalized engagement for their customers. AI is key to make it a reality."

Antonio Figueiredo[232], **RVP Salesforce**

---

[232] https://www.linkedin.com/in/afigueiredo/

Face recognition

Face recognition is about recognizing human or other faces. This AI feature can be used to recognize someone and then take some action. Face recognition can be used for any security or authorization systems to allow access. One of the key examples of face recognition is Microsoft's Windows Hello feature, introduced back in 2015 with Windows 10, for you to log into your PC or a laptop using your face instead of a text password or some other security authorization mechanism. Windows Hello uses AI to recognize your face and uses that as the primary method of logging you into your laptop/PC. Microsoft Azure also offers pre-built face recognition API that developers can use immediately for building customized applications requiring face recognition capabilities.

Customer Story	**Uber,** a global personal transportation organization is utilizing Face API from Azure Cognitive Services to improve safety of the passengers along with reducing fraud. Using the Azure AI services Uber development team saved months of development work that they are utilizing elsewhere on business-critical projects. This service is being utilized by more than one million customers and partners globally. Read the entire story[233]

---

[233] https://customers.microsoft.com/en-us/story/731196-uber

---

Chatbots

Chatbots are primarily the AI-based virtual customer service and support assistants that you find on many websites and other systems that you interact with on the Web. These chatbots are used to answer common questions and queries that the site visitors may have about your site, products, and services. Using a chatbot is a great way for you to provide customer support on your site, around the clock without the need for humans to answer all the questions that the site visitors may have. There is also capability that you can build in your chatbots to direct the site visitor query to an actual human being, if it cannot answer a particular question that a site visitor may have. Azure offers services to build simple no-code to highly customized chatbots.

Virtual assistants

Virtual assistants are the intelligent AI-based systems which we find in many of our home devices including the smart phones, smart speakers, smart TVs, and many other IoT devices that exist in our homes. Some typical examples of consumer IoT devices examples include thermostats, electrical switches, door openers, etc. Majority of virtual assistants in all these devices are all AI-based and use NLP capability to listen, interpret, and then execute the command that you have given them.

Industry Statistics

4.2B

Digital voice assistants being used in devices around the world in 2020. Forecasts suggest that by 2024, the number of digital voice assistants will reach 8.4 billion units – a number higher than the world's population according to a Statista report[234].

Some of the advanced virtual assistants such as Alexa, Siri, Google Assistant, and Cortana also learn over a period and become smarter by making recommendations to you considering the commands you have given to them previously. An extension of this AI and IoT device combination in the commercial world is edge computing where IoT devices either have embedded AI system or communicate with a physically close-by edge device with ML/AI capability to take some action. Edge computing is discussed in detail in chapter 3 and in chapter 6.

---

[234] https://www.statista.com/statistics/973815/worldwide-digital-voice-assistant-in-use/

Customer Story	**Telefonica,** a multinational telco used Azure Cognitive Services and Azure Bot services to build their own customized, conversational, and multilingual virtual agent to help customers with various services including managing their provisioned products, get real-time support, or change TV channels. This has helped Telefonica launch their agent in six countries and on four separate channels.
	Read the entire story[235]

Optical character recognition

Optical character recognition (OCR) is the science of recognizing hand-written and typed text. There are many applications and uses of OCR in the commercial world including the conversion of hand-written business documents to typed text, depositing checks via an automatic teller machine (ATM), checking the authenticity and information capturing from the passports at national borders, recognizing the vehicle number plates at the toll passes, conversion of a physician's handwritten notes or prescription to typed text and many more. Azure offers the Computer Vision API, which includes OCR capability, that a developer can use to create customized OCR applications.

---

[235] https://customers.microsoft.com/en-us/story/726906-telefonica-media-telco-cognitive-services-azure

Robotics

Robots are already used in some industries to automate and accelerate the production on the assembly lines. Robots are also utilized in industries and in manufacturing processes where it may be hazardous for humans to be always present at the assembly lines. Auto industry in one example of an industry which heavily relies on robotics for its manufacturing assembly lines. Other major industries that use robotics include electrical/electronics, metal, plastic, and chemical products manufacturing industries. Robotics have been used for decades in the manufacturing sector but with the advent of AI usage in combination with the robotics has breathed a new level of intelligence into the manufacturing robots to adapt and make autonomous decisions, with changing assembly line conditions and environment, without constant human intervention.

Healthcare industry applications

AI is and will continue to play a key role in healthcare systems. There are many uses of AI in healthcare but the one significant to call out is the use of AI to help doctors with accurate diagnosis of patients from the output of x-rays, ultrasound, magnetic resonance imaging (MRI), and other such similar scans which are performed on the patient. The output produced from such medical scans can be analyzed by an AI system to help classify these images or recognize any potential risks and issues for the patients. These AI-based systems analysis and results can be used by the physicians to confirm their diagnosis of the patient. In many studies performed in the last few years, these AI systems have outperformed the physicians in accurately diagnosing the patient compared to the physicians. Azure AI services offer both

---

classification and custom vision capabilities for developers to build such intelligent systems for healthcare use.

Finance industry applications

AI systems have been used in the finance industry for some decades now utilizing highly customized systems. Various common tasks in this industry such as credit card fraud detection, automated loan processing, and stock trading are being handled with AI systems. These systems can help detect possible fraud on credit card transactions, make decisions on consumer and commercial loan applications or predict variations on stocks prices over a certain timeframe. Fraud detection and loan processing systems use AI, which utilizes anomaly detection machine learning algorithms. Stock variations and stock predictions AI systems typically use time-series ML algorithms or complex deep learning algorithms. Azure offers an Anomaly Detector API that developers can use to start creating applications which need to catch unusual occurrences and take some action.

Industry Statistics

$10B

Spending on AI systems between Retail and Banking industries, each of which invested more than $5B in 2019. This number will continue to grow in the upcoming years. Nearly half of the retail spending will go toward automated customer service agents and expert shopping advisors & product recommendation systems according to an IDC report[236].

Customer Story

KPMG, a professional services organization, utilizes Azure Cognitive Services for their risk analytics solution for their financial institution customers. The solution uses AI for call transcription, translation, and fraud analytics. This has led to **80% reduction** in time and cost for them.

Read the entire story[237]

---

[236] https://www.idc.com/getdoc.jsp?containerId=prUS45481219
[237] https://customers.microsoft.com/en-us/story/754840-kpmg-partner-professional-services-azure

AI STRATEGY & PLANNING

Utilizing AI for revenue growth, automation, efficiency improvements, customer service enhancements, competitive advantage by offering groundbreaking products and services are some of the key reasons why AI has become critical in digital transformation journeys of many organizations. In the following sections, we review some core AI digital transformation strategy factors including vision, ROI, how to build and implement, overall impact to the organization, privacy/security, and the required AI tools & services.

Industry Statistics	**75%**

C-suite executives believe that if they don't scale artificial intelligence in the next five years, they risk going out of business entirely according to Accenture[238].

---

[238] https://www.accenture.com/us-en/insights/artificial-intelligence-summary-index

Define vision, ROI, and success metrics

An organization's top leadership needs to have a clear vision on why and how AI will be used to transform the organization. This vision is typically driven from the need to enhance operational agility, to automate, or to compete in the market. To build a well thought-of and informed AI vision requires a thorough analysis of the current business use cases and additional uses cases which can be unlocked by using AI. At the end of the day, the vision should lead to a strategy that is aligned with the overall goals of the organization.

Industry Statistics **73%**

Executives believe that AI will help them evolve their business model by enhancing the ability to introduce new products/services or by creating new businesses in the next three years according to a Cognizant report[239].

Creating a clear vision typically involves the CEO or the CIO working closely with the all the business units in an organization to get alignment across the whole organization. IT unit usually takes the lead in technology selection, installation, configuration, and maintenance. Most of the time it is the IT unit that takes on bold technical initiatives, thus the role of a CIO is important in understanding how any technology, including AI, will help the organization in meeting its business goals.

---

[239] https://www.cognizant.com/artificial-intelligence-adoption-for-business

A clear vision along with an ROI defined upfront is a recipe for success. Any digital transformation initiatives which involve AI should also have success metrics defined upfront. These AI-based systems, with telemetry configured properly, can provide insights, and required metrics to quantify the ROI. Once the vision is clear, it is important to communicate that to all the layers within the organization. AI-based systems can be quite disruptive to the usual way of how work is done in any organization, and it is important that everyone in the organization understands why AI is being used and how it is going to benefit the internal employees, customers, or the organization.

Industry Statistics

22%

of the businesses in 2020 reported at least **5%** EBIT (Earnings Before Interest and Taxes) because of AI according to a McKinsey report[240].

Build, buy, outsource, or partner

After the vision and ROI have been clearly defined and communicated through all the layers of the organization, a decision needs to be made if you should build, build, partner or outsource the AI system.

Build – Customized

If the proposed initiative will be unique to the organization's needs and there is already an in-house

---

[240] https://www.mckinsey.com/Business-Functions/McKinsey-Analytics/Our-Insights/Global-survey-The-state-of-AI-in-2020

data science, machine learning/AI developer, and other required resources available, then you may want to build your own customized AI system utilizing these resources. Depending on the scope of the AI initiative the AI team will have to collaborate across various units of the organization. Building a customized in-house solution is the most flexible option available, but usually is the most expensive to maintain for the long-term since you must retain the data scientists, ML/AI development engineers, and other resources.

Build – No-code & Low-code

All the top cloud providers are offering many no-code/low-code AI building tools and services, such as the Azure Machine Learning designer, as part of Machine Learning Studio. These tools can be used to quickly start a prototype and build a production AI/ML-based system. These tools typically don't require deeper machine learning expertise and, in some cases, no coding experience either. This ease of use, however, comes with minimal flexibility in building a fully customized system. While utilizing these tools, machine learning and AI developers can tweak the code, a data scientist may still be required to build a fully customized AI system.

Buy

There are certain common business use cases AI applications and services available that can be purchased and easily customized to suit an organization's needs. These out of the box AI solutions can be purchased and with minimum configuration, you are ready to go. Although such solutions may work initially, as you or your customers use them, there may be a need to customize them in the long run. This is the least flexible solution since there is very little customization that is allowed for such AI-based systems. For any extensive customization, if it is allowed, you may have to work with the original vendor who created the AI system/service or bring in external consulting vendor who is experienced with this AI system.

Outsource

Outsourcing will be an option if the organization lacks both the availability of data science and ML/AI development talent and other necessary skills to, build, deploy, and maintain AI systems. This is the costliest of all the options for creating AI systems and applications. This is the best option to get started quickly while you can work on hiring data science, ML/AI developers and other resources to help with the long-term management and maintenance of the system.

Partnering

This is another option to consider if you are part of a large organization. You may be able to partner across the units in an organization and combine your resources to build an AI system. One unit may be able to help with developer resources, while another unit can help with data science requirements and yet another unit can help with the overall program and project management of the system. This kind of cross team and cross organization collaboration is very common in a large enterprise where resources and talent are spread across various units of the organization. This option, however, is hard to manage because of you working across different units and hard to sustain for the long run.

Assess the impact on people, processes, and technology

Before you bring in an AI-based system, either internally or to your customers, you should carefully assess the impact on the three key pillars of IT: people, processes, and technology.

People

AI systems are generally perceived as something which will replace all jobs and that is not true at all. While most of the AI systems look to automate most of the manual tasks within an organization and improve operational efficiencies, they are also responsible for creating many jobs for managing and maintaining these new systems. An AI strategy should carefully examine the impact of AI to people, including both internal employees and external customers. Such an assessment should include jobs losses that may occur, jobs creation and any retraining that needs to be done. Retraining your current workforce is good way to minimize the number of job losses which may result from the introduction of an AI system within an organization. The retrained workforce can be utilized to manage and maintain the AI systems along with possibly building the next version of the current AI system.

Industry Statistics

2.3X

The respondents at high AI performing companies are 2.3X more likely than others to consider their C-suite leadership very effective according to a McKinsey report[241].

Processes

Two of the key reasons why AI-based systems are built are to improve the operational efficiencies and to bring agility to the current manual processes. One of the fundamental advantages of AI is the automation of manual processes which may have existed before the AI system was built. With AI, there will be significant gains in efficiency in processes leading to faster business results. This will also lead to shift in business culture because AI-based systems will bring in new ways of doing older tasks. There may be some resistance to this new way of accomplishing tasks. Communicating to the workforce on how the AI system will make their jobs easier and faster along with training them to use it properly will reduce any friction in adopting the new AI system. Externally, the customers will appreciate the agility and automation you have built using AI in your products, services, and digital experiences.

Technology & tools

For building and maintaining an AI-based system, you will need to decide on tools, software, and any necessary technology. Traditionally, AI systems use machine

---

[241] https://www.mckinsey.com/Business-Functions/McKinsey-Analytics/Our-Insights/Global-survey-The-state-of-AI-in-2020

learning and deep learning, under the covers. For building, training, and deploying the underlying machine learning and deep learning models in an AI-based system, you will have to decide on tools and services required for those tasks. All this can add up to huge upfront capital cost to procure all this required software and hardware. An alternative to setting up your own infrastructure and getting a disparate set of tools and software from different vendors is to use cloud providers for all your AI needs. Major cloud providers offer machine learning and AI tools, services, and compute infrastructure to build, deploy, and maintain these AI systems. Azure Machine Learning, Azure Cognitive Services, Azure Bot Services and Azure Cognitive Search Services are examples of such tools and services from Microsoft. Going with one cloud vendor for all your ML/deep learning/AI needs will reduce the administrative effort of managing relationship with multiple vendors.

Privacy and security

Security and privacy of data used by an AI system are critical parts of any AI system and essential elements to be considered in building, deploying, and using an AI system. Depending on where globally the AI system is being built and will be utilized, consider the local privacy and data protection laws such as General Data Protection Regulation (GDPR) and other regulations. Other strict US regulations such as California's Consumer Privacy Act (CCPA) call for anonymizing the data and removing other personal information. While the data is still useful and can be used in training a machine learning model, it may not be that helpful in training the AI system because of missing personal information data.

Most of the AI system use machine learning and deep learning models which require data to be continuously fed into these systems to help the models to become more and more intelligent in accurately responding to queries or making predictions. Some of the data is private in nature, such as medical diagnosis data, for an AI-based healthcare system. It is important that you have proper consent from the users, from which this data has been obtained. The personal nature of this data also makes it more susceptible to theft and breaches. Once proper usage consent is obtained, make sure that this data is properly encrypted while at rest or in transit as it gets utilized for training and building the machine learning models. When the AI system is in production and is being utilized with additional input from users and producing output, all that data is still required to be secured via encryption and other cybersecurity techniques.

AI tools and services

Many companies are offering AI services and tools. There are very few companies out there which might offer end-to-end tools and services to fulfill all your requirements. Cloud providers are examples of companies which can offer end-to-end AI tools and services. It is worth considering them, so you have one vendor for all your tooling and AI services rather than going with multiple vendors. Vendor, tools, and AI services management will become an issue if you go with multiple AI vendors.

Cloud providers like Microsoft, Google, IBM, and Amazon are trying their best to commoditize AI and give developers the tools, services, and ability to build and deploy AI-based systems quickly and easily. Each cloud provider has their machine learning offerings, AI services, and tools. In the following section, we are going to examine and explore Microsoft Azure's AI platform. Although Microsoft categorizes Azure Machine Learning as part of Azure AI platform, but because of the scope and importance of machine learning we dedicated a full chapter on it. We discussed Azure Machine Learning in detail in chapter 4.

AZURE AI PLATFORM

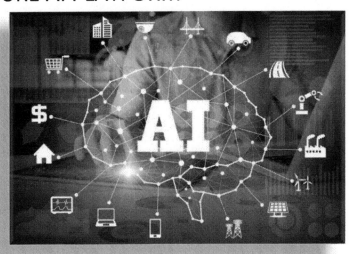

Azure AI platform is an umbrella category that Microsoft uses to classify the various AI services and tools it offers to its customers. Primary components of Azure AI platform include Azure Machine Learning, Azure Cognitive service, Azure Bot service, Azure Cognitive Search and Azure Databricks. All these services are built and provided to make a developer's life easy when building AI apps. Microsoft has considered the most common business use case scenarios and created easy to use API endpoints that developers can very quickly use in their apps to build amazing AI experiences. See **Figure 5-1** to get a high-level view of the Azure AI platform offerings.

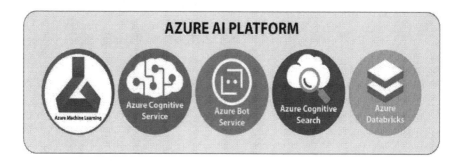

Figure 5-1

In the following sections, we are going to explore the main components of the Azure AI platform in some more depth to fully understand the features and capability of each component. We will differentiate Azure Machine Learning Services and Azure Cognitive service and the differences of pre-built vs. customized AI.

Azure Machine Learning

Azure Machine Learning[242] services are available for organizations to bring their own datasets to create, train, and implement customized machine learning models using various tools and services available in Azure Machine Learning Studio such as Designer, AutoML and Azure Notebooks. These Azure Machine Learning tools and services are part of the **Custom AI** offering from Microsoft for giving the freedom to developers to build intelligent apps using highly customized machine learning models. Azure Machine Learning services and related tools were discussed in detail in chapter 4.

---

[242] https://docs.microsoft.com/en-us/azure/machine-learning/

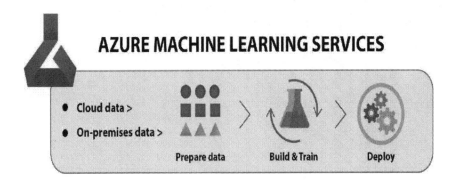

Figure 5-2

Azure Cognitive Services

Azure Cognitive Services[243] provide API endpoints for different cognitive domains including vision, speech, language, and decision. These API are available for developers to pick up and start using immediately in their applications without any machine learning experience. These pre-built API have been created using machine learning models that Microsoft built, trained, and deployed for developers to start utilizing without having any knowledge of the underlying machine learning models. These Azure Machine Learning tools and services are part of the **pre-built AI** offering from Microsoft.

---

[243] https://docs.microsoft.com/en-us/azure/cognitive-services/what-are-cognitive-services

Expert Opinion	"The state-of-the-art AI models underlying cognitive services will help customers around the world gather actionable insights from their data in multiple languages. These cognitive services are designed to help business users quickly start with building AI applications and allow tuning these models in some case with their domain specific data. These cognitive services are available globally for use and we keep adding new capabilities based on customer feedback."
	Parashar Shah[244], Azure Cognitive Services program manager

Azure Cognitive Services are classified into four categories of cognitive domains: vision, speech, language, and decision:

AZURE COGNITIVE SERVICES

VISION   SPEECH   LANGUAGE   DECISION

Figure 5-3

In the following sections we will review each of these cognitive domains and the associated services that Azure

---

[244] https://www.linkedin.com/in/parashar/

offers. The services for each of these cognitive domains have been created considering many common business use cases that exist. As other common use cases and scenarios are recognized, Microsoft for sure is going to build other services for each of these domains.

Vision

Azure Cognitive Services for vision will help you recognize and explore content within videos and images. As of the writing of this book there are five services available for vision.

Computer Vision

For analyzing content in videos and images. This service is available via an SDK and as a pre-built API for multiple development languages.

Custom Vision

For building, training, and deploying a vision API service when working with your own custom images recognition to fit your business needs. This service is available via a web portal[245] or by a custom vision software development kit (SDKs).

Face

For detecting and recognizing people and their emotions in images. This service is available via an SDK and as a pre-built API for multiple development languages.

Form Recognizer

For extracting text, key-value pairs, and tables from documents. This service is available as a pre-built API or by you building a customized machine learning model built by training with your specific data.

---

[245] https://www.customvision.ai/

Video Indexer

For examining the audio and visual channels of a video and indexing its content. This service is available as a pre-built API or by utilizing a <u>Web Indexer portal</u>[246].

Speech

Speech to Text

For recording audible speech into readable and searchable text. This service is available via an SDK and as a pre-built API for multiple development languages along with an option to build, train and create a customized machine learning model using the Azure Cognitive Services <u>Speech Studio portal</u>[247].

Text to Speech

For converting text to speech for natural language interfaces. This service is available via an SDK and as a pre-built API for multiple development languages along with an option to build, train and create a customized machine learning model using the Azure Cognitive Services <u>Speech Studio portal</u>[248].

Speech Translation

For creating real-time speech translation available in around 30 languages. This service is available via an SDK and as a pre-built API for multiple development languages along with an option to build customized neural machine translation (NMT) systems using the Azure Cognitive Services <u>Custom Translator portal</u>[249].

---

[246] <u>https://www.videoindexer.ai/account/login</u>
[247] <u>https://speech.microsoft.com/portal</u>
[248] <u>https://speech.microsoft.com/portal</u>
[249] <u>https://portal.customtranslator.azure.ai/</u>

Customer Story	**Volkswagen,** a global car manufacturer works with more than **40** languages when it comes to customer manuals, apps, web content, and the infotainment systems built into their cars. Over the period of years, they have also built their translation memories database that contains the text along with its translation. To meet customer expectations of quick turnaround times, they cut down on the manual effort to do human translation and to reduce the overall cost of using the current portal they were using, they decided to go with Azure Cognitive services for their translation needs.

Read the entire story[250]

Speaker Recognition (Preview)
For identifying and confirming the people speaking based on their audio. As of the writing of this book, this service was in preview and not released as a production service. This service is available via an SDK and as a pre-built API for multiple development languages.

Language

Immersive Reader
For assisting readers of all abilities understand text using audio and visual clues. This service is available via an SDK and as a pre-built an API call for multiple development languages.

---

[250] https://customers.microsoft.com/en-us/story/779468-volkswagen-azure-automotive-en

Language Understanding

For building natural language understanding into bots, apps, and IoT devices. This service is available via Azure Cognitive Services Language Understanding portal[251] to build, train, and deploy a customized machine learning model which can be utilized in your apps, bots and IoT devices.

QnA Maker

For creating a conversational question and answer layer over your data. Data can be semi-structured content, including FAQs, manuals, and documents. This service helps you build a knowledgebase of questions and answers. Once the knowledge base is built using this service, you can extend it further by building a chatbot application. The service is available via the Azure Cognitive Services QnA Maker portal[252].

Text Analytics

For detecting and analyzing sentiment, opinions, and key phrases. This service is available via a pre-built API and a client library for multiple development languages.

Translator

For identifying and translating more than 60 supported languages. This service is available via an SDK and as a pre-built API for multiple development languages along with an option to build customized neural machine translation (NMT) systems using the Azure Cognitive Services Custom Translator portal[253].

---

[251] https://www.luis.ai/
[252] https://www.qnamaker.ai/
[253] https://portal.customtranslator.azure.ai/

Decision

Anomaly Detector

For detecting unusual occurrences in the data and for identifying any potential problems quickly. This can help you take actions to rectify any issues that are about to occur in your business process or devices. This service is available via a pre-built API for multiple development languages. It is as simple as passing your time series data to the API to identify the anomalies in the data without any knowledge of the underlying machine learning model utilized by the API. This service can be used by for detecting anomalies within IoT data.

Customer Story	TIBCO, a software and data analytics provider, is utilizing Azure Cognitive Services in their customized solutions, for their customers, for anomaly detection. The solution detects anomalies, provides root cause, and suggest actions. Read the entire story[254]

Content Moderator

For detecting and moderating content to identify offensive images, profanity, undesirable text, and adult video content. This service is available via a pre-built API for multiple development languages along with a review tool[255] for humans to add additional layer of accuracy and audit to the process of content moderation.

---

[254] https://customers.microsoft.com/en-us/story/811324-tibco-partner-professional-services-azure
[255] https://contentmoderator.cognitive.microsoft.com/dashboard

Personalizer

For creating personalized experiences in your applications by choosing the best content (text, images, URL, email or whatever you want to select from and show the users) is shown to the user to show to the users. This service is available via a pre-built API for multiple development languages. Personalizer API is built from a reinforcement machine learning model which is continuously learning and getting better in accurately picking or recommending the best option for the application user.

Metrics Advisor (Preview)

For analyzing your time series data, identifying anomalies, sending alerts, and identifying the root cause of the issue. It is a great service to use to monitor your business operations data. As of the writing of this book, this service was in preview and not released as a production service. This service is available via a web-based portal and client libraries, for multiple development languages. Features include data ingestion, anomaly detection, alert notification, and root cause analysis.

Azure Bot Services

Enhance your customer service experiences by building and deploying intelligent bots that understand and communicate in a human-like natural language. With Azure Bot Services[256] you can build these bots either using no-code or a fully customized bot solution.

Azure Bot Framework provides the ability to start building a simple bot to answer documented and common questions from your customers and then evolve it into an

---

[256] https://docs.microsoft.com/en-us/azure/bot-service/?view=azure-bot-service-4.0

advanced your custom branded virtual assistant. You can continue to improve these bots by extending their skills. Azure Bot Service also provides the ability to seamlessly transition from bot to a human agent for those special and complex scenarios where the bot is not able to help your customers.

Considering the current COVID-19 pandemic and the importance of healthcare, Microsoft has also recently introduced Azure Health Bot, which can be utilized by healthcare organizations to build their own bots which can help with common health related tasks such as triaging symptoms, answering lab questions, providing answers to COVID-19 related questions, locating all healthcare facilities, and responding to inquiries on COVID-19 vaccines.

Azure Cognitive Search

Formerly known as Azure Search, Azure Cognitive Search[257] is Microsoft's Search provider service which can be used to index various content sources from within an on-premises environment or the web and then provides API capability to the developers to build rich search solutions in their apps and websites using these indexes. Along with basic indexing feature that any search provider offers, it has rich set of features which utilize Azure's speech, vision, and language cognitive services to transform your unstructured information into searchable content. As discussed in the Azure Cognitive Services section, these cognitive services offer capabilities such as OCR, translation, key phrase extraction, location, people, and organization detection. After Azure Cognitive Services have identified all the different aspects of your raw, unstructured data, as

---

[257] https://docs.microsoft.com/en-us/azure/search/search-what-is-azure-search

mentioned, it then gets indexed. You can then query this indexed data and offer it in your applications and websites via different search facets.

Azure Databricks

Azure Databricks[258] is an open-source Apache Spark-based analytics platform for your AI applications. You can use Azure Databricks for processing and transforming your data. It is a fully managed solution with on-demand or scheduled scalability to meet varying processing needs. It can be used for big data analytics, real-time analytics, or Machine learning models training and building. It supports all popular data science languages including Python, Scala, R, Java, and SQL, as well as frameworks and libraries including TensorFlow, PyTorch, and scikit-learn.

◆ ◆ ◆ ◆ ◆ ◆ ◆ ◆ ◆ ◆ ◆

---

[258] https://docs.microsoft.com/en-us/azure/databricks/scenarios/what-is-azure-databricks

---

AI CHALLENGES

There are several challenges that exist for AI systems from shortage of talent, high costs for the required talent, data and machine learning algorithm considerations when using the AI systems, compute infrastructure costs, AI bias, and the lack of transparent AI systems. We review these challenges in detail in the following sections.

High-priced and scarce expertise

AI doesn't come cheap, if I were to sum it up when it comes to having the required personnel to build and maintain AI systems. A traditional AI team has one or multiple data scientists and DevOps or AI development engineers. Data scientists are well versed and experts in the field of math and statistics and are required to work with the underlying machine learning and deep learning algorithms. Whereas AI developers and DevOps professionals are required to help with the complex coding to train, deploy, and maintain the models. As previously discussed in the machine learning chapter, data scientists don't come that easy. These folks typically hold PhD degrees, are high in demand and thus have a high price tag associated with them. In the last few years, most of the large enterprises have swept them and are utilizing them for the AI tools and services they are building for their internal and external customers. DevOps professionals and AI developers on the other hand are easy to come by and help the data scientists with any coding needs as a part of the AI tools and services creation. They are proficient in one or more of the traditional machine learning languages such as R, Python, Scala, Java et. al along with CI/CD (continuous integration/continuous delivery) skills to maintain the models. Smaller to mid-sized companies that want to break into the AI realm may not be able to afford the high-priced data scientists. Instead, they can consider outsourcing to build their AI systems.

Industry Statistics **28%**

of AI/ML initiatives have failed. Lack of staff with necessary expertise, lack of production-ready data, and lack of integrated development environment are reported as primary reasons for failure according to an IDC report[259].

Another approach that small to mid-sized organizations can take is to experiment and innovate to create simple AI systems by utilizing the tools and services provided

---

[259] https://www.idc.com/getdoc.jsp?containerId=prUS46534820

by many AI technology providers. All the top cloud providers are part of these AI technology providers and are trying to commoditize ML and AI by offering various services and tools which can be utilized by both developers and non-developers who don't have deep data science expertise. Automated ML in Azure Machine Learning is an example of one of those services where the service doesn't require the user to select or tweak the underlying machine learning algorithm and does that for you. AutoML was discussed in chapter 4 of the book.

Data and algorithm concerns

Data is an essential ingredient of any AI system, and it is important to understand the challenges around data primarily around quantity, quality, relevance, and regulatory compliance before you start utilizing any data for your machine learning models. There are many public data sets[260] which can be used to experiment with ML and AI but they should never be used for training your production systems.

Expert Opinion	"AI is more data-hungry than ever, however organization are still struggling to break their silos and unlock the data to feed AI processes and models."
	Antonio Figueiredo[261], RVP Salesforce

---

[260] https://lionbridge.ai/datasets/the-50-best-free-datasets-for-machine-learning/
[261] https://www.linkedin.com/in/afigueiredo/

Key considerations for data include:

- For larger organizations, the data may be dispersed and available in various systems with different units. Consolidating and bringing this data together may take development work and time.

- Data may need to be pre-processed and cleaned up before it can be fed into a ML or deep learning model. This also where a data scientist spends lot of their time.

- There should also be enough data available for training your model. Utilizing a limited amount of data to train the system will lead to an AI system which doesn't provide accurate results once it is deployed.

- For building a realistic and accurate AI system for your specific business use case, actual relevant data is required to train your underlying ML or deep learning model. You cannot use generic or public data available for this purpose. For some AI systems, data set may be available from a third-party vendor who keeps and maintains such required data. Azure Custom Vision and Custom Speech are examples of services from Azure Cognitive Services offering, which lets you bring your own relevant data to train the models.

- Data may be protected by local or global regulations and compliance standards and those should be considered first before you utilize that data for your models. Healthcare data is a prime example of such a data set.

Expensive and non-scalable compute infrastructure

Any AI system requires compute power to train and build the underlying machine learning model. ML and deep learning models use complex and compute-intensive algorithms which typically require dedicated compute infrastructure. Small and mid-sized organizations may be able to run experiments on some unused hardware lying around or going to a cloud provider and signing up for their time limited trials to do a quick proof-of-concept experiment but training and building a production system is a different story.

Dedicated infrastructure is required not only to train and build the models but also to maintain and manage them in the long run. As an example, historically many financial services organizations, which have been using AI systems for a while, have used their dedicated on-premises infrastructure for the required compute power required for their AI systems. It was hard for small and mid-sized businesses to break into the AI world because they couldn't afford to dedicate infrastructure for the AI compute needs. Now, with the advent and availability of ubiquitous cloud computing, organizations of any size can provision and utilize the on-demand and pay-as-you-use compute infrastructure from the cloud providers for their AI compute needs. The providers also offer the ability of scaling out the compute infrastructure on-demand or scheduled basis depending on the varying needs of the AI system.

Microsoft CEO Satya Nadella said at <u>MIT's AI and the Work of the Future Congress 2020</u>[262] that he is amazed

---

by the ability of cloud computing to provision massive computing power. "The computing available to do AI is transformative," Nadella said.

Bias and ethical issues

One of the key arguments against AI systems is that it can provide output, predictions or decisions which are biased against certain groups, minorities, and marginalized communities. They can produce unintentional output which can lead to humans, using these AI systems, to make decisions which can reinforce some of the already existing societal biases around age, gender, sexual orientation, ethnicity, race, religion, disability, and socioeconomic status. There are many examples of AI systems that have led to biased decisions.

Expert Opinion	"Underrepresentation is by far the largest ethical and practical weakness of AI/ML." Johannes Drooghaag[263], CEO Spearhead Management

One example was the AI-based recruitment tool which favored male resumes over female resumes. This AI tool had been trained on a data set for 10 years of resumes submitted to Amazon primarily from white males. Amazon decided to stop using this recruitment tool[264] in 2018.

---

[263] https://www.linkedin.com/in/johannesdrooghaag/
[264] https://www.theverge.com/2018/10/10/17958784/ai-recruiting-tool-bias-amazon-report

---

Another recent example during the COVID-19 pandemic was AI grading system used by UK's Office of Qualifications and Examinations Regulation (Ofqual) to assign grades to students for university admissions, since the official A levels exams were cancelled due to the pandemic. A-level exams are the formal exams considered by many universities across UK to give admissions to students. The AI grading system was ditched[265] after it was accused of being biased to students from poor backgrounds.

Data used for training the AI systems is one of the key reasons for them making biased decisions. Two aspects of the data are leading to these unfair AI systems – one is that the data is influenced by the historical societal biases and second is unrepresentative and non-holistic data. Amazon's recruitment tool is an example of a system which favored males over females for jobs in Amazon since the system had majority of male resumes compared to female resumes and thus considered males more fit for the positions than females. Ofqual's AI system is an example of a system which did not fully consider the students from poorer background because it was primarily trained in a data set which was unrepresentative of such students.

Such biases attributed by AI systems can lead to unfair and unethical decisions. Thus, it is important to make sure that the AI system being built doesn't have bias built into it either due to the data which was used to train the underlying machine learning model or intentionally by the data scientists or the machine learning developers.

---

[265]https://www.theverge.com/2020/8/17/21372045/uk-a-level-results-algorithm-biased-coronavirus-covid-19-pandemic-university-applications

Some cloud vendors, such as Microsoft, IBM, and Amazon, which offer AI technology are trying to deter some unethical practices and mandating that their AI tools and services be not used for certain scenarios. Specifically, where AI systems, utilizing their technology, are leading to biased and unethical decisioning and actions such as police brutality and racial profiling. In mid-2020 Microsoft announced[266] that its facial recognition in Azure Cognitive Service may not be used by Police departments or by customers building AI systems for the police departments in the United States.

Lack of trustworthy AI

Imagine an AI system utilized by a physician which can perform an automated diagnosis on providing patient data input to it. The physician can use the system to see what diagnosis the AI system makes about the patient. This is critical in having the physician take the next course of action, including prescriptions and treatments.

While this situation is very helpful for the physicians to make quick decisions but at the same time, they also need to understand why the AI system reached a specific decision about a particular patient's diagnosis. Blind trust in such an AI system, without understanding the reasoning on why and how the AI system reached this decision, can be disastrous for the patient. Such situations of AI usage have led to the advent of explainable AI (xAI).

---

[266] https://www.washingtonpost.com/technology/2020/06/11/microsoft-facial-recognition/

The whole concept of xAI stems from the belief that an AI system should not be a black box and any solutions or decisions made by the AI system could be explained by the system. xAI is also sometimes referred to as explained AI, interpretable AI, or transparent AI. Transparency of how and why the AI is making certain decisions and conclusions is important to understand for users of these AI systems. Automated ML in Azure Machine Learning as discussed in chapter 4 of this book, offers the AI explainability feature which helps the data scientist, or the ML developer understand why it picked a specific or a combination of algorithms for building a ML model.

An AI system that doesn't offer any transparency on how it is reaching its decisioning and conclusions will also end up making biased and unethical decisions which will be hard to analyze and understand without the xAI features in the system. Not all the AI systems built nowadays offer xAI features. You want to make sure that any AI-based system you buy, build, or outsource has xAI features and provides the transparency on all the decisions or predictions it is making for your business use cases.

AI FUTURE

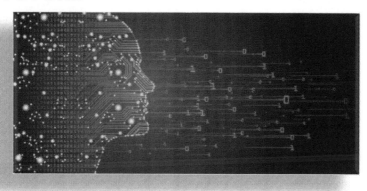

Future trends of AI will see organizations, big and small, using combination of ML and AI to automate and build products and services which improve customer experiences and enhance operational efficiencies. Organizations are also going to be driven by the motivation to evolve their business models with revenue generation prospects by building AI products and services. With the cloud providers trying to democratize and provide ML/AI tools, services, and compute power to help organizations realize their business use cases, we are going to see an explosive growth of AI utilization by organizations.

Industry Statistics **$97.9B**

Spending on AI systems in 2023, which is more than two and one-half times the amount that was spent in 2019 according to an IDC report[267].

---

[267] https://www.idc.com/getdoc.jsp?containerId=prUS45481219

Democratization of AI

Cloud providers see a huge opportunity for key technologies like ML and AI and that is why they are trying to democratize both ML and AI. They are not only trying to simplify technologies but also offering tools, services, online training, and other products to make sure that they can have data scientists, developers, and other IT professionals to starting using ML/AI technologies quickly and easily.

Taking Microsoft as an example, for developers they offer free online learning courses, free IDE tools such as Visual Studio Code for multiple platforms (Windows, Mac, Linux), and pre-built AI API for them to quickly build intelligent AI apps. For IT professionals, with minimal data science and developer skills, they have Azure Machine Learning Studio within the Azure Machine Learning portal. Using the machine learning studio, IT professionals can quickly and easily build ML models which can be incorporated within the AI applications.

For data scientists and hybrid developer/data scientist roles, they offer ML/AI compute infrastructure and scaling ability to handle compute intensive machine learning models which may be using large training data set and utilizing complex machine learning algorithms.

AI governance framework

Organization considering and building AI-based systems should consider creating an AI governance framework to make sure that they are using the technology to benefit both businesses and humans. Responsible AI principles should be core part of your AI framework. Responsible

AI ensures that fair, ethical, transparent, and accountable practices are followed for creating and maintaining AI-based systems.

An AI framework should consider the following key elements of the AI technology:

Fairness

Any AI system should treat all people fairly and should not be favorable or negatively biased to certain groups or types of people. There are already examples of AI-based systems in criminal justice, recruitment and finance industry which have not treated people fairly because of the data and the algorithms used behind them. Any system built should be fully tested to make sure that it doesn't intentionally or unintentionally is biased against certain groups or people.

Reliability & safety

The AI systems which are being build are going to be reliable and safe and not going to harm the user of the surroundings where they are deployed. Imagine an AI system installed in a chemical factory that can predict the ambient toxicity levels of chemicals. Even if there are some negative repercussions that may exist from the use and the maintenance of such systems, they should be documented and disclosed to the potential users of these AI systems.

Inclusiveness

This principle speaks to the inclusion of all the underrepresented and marginalized communities in our society and ensures that we include people of these communities to not only help us build the AI systems but also assist in testing to make sure that such systems are going to work well for all communities in our society including minorities, migrants, people with disabilities, etc.

Accountability

An organization building an AI system is accountable for the implications, both good and bad, that their AI-based system may have on people, society, and the environment. This same accountability should also be passed on to the partners and resellers who may be using your AI technology in their products and services.

Human assessment

All ML/AI processes, and models should be reviewed by humans to assess the accuracy of the results and predictions that a model may be making. This stems from the fact that models are not perfect, and we want to ensure that they are reviewed by humans for accuracy of the results and predictions they are making. This is where a data scientist or business analysts can double check the results produced by machine learning models rather than putting their blind trust in the machine learning model results.

Bias detection and evaluation

There should be processes setup in your organization to detect, understand and continuously monitor the machine learning and deep learning models for bias. These models are the underlying technology in the AI-based systems. As discussed in the machine learning challenges section in chapter 4, Machine learning data sets and algorithms are the two biggest sources for introducing bias into the models. Business analysts and data scientists need to deeply understand the data set and how it can introduce bias in a machine learning-based system. Along with that the data scientists need to understand the context is which the model is going to be used so they can accordingly adjust the algorithm.

Displacement strategy

This aspect of AI considers and fully documents how AI-based systems will affect the human workforce. Will there be job losses or new jobs created because of the creation of an AI system(s) in the organization? What processes are in place or need to be created to mitigate the effect of any possible human workforce job losses. What training should be considered to minimize the effect on the human workforce?

Practical accuracy

Practical accuracy is achieved by making sure that the underlying machine and deep learning models are producing reproducible results regardless of using different training data sets, moving your models from development to production environments, or scaling your AI system. Ensure that the AI systems are producing accurate results in all the applications where the AI system is going to be used.

Regulatory compliance

Depending on your industry or global region, you may have to maintain certain compliance standards for your IT systems. Make sure that the AI systems are compliant with all the regulations of your industry and region where the AI system is going to be deployed. Create and maintain documentation on how the AI system is fully compliant for your industry and global requirements. You will also need processes in place to monitor for newer regulations along with making sure that you are renewing any required compliance certifications periodically.

Technical advancements

There have been a few notable technical advancements in the field of AI that are going to affect us personally and professionally alike in the future. These include the availability of the next version of the generative transformer, usage of deep learning in the next generation of AI systems, and deepfakes.

GPT-3

Generative Pre-Trained Transformer (GPT-3) is one of key advancements which have been made in the AI in 2020 and will surely affect us and will transform AI for many years to come. It is called generative since it can generate human like coherent output. It has been trained with an over excessive amount of data from the Internet. Along with that it has multilingual capability which will help with global use. From data scientist perspective, GPT-3 is highly advanced and complex with around 175 billion algorithmic parameters compared to 1.5 billion parameters from its predecessor GPT-2. The advanced nature of GPT-3 makes it highly advanced and very closely mimicking and providing human like response. There is a waiting list available if your organization wants to test out GPT-3's API for use in your products and services. OpenAI, the creator of GPT, has also exclusively licensed it out to Microsoft to use in its AI products and services. The key thing to understand about GPT-3 is its general-purpose nature and compared to other AI models out there that enable one off use cases, GPT-3 can be used for various general scenarios. Some of the key and obvious scenarios include:

- Chatbots
- Language translator
- Create content (blog post, book, poem, etc.)

- Customized search
- Write developer code.

The above list will surely grow as the API is made public and organizations start enabling other business uses cases involving general input and output.

Deep learning

As discussed earlier deep learning is a form of machine learning but much more advanced since it tries to mimic the human brain. Instead of just one machine learning model between the input and output of a typical AI/ML system, deep learning uses neural networks, very similar to a human brain. One of the key requirements for building and training deep learning models, is the need for massive and persistent compute power for the models to get trained and run. This has been a hindrance for small to mid-sized organizations to use deep learning for their AI products and services. The cloud providers are now trying to solve that problem by offering hyperscale and globally available compute power and infrastructure. Although the current growth is slow for organizations using deep learning in their AI systems, we are going to continue to see the growth of deep learning in AI systems to improve the accuracy of the output and to emulate human-like behavior of their systems.

Industry Statistics **16%**

of the respondent organizations reported that they have moved from their pilot stage to production state for utilizing deep learning for their AI initiatives according to a McKinsey report[268].

Deepfake

The term deepfake comes from the combination of "deep learning" and "fake". In simple terms, it is when you can create a falsified video by utilizing deep learning. You can use someone else's face, as an example, in an original video of somebody else. While this kind of visual effects have already been utilized in the movie and entertainment industry for a long time, availability of almost unlimited compute and scalability from cloud providers is now making it possible for enthusiasts, hobbyists, small and mid-sized organizations to also create AI systems utilizing deep learning. The technology behind deepfake is not simple to use and automated in any way and in some cases may take multiple days to train the deepfake AI model. Tools and services, however, are popping up to simplify and automate the deepfake system. Deepfake is dangerous in nature and can be used in nefarious ways. For this reason, many tech companies, including Microsoft, are coming up with tools to detect such deepfake systems.

◆ ◆ ◆ ◆ ◆ ◆ ◆ ◆ ◆ ◆ ◆

---

[268]  https://www.mckinsey.com/Business-Functions/McKinsey-Analytics/Our-Insights/Global-survey-The-state-of-AI-in-2020

SUMMARY

In this chapter we discussed artificial intelligence, its importance to organizations of all sizes and some common business cases. We also assessed the various factors to be considered for building an AI strategy. Azure AI services section looked at the core AI services and tools available as part of the Microsoft's Azure AI platform including Azure Cognitive Services, Azure Bot Services, Azure Cognitive Search and Azure Databricks. Key business and technical challenges in using and adopting AI in your organizations were examined along with the future predictions and assessments of AI.

In the next chapter, we will review another important prolific technology, Internet of Things (IoT), which also works in tandem with ML/AI for some use cases, and is very quickly making waves in the consumer, commercial, and industrial world with accelerated adoption.

CHAPTER 6:

INTERNET OF THINGS

IOT OVERVIEW

Internet of things or IoT is a network of "things" which typically are smart devices with certain sensors and software and connected to the Internet. Common sensors found on these devices include temperature, humidity, pressure, gas, smoke, proximity, accelerometer, gyroscope, optical and infrared. These sensors are constantly measuring the required metric and sending the data back to the central location. These devices have been used for consumer, commercial, and industrial purposes for decades.

IoT is enabling controlling, managing, and maintaining these devices remotely over the Internet. All these devices are generating data utilizing the sensors. This data can now be sent back to the cloud for analysis, storage, and triggering business or operational actions. Other emerging technologies such as ML and AI are used with IoT to help analyze the constant stream and large amount of data to make business decisions, predictions, or initiate other actions.

Thus, IoT is driving deeper insights and predictions on the devices along with helping businesses automate many of the tasks related to actions they need to take for their business processes. See **Figure 6-1** for an all-up view of separate phases of an IoT system from devices to connectivity to the cloud for processing/analysis and storage, generation of insights, and eventually leading to actions being taken.

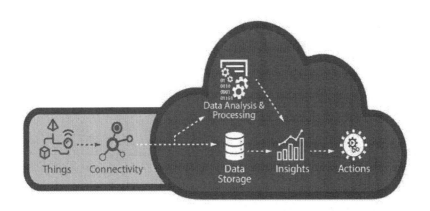

Figure 6-1

An example from consumer domain is a smart motion detector in a house that detects some movement in the house and can send that data back to the cloud, which is quickly analyzed and then an action is triggered to inform the homeowner of this movement detection via an application, automated phone call, or an SMS text message.

Industry Statistics
8.2%

IoT spending growing year over year to $742 billion in 2020 down from 14.9% growth forecast in the November 2019 according to the IDC report[269].

Although the spending for IoT was down in 2020, primarily due to COVID-19 pandemic, IDC is predicting that IoT will bounce back in 2021 and will achieve a compound annual growth rate (CAGR) of 11.3% from 2020 to 2024.

For the industrial use case, consider a manufacturing facility where certain temperature needs to be maintained for operations to continue. Temperature sensing IoT devices can be used in this scenario to monitor the temperature. If the temperature changes from the pre-configured threshold, these devices are sending all their sensor measurements back to the cloud for quick analysis and operational action can follow. The floor supervisor can be notified, or a field technician can be dispatched to the manufacturing facility to review, troubleshoot, and fix the issue.

In the recent few years, we have seen the world of edge computing that has flourished around overall IoT

---

[269] https://www.idc.com/getdoc.jsp?containerId=prUS46609320

systems. Edge computing enables the partial processing of IoT devices generated data close to the IoT devices, by utilizing additional edge devices, rather than sending it all the way back to the cloud for processing. Thus, edge processing reduces latency and allows for real-time actions. IoT data can still go back to the cloud for storage, deeper analysis, and insights.

Expert Opinion	"Edge technology delivers on solving the main weaknesses of cloud technology: latency and bandwidth restrictions. It also reduces the dependency on internet connectivity, which enables higher adoption of cloud technology in industrial environments. For many organizations, the gap between cloud and on-premises is too large and edge technology can reduce that gap."
	Johannes Drooghaag[270], CEO Spearhead Management

Edge computing is enabled via the availability of special edge devices. Most of the top cloud providers offer these devices as part of their IoT services offerings. Amazon, for example, has AWS Snowball and Snowcone devices[271] while Microsoft has Azure Stack edge devices[272]. All these devices can be used for varying level of data storage, analysis, and machine learning processing. See **Figure 6-2**. Machine learning models in these devices process the data coming from the IoT devices and make predictions, decisions and trigger appropriate real time actions.

---

[270] https://www.linkedin.com/in/johannesdrooghaag/
[271] https://aws.amazon.com/snow/
[272] https://azure.microsoft.com/en-gb/products/azure-stack/edge/

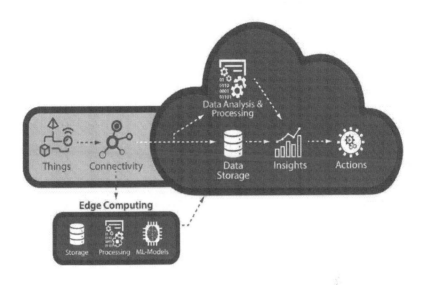

Figure 6-2

How IoT works

IoT is not a single technology solution but a complex combination of hardware, software, cloud services, and technologies which enable the various phases of IoT including data collection, analysis, insights generation, and actions. Top Cloud providers such as Amazon, Microsoft, and Google offer IoT and a suite of related services to make sure that your organization can enable their IoT business scenarios. Due to the number of technologies and the corresponding complexity that comes with it, typically cloud provider's partners may be required to complete and end-to-end implementation of all IoT solution.

Things and devices

IoT things or devices typically refer to a device with electronic circuit boards with microcontrollers and sensors installed and connectivity to the Internet via a Wi-Fi connection. The sensors are monitoring and generating data, which can be processed by the local microcontroller and then is sent to the cloud via a Wi-Fi, Bluetooth, or other networking technologies. There are many OEM (Original Equipment Manufacturers) who create these devices and all these devices must be certified by the cloud providers so they can work with provider's IoT services.

Industry Statistics	**13.8B**
	Total projected Internet of Things (IoT) devices connected worldwide in 2021 is projected to go up to 30.9 billion units by 2025 according to a Statista report[273].

Connectivity

All the devices for a typical IoT scenario are connected to the on-premises network of an organization owning the devices. First step to connecting them to the Internet is to extend the on-premises network to the cloud so the devices are visible to the public cloud. There are, however, other business use case scenarios where the devices are connected directly to the cloud via wireless networking including cellular and satellite.

---

[273] https://www.statista.com/statistics/1101442/iot-number-of-connected-devices-worldwide/

Cloud IoT services

Once the devices are connected to the public cloud, the cloud provider's IoT services can be utilized to enable all the other phases of the IoT including data collection, analysis, storage and triggering of actions. Various public cloud providers offer IoT services to help organizations enable their IoT scenarios. Amazon offers AWS IoT[274], Microsoft has Azure IoT[275], and Google IoT is called Google Cloud IoT Solutions[276].

Processing and analysis

All the data flowing from IoT devices either must be analyzed close to the devices using one of the edge devices or sent back to the public cloud for analysis and processing. In the early days to IoT all the data was sent back to the cloud for processing. This introduced latency in the IoT system and subsequently led to delays in triggering real-time actions. As mentioned before, this is where edge devices can be used to perform partial processing of data close to the IoT devices and send the rest of the data back to the cloud for additional deeper analysis and data storage. Edge's proximity processing will reduce any latency and will trigger real time actions. For majority of the scenarios, processing and analysis will involve using ML/AI to analyze the stream of data and make decisions or predictions from it.

These edge devices also enable no connectivity scenarios where the IoT devices are disconnected from the cloud. For these disconnected scenarios, these edge devices provide storage and processing of data and later can transmit the required data back to the cloud once the connection is restored to the cloud. An example of that

---

[274] https://aws.amazon.com/iot/
[275] https://azure.microsoft.com/en-gb/overview/iot/
[276] https://cloud.google.com/solutions/iot

---

would be a container ship that may be travelling across the ocean where there may not be any cloud connectivity.

Industry Statistics

61%

IoT projects utilizing AI and ML to build an intelligent and automated system according to a McKinsey report[277].

Customer Story

RXR Realty, is the third largest real estate owner in New York City. They were looking for safety measures, due to COVID-19 pandemic, after the buildings reopened. They settled on using Azure AI and IoT because of all their data, analytics, and security requirements which only Microsoft can deliver.

Read the entire story[278]

Storage

All the data from IoT devices can either be analyzed by using any analytical service or stored in the cloud for archival or on-demand processing later down the timeline. As an example, for an Azure Cloud IoT system, Azure Blob Storage, Azure SQL, Azure SQL Data Warehouse or Cosmos DB can be used depending on the

---

[277] https://www.mckinsey.com/business-functions/mckinsey-digital/our-insights/ten-trends-shaping-the-internet-of-things-business-landscape
[278] https://customers.microsoft.com/en-us/story/843823-rxr-realty-reopens-for-business-using-azure-iot

structure of the data. As an alternative, Azure Data Lake can be used for both analysis and storage.

Communication

Various communication technologies can be utilized for enabling IoT scenarios. While a typical network of IoT devices is connected to the cloud via a dedicated telco connection, satellite networks are used in other remote locations such as deserts, rural areas, and oceans to connect to the cloud. With the advent of faster and reliable 5G networks being offered by various telcos, many IoT enablement scenarios are surely going to benefit from this technology. 5G however, is far from being a mature technology and it will take a couple of years before we see widespread use of this technology with IoT systems. For intermittent cloud connectivity or no connectivity to the cloud, edge devices can be utilized.

There are various types of IoT devices that exist in the consumer, commercial, and industrial domains. We are going to review some of these devices in these specific markets and their basic functionality in the following sections.

Consumer IoT (CIoT)

Consumer IoT or CIoT refers to the devices which are used by consumers to simplify and automate many of the previously manual tasks. CIoT can be further classified into sub-categories of **personal devices**, **wearables**, and **smart home devices.**

Personal devices

A smart phone is a key example of personal device which is used for anything we do in our daily life from productivity, communication, social media, gaming, travelling, maps, GPS, and the list goes on. There is an application for most of the common personal tasks we have in our daily lives. Other common personal devices examples include smart stress management, vital signs monitoring, elderly care management, smart body analyzer, pet trackers, and physical asset trackers.

Wearables

Smart watches are one of the core examples of wearables. These smart devices monitor your physical activity, movements, and provide basic health metrics. Apple, Fitbit, and Samsung are three companies which are leading the pack on smart watches. Smart clothing/belts with devices to monitor temperature, heartbeat etc. are also available in the market for personal use. Smart hearing devices or **hearables** are available to help you with listening to any audio along with improving your ear's listening powers.

Smart home

One of the biggest and the hottest markets in the IoT domain is around smart homes. Now you can remotely monitor, control, and manage a range of home devices. Some key examples include kitchen appliances, home security systems, thermostats, fire alarm systems, door lock/unlock systems, house lighting, smart electrical plugs, and digital voice assistants such as Amazon Echo and Google smart speakers.

Customer Story	**Sub-Zero Group**, a kitchen appliances provider of refrigerators, ovens, dishwashers, and microwaves, etc. wanted to build new consumer customer experiences when it came to controlling, managing, and maintaining these appliances. They turned to Microsoft Azure to build a secure mobile app experience for their customers by utilizing Azure IoT technologies. Read the entire story[279]
Expert Opinion	"Over the past decade, IoT as we know it today was a solution looking for problem, and generally experienced a prolonged infancy stage. As we are now seeing exponential growth in the segment, IoT is playing a bigger role in the advancement of "smart" devices, such as watches, appliances, automobiles, and various everyday objects. Consumers and businesses are now finding real-world practicality, where IoT actively enables multi-channel health monitoring, automated inventory and resource management, real-time quality-control feedback, and a multitude of other scenarios. We are only beginning to scratch the surface, but it is clear that beneficial change will one day be democratized for everyone." Mark Gerban[280], Digital Strategy Lead at Mercedes-Benz AG

---

[279] https://customers.microsoft.com/en-gb/story/781398-sub-zero-consumer-goods-azure-iot
[280] https://www.linkedin.com/in/markgerban/

Industrial IoT (IIoT)

Industrial IoT is a network of devices which traditionally have been used in manufacturing, industrial robotics, and the energy sector. There are now various non-manufacturing industries including supply chain, agriculture, healthcare, financial services, retail, and advertising which are also utilizing IoT as part of their digital transformation. The main goal of organizations in utilizing IoT is to improve productivity and enhance operational efficiency. By utilizing IIoT, organizations are closely monitoring devices, processing the data generated from them, and then making quick business decisions around processes, personnel, and their equipment.

Smart cities

Cities which use information and communication technologies and primarily IoT to collect data from various assets in the city including commercial buildings, schools, libraries, hospitals, parking lots, parks, public service facilities, traffic systems, city surveillance systems, and other public systems are typically referred to as smart cities. The data collected from all the devices and assets is then analyzed for trends, anomalies, and relationships and actions are taken or business decisions are made to improve the operational efficiency of the city and improving the quality of life of the people residing in the city. IoT data analysis also helps in making decisions on any future enhancements and expansion plans for the city. Some of the key technologies utilized in creating smart cities include cloud computing, IoT, ML, AI, analytics dashboards, and mesh networks. According to the Smart

City Governments[281] ranking of the top global smart cities in the world Singapore, Seoul, London, Barcelona, and Helsinki lead the pack as the top five smartest cities in the world.

◆ ◆ ◆ ◆ ◆ ◆ ◆ ◆ ◆ ◆ ◆

---

[281]  https://www.smartcitygovt.com/

BUSINESS USE CASES OF IOT

In this section, we will explore some commercial and industrial IoT use case scenarios to highlight how organizations are digitally transforming using IoT and related technologies.

Real-time analytics, anomaly detection, suggesting predictive maintenance, providing quicker real-time response actions, delivering deeper insights on the detected issues, and recommending corrective measures are some of the key things that an end-to-end customized IoT solution can provide. We will also review some key industries which are already reaping the benefit of utilizing IoT to reduce costs and improve operational efficiencies.

Industry Statistics

61%

Enterprises now have achieved high level of IoT maturity according to a Gartner report[282].

Commercial use

There are many examples of commercial IoT solutions. In the following sections we discuss some common commercial scenarios including car park monitoring, traffic management, temperature monitoring, and elevator management.

Car Park monitoring

The use of IoT in parking garages helps vehicle users know the availability of a parking spot's availability through visual electronic boards in the parking garages and smart phone applications. Sensors and controllers are placed for each parking spot to see if it is occupied or not. Data is sent periodically to the electronic board in the parking garage and to the cloud to a customized IoT solution utilizing an IoT hub. This IoT solution has a consumer mobile application. The consumer uses the mobile application to see which parking spots are open in the parking garage. Such an IoT solution helps consumer pre-planning before visiting the parking garage, avoiding traffic congestion in the garage along with avoiding customer irritation. It also improves customer experience and satisfaction along with your organization living up to customer expectations.

---

[282] https://www.gartner.com/en/information-technology/insights/internet-of-things

Traffic management

Monitoring traffic in a city via cameras integrated with an intelligent IoT system can help local governments with traffic management, plan future road and other related construction, respond quickly to traffic accidents along with observing and reacting to any criminal activity. Responding to traffic incidents and sending emergency response teams, in near real-time, is one of the most common use cases and helps not only in saving lives and long-term injuries but an IoT system can also recommend detours for the other drivers to avoid subsequent traffic jams thus improving the efficiency for all the drivers close to traffic incident scene.

A typical traffic monitoring system will include IoT enabled cameras and traffic lights along with an IoT backend that can analyze the video feed and utilizing an AI-based video analysis can predict the traffic issue, along with immediately triggering a dispatch of emergency response teams to the scene.

Temperature monitoring

Temperature monitoring is one of the most common scenarios in commercial and industrial IoT domains. One common commercial scenario is the monitoring of temperature inside a data center. Computers and electronic circuitry inside the computers must have certain ambient temperature to be maintained around them. If the ambient temperature inside one part of the data center in a computer rack goes up above a certain threshold, it can lead to the electronic circuitry failure, leading a single computer or multiple computers failures in the rack.

To avoid this catastrophic situation, a data center may have ambient temperature monitoring IoT devices in different parts of a data center, within the racks, and inside large sized computers. The data from the IoT devices gets analyzed in real-time and if an anomaly is detected from one of the devices, it can be quickly identified. A technician is dispatched to fix the issue or the computer/rack failovers to another computer/rack in a different part of the data center or to different regional data center. Anomalies in data in this case is defined as any temperature above the pre-configured temperature threshold that was setup initially when IoT devices were configured for the data center.

A similar example of temperature monitoring is IoT devices in a cold storage warehouse where all the stored products must be kept at certain temperature. Another common everyday scenario is in grocery stores where IoT devices may be used to monitor the frozen food sections. This monitoring avoids food spoilage and improves shelf life for the frozen items. IoT systems can alert the store employees to take corrective measures as soon as the temperature goes above the pre-configured threshold.

Elevator management and monitoring

Elevator management and monitoring is another prime candidate for utilizing IoT devices within the elevator. These devices can be used not only to monitor the performance of the elevator but also manage it remotely. If one of the monitored parts of the elevator starts sending anomalous data, that can be used to trigger predictive maintenance and alert the field technician to perform preventive maintenance on the elevator. Such predictive maintenance avoids long term permanent damage to the elevator which may be costly to the company owning the building compared to just getting preventive maintenance performed on the elevator. Along with cost savings, IoT devices in an elevator will also help with avoiding any potential safety incidents with the elevator. There may be various IoT devices installed in an elevator monitoring various main components of the elevator.

Customer Story	**ABB**, a software vendor, and a Microsoft partner built an aquaculture solution for one of its key customers, Norway Royal Salmon (NRS), utilizing Azure AI platform and Azure IoT. Using these technologies, they were able to help NRS manage and optimize their aquaculture business along with employees' well-being. Read the entire story[283]

Industrial use

There are certain key industries which are currently going through digital transformation to reduce operational costs, improve customer satisfaction, or potentially grow revenue via new services. These industries include manufacturing, energy, healthcare, retail, and transport & logistics.

Manufacturing

In the manufacturing industry IoT devices are being used along with the manufacturing equipment to not only manage the manufacturing devices but also enhance the manufacturing devices' reliability and longevity via predictive maintenance. An IIoT-based system can have

---

[283] https://customers.microsoft.com/en-gb/story/769806-abb-partner-professional-services-azure

a central dashboard which can be used to monitor, in real-time, the key performance indices (KPI), view alerts and warnings, examine the details of the monitored equipment, along with identifying the equipment anomalies and possible solutions to them.

Energy

The energy sector is another key area where IoT is being utilized for optimizing operations and reducing costs both for the energy organizations and their customers. Some common scenarios for the energy industry include - electrical grid management to provide holistic oversights, trigger predictive maintenance, and provide safety measures for the workers. Electrical vehicle (EV) charging stations can be remotely monitored and serviced. As a manufacturing facility, you can monitor your emissions along with working on initiatives to reduce emissions levels to go above regulated thresholds or other internal sustainability targets. Grid operators can also use IoT devices to monitor and balance supply demand for electricity and avoid severe power outages.

Healthcare

The healthcare industry has many use cases for IoT. Using IoT you can now monitor patients remotely. This was one of the most common scenarios that the healthcare industry used during the COVID-19 pandemic. Availability of personal IoT devices which perform various health monitoring tasks including vital signs checking are already available to many consumers. Most of the hospitals which have embarked on digital transformation journeys have also upgraded several of their regular patient care equipment, which is now IoT enabled and helping them manage and monitor this equipment efficiently. IoT devices are now being utilized in certain hospitals to allow for safe and efficient experience for all staff and patients. IoT devices are also used in the medical storage facilities for inventory management and for medical supply chain management to avoid medicine spoilage. The healthcare manufacturing sector is also utilizing IoT to build healthcare devices, products, and medicine with highest quality along with complying with any regulations.

Customer Story	Rancho Los Amigos National Rehabilitation Center, worked with Sensoria Health to build a hardware and software solution for diabetic patients at elevated risk of lower limb amputation. The secured solution was built utilizing hardware, AI, mobile applications, cloud, and IoT. It uses key technologies from Microsoft such as Azure IoT Central and Azure API for FHIR (Fast Healthcare Interoperability Resources). Read the entire story[284]

Retail

The retail industry is also utilizing IoT in different ways to reduce costs, enhance efficiency, and delight customers with in-store, mobile and web experiences. IoT is being used in fulfillment centers, distribution warehouses, and brick and mortar storefronts to automate the supply chain processes. IoT is allowing not only the tracking of products from the manufacturing facility to the retail outlets but also allowing customers to track their shipments in air, on water or on land. Inventory management is also being automated for both physical

---

[284] https://customers.microsoft.com/en-gb/story/779843-rancho-los-amigos-health-provider-azure

and web storefronts via IoT devices. To protect the customers and store employees, IoT is allowing for digitally securing the data and the physical storefronts. Store analytics and insights from IoT devices can be used in conjunction with provided mobile applications to make recommendations to customers considering their previous purchase history, demographics, and ML models.

Transport and logistics

This industry is also reaping the benefits from IoT. You can use IoT devices on vehicles to understand traffic and congestion and route the logistics fleet vehicles or public transportation vehicles to an alternative route for improved efficiency and on-time operations. Supply chain operations are also being automated with near to real-time tracking from the product supplier to the warehouse, to the distribution center, and eventually to the customer.

IOT STRATEGY & PLANNING

Cloud-enabled IoT implementation is one of the key digital transformation initiatives considered by many organizations. Reducing costs, growing revenue, enhancing operational efficiency, and improving safety are some of the key objectives for organizations to initiate IoT-based digital transformation initiatives. Fundamental requirements of your strategy will involve understanding your requirements, running a pilot, deciding on out-sourcing, choosing the right solution, and considering edge computing.

Industry Statistics

47%

Organizations will increase IoT investments despite COVID-19 pandemic according to a Gartner report[285].

Understanding the requirements

An organization's vision will drive the IoT strategy and will also help in landing the requirements for the IoT initiative. There are some basic questions and considerations that need to be addressed upfront so the right IoT system can be built which will fulfill the organization.

- Is there already an existing IoT network?
  - Are the devices compatible with the selected cloud provider?
  - How good is the security of all the components?
- Is there a need to generate real-time actions from your IoT system?
- Is there a requirement to store all the IoT devices generated data for future analysis and insights?
- Does the planned IoT system require customized development?
- Is there in-house expertise to setup and maintain the IoT system?
- Is there a requirement to create a digital twins system for the physical IoT system?

---

[285] https://www.gartner.com/en/newsroom/press-releases/2020-10-29-gartner-survey-reveals-47-percent-of-organizations-will-increase-investments-in-iot-despite-the-impact-of-covid-19-

---

Once these basic questions have been answered, they will help in building the right strategy for your IoT system.

Pilot to production

Assuming there are internal IT resources available or even if has been decided to out-source the IoT implementation to an external vendor, it is recommended to do a pilot for the eventual production system that needs to be built. Doing such a pilot will not only help you understand the end-to-end system but will expose some additional considerations and requirements that may have to considered as part of your overall strategy.

During the pilot phase, the cloud IoT services can be configured with a set of experimental devices. Not all current IoT devices or the new devices which need to be connected to the IoT infrastructure may be compatible with the selected cloud provider. Each cloud provider keeps a list of compatible devices, which have been certified for their cloud, and this compatibility should be checked upfront.

Security is always a key area of consideration for an IoT system, and all aspects of security should be considered and understood in the pilot phase. This will include devices, IoT infrastructure, edge network, on-premises network, and the cloud infrastructure, and IoT cloud services.

In-house or out-source

Depending on the complexity of your IoT system and the availability of IT resources, a decision needs to be made whether to build the IoT system utilizing internal resources or to out-source the initiative to a third-party vendor. IoT systems are generally very complex in nature and have many components. While your IT staff may understand some parts to the IoT system, they may not understand all the components or how the system functions end to end. For this reason, it is recommended to work with a certified vendor with experience in multiple IoT implementations. Assuming you are going with a cloud provider to use their IoT services, the cloud providers keep a list of partners who can help other customers with IoT implementations. One of these partners can be considered for your IoT implementation. If there is already a vendor of choice, who is maintaining your current IoT system, you want to ensure that they are fully certified to do cloud implementations.

Customer Story	**Mars Inc.**, makes candy bars such as Mars bars, Milky Way, M&M, Skittles, Snickers, and Twix. They were looking for a solution to track their displays and interaction with customers during the huge sales moment around Halloween. They worked with Footmarks, a Microsoft partner, and Microsoft to land on Azure IoT for helping them track their displays from creation to end of life. Read the entire story[286]

One practical approach to consider would be to bring in a partner for initial assessment and deployment along with retaining them in the long term for helping with complex maintenance issues. While you are going

---

[286] https://customers.microsoft.com/en-gb/story/776730-mars-inc-consumer-goods-azure

through the assessment and deployment of the system, train your internal IT staff to understand the system so they can manage and maintain it in the long run.

Type of solution

Before a solution is chosen from a cloud provider, there are some key questions that need to be answered upfront to help pick the right solution offered from the cloud provider.

Basic infrastructure decisions that should be made upfront include:

- Are you utilizing your current IoT vendor's infrastructure for managing your existing IoT network?
- Do you want to setup your own IoT network and connect it directly to your cloud provider?
- Do you want to connect your own IoT network to your on-premises infrastructure in the middle and then connect to the cloud provider?

| Customer Story | **Bentley systems**, a software and systems provider, helps its customers with large infrastructure projects anywhere from commercial and industrial plants, public utilities, to road & rail networks. They decided on Azure digital twins to help their customers visualize and make sense of the data from large infrastructure projects. They used Azure Digital Twins, Azure IoT Hub, and Azure Time Series Insights and related services for their iTwin product. Read the entire story[287] |

---

[287] https://customers.microsoft.com/en-gb/story/806028-bentley-systems-partner-professional-services-azure

---

Cloud providers offer various types of IoT solutions for their customers. Microsoft Azure Cloud as an example provides Azure IoT Central which is a SaaS solution and can be used for low to mid complexity IoT systems. Microsoft Azure also offers wide range of IoT services which can be combined to build a fully customized solution. These options will be further described in the Azure IoT products and services section in this chapter. Azure IoT Central can be a great option for organizations who do not have developers or limited developer resources to work on the IoT initiative but want to get started quick on a basic IoT system. While easy to setup and configure without developer experience, this solution, however, does not have the flexibility to be customized for all your requirements.

Expansion and scalability

If you are going to expand your business globally and with that your IoT network in those regions, one of the first consideration should be if the cloud provider can support you with IoT services in the new global region. If there is a plan to start small with some IoT devices in one region but to grow big in the future, make sure that the cloud provider can offer the required scale in their IoT services to support the future expansion of IoT devices and infrastructure.

One of the key features of cloud computing is that it offers both scale and global expansion capability as the organization's requirements grow. While a small network of IoT devices can be supported and managed via an on-premises or a third-party vendor network using a proprietary IoT solution, growing this IoT system may not be possible. Cloud IoT services can help you to scale the system and to support hundreds or thousands of devices, expand the IoT network globally, or to create a new global IoT infrastructure. With IoT services available in all the key regions of the world, cloud providers can come to the rescue to sustain your global IoT expansion.

Enabling edge computing

If an IoT use case is going to include temporarily disconnected IoT devices along with a requirement to take real time business critical actions, then an edge network should be setup. Edge computing and its relevance to IoT was covered in the IoT overview section previously in this chapter.

Edge computing is a newer development in the IoT world and typically applies to an already existing mature or advanced IoT implementations with a need for real time actions. Enabling edge computing will significantly reduce or eliminate the latency in sending all the IoT data back to the cloud for processing and analysis. See **Figure 6-2**.

Edge computing allows for close-by processing of data on the edge devices which leads to real-time actions getting triggered from the system. Edge devices typically have ML models in them which are used to process IoT data and trigger actions. For temporarily disconnected devices, edge devices offer storage and the ability to upload to the cloud upon network connectivity restoration.

AZURE IOT PRODUCTS AND SERVICES

Microsoft Azure offers a collection of services which can be utilized for the various phases of an end-to-end IoT system, from IoT devices generating data to ingesting that data for processing and analysis, leading to insights to triggering actions from insights. **Figure 6-3** is a typical representation of an end-to-end IoT system utilizing Microsoft technologies for each major phase of an IoT system including devices, edge connectivity, insights, and actions.

In the following sections, we review Microsoft products and services which can be utilized for all the major phases of an IoT solution. We also explore Azure IoT Central, a SaaS IoT solution and compare it with a fully customized IoT solution.

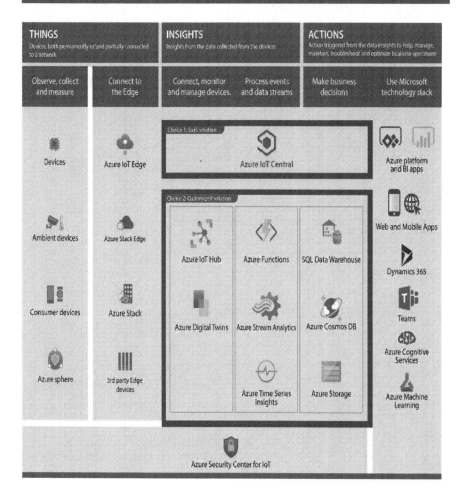

Figure 6-3

Things: devices and things

Azure supports consumer, commercial, and industrial IoT devices. Microsoft has a <u>device certification program</u>[288] which can be used by device manufacturers to certify their IoT devices. Once certified, these devices can be used safely with Microsoft Azure and all the relevant IoT

---

[288] <u>https://www.microsoft.com/azure/partners/azure-certified-device</u>

services. Microsoft also offers various IoT devices services and software.

Azure Sphere

Microsoft offers Azure Sphere[289], a Linux-based microcontroller unit (MCU) which can be used for IoT or edge computing devices. This MCU provides a cloud-based security to make sure that the IoT devices have the latest and greatest security updates pushed from the cloud to them.

Azure RTOS

Azure has a real time operating system[290] (RTOS) for IoT and edge devices utilizing microcontroller units. RTOS is typically used in devices required for real-time processing, with low power and small memory requirements. Combination of Azure Sphere with Azure RTOS can bring top rated real-time processing with stringent security requirements in one device.

Windows for IoT

Microsoft also provides small footprint Windows operating system, such as Windows for IoT[291] which can be utilized in IoT and edge devices to provide the same familiar platform to developers to build intelligent applications, with top notch security features, availability of tools and enterprise level support from Microsoft for their operating system.

---

[289] https://azure.microsoft.com/en-gb/services/azure-sphere/
[290] https://azure.microsoft.com/en-us/services/rtos/
[291] https://www.microsoft.com/en-ww/windowsforbusiness/windows-iot

---

Edge connectivity: IoT Edge

As mentioned earlier in this chapter, edge computing has become extremely popular with the requirements to process IoT device data close to the device rather than sending to the cloud, thus reducing latency in processing, and triggering quick actions from the insights from the device data. There are various Microsoft products and service which are enabling edge computing.

Azure Stack Edge

Azure Stack Edge is a set of intelligent physical devices which can be utilized in the edge, close to the IoT devices. They can process IoT device data, store data to upload to the cloud for thorough analysis, and AI capability to detect anomalies in the IoT data to trigger actions. Currently, Azure is offering three devices depending on the portability, climate endurance and AI capability:

- Azure Stack Edge Pro – GPU
- Azure Stack Edge Pro R
- Azure Stack Edge Mini R

Azure also works with other certified third-party appliances in the edge environment.

Azure IoT Edge

Using Azure IoT Edge services, developers can utilize containers to package business logic needed to analyze and take actions on all the IoT data getting generated by the IoT devices. These containers can be deployed into the edge devices to analyze the data and take any required action if there are anomalies found in the data.

This saves huge costs by not transferring large amounts of IoT device data back to the cloud for analysis.

Azure Stack Hub

Azure Stack Hub allows you to run your own private cloud in your on-premises infrastructure, just like the public Azure Cloud. Azure Stack Hub is typically installed on certified OEM devices. Dell, HPE, Lenovo, Cisco, and Fujitsu to name a few key OEMs offering Azure Stack Hub devices. Azure Stack was covered in chapter 3 when we reviewed Azure cloud services. Azure Stack Hub devices can also be installed in the edge environment.

Insights and actions

When it comes to building an end-to-end IoT solution, Azure offers several choices for organizations to consider. One is to use a SaaS solution, while the other is to build a customized IoT solution using various IoT services and components and the third is to use IoT solution accelerators to get started with IoT templates for some common use cases. Due to the complexity of IoT projects, it is recommended that you work with a Microsoft Azure partner who has experience with IoT implementations. While it is easy to pilot using Azure IoT Central or setting up a an IoT system using the solution accelerators, any customization will require developer resources and an experienced partner to assess, develop, and implement a production IoT system.

Insights and actions: IoT SaaS solution

Azure IoT Central[292] is an example of an end-to-end IoT solution with a web interface that lets you get started quickly and easily to connect devices, collect, process, analyze and then act on the data insights. See **Figure 6-3**.

Azure IoT Central is an enterprise level IoT application platform that allows you to quickly setup, configure, customize, and then start managing and maintaining your IoT solution. It requires almost no development experience to setup and to start using this IoT system. You can quickly start by using the web UI to create a new IoT application or use one of the industrial templates available to you: retail, energy, government, or healthcare. Utilizing the insights from the analyzed data you can interface with other products from the Microsoft products stack, such as Power Apps or Power BI to create additional applications and dashboards. Azure Security Center for IoT is used to secure the Azure IoT Central solution from end to end.

Insights and actions: IoT customized solution

When it comes to building a fully customized IoT solution, Azure offers various components to build a flexible solution built fully to your requirements. A customized solution typically contains various components which Microsoft has provided for the sole purpose for organizations wanting to build fully

---

[292] https://azure.microsoft.com/en-gb/services/iot-central/

customized and complex IoT solutions per their requirements. See **Figure 6-3**.

<u>Azure IoT Hub</u>[293] is an IoT connector between the IoT devices and the Azure Cloud and is used for a two-way communication between the IoT devices and the Azure Cloud. It is a fully managed, scalable, and secure service capable of managing communication from millions of IoT devices.

<u>Azure Digital Twins</u>[294] is the digital representations of all assets in an IoT solution or environment. An IoT solution can be for various industries such as for agriculture, manufacturing, energy, healthcare, retail or for an entire smart city. Azure Digital Twins allows you to build a digital model of the complete environment. By understanding and analyzing the behavior of the digital twins, it is possible to predict the behavior of the actual physical devices and assets and address any issues before they occur.

For IoT data processing and analysis various services such as Azure Stream Analytics, Azure Time Series Insights, and Azure Functions can be utilized.

<u>Azure Stream Analytics</u>[295] is a secure and a scalable service which can consume data from an Azure IoT Hub or other sources to process and provide real-time analytics. It is capable of ingesting and processing large volume of high-speed streaming data concurrently from multiple sources. Azure Stream Analytics can analyze data and recognize patterns, relationships, and anomalies in the data to trigger actions. Actions can be triggered

---

[293] https://azure.microsoft.com/en-us/services/iot-hub/
[294] https://azure.microsoft.com/en-us/services/digital-twins/
[295] https://azure.microsoft.com/en-us/services/stream-analytics/

using Azure Functions and using other business logic. Azure Stream Analytics is also available for Azure IoT Edge and the Azure Stack Hub. Azure Stream Analytics can further be connected to other Microsoft stack products to build other applications and services.

Azure Time Series Insights[296] is a fully scalable, secure and a cloud managed storage, analytics, and visualization service for IoT data. Its main difference from Azure Stream Analytics is that it provides storage for IoT data and then provides visual analytics.

An IoT device can be stored for later analysis to various storage options that are available in the Azure cloud including Azure Blog storage, Azure SQL, Azure SQL Data Warehouse, or Azure Cosmos DB. Azure Blob Storage is used for storing large amounts of data for a low cost. This data can be loaded into Azure SQL and Azure SQL Data Warehouse on demand as needed for analysis. Azure SQL and Azure SQL Data Warehouse can be used if the data can be analyzed and saved with relationships to a relational database. If the IoT device data is in JSON (JavaScript Object Notation) key/value format pair, then Azure SQL can be used for storing that data. Azure Cosmos DB can be utilized for storing semi-structured and non-relational data. For securing a customized IoT solution, Azure Security Center for IoT is utilized.

Action: Build value-add applications

As we learnt in the previous section that all IoT data can either be processed and analyzed and actions can be triggered along with the option to save the IoT data for future analysis.

---

[296] https://azure.microsoft.com/en-us/services/time-series-insights/

For real-time actions, you can further integrate other Microsoft products to create other applications to build rich experiences for your customers, partners, and internal employees. These applications include the traditional web and mobile applications along with low-code/no-code application utilizing Power Apps and Power Automate. As an example, a triggered action from the IoT data analysis can be fed into a Power Apps application and using Power Automate, you can create a business flow to email or call someone.

The triggered actions and IoT data can be integrated into customer engagement and back-office applications to provide customers with the latest and up to date information. As an example, if you are monitoring the temperature inside the vending machines in a city using an IoT solution. If the IoT data analysis indicates that the temperature went above a certain set threshold for one of the machines, it can automatically create a ticket for a field technician in a customer engagement application like Dynamics 365 Customer Service.

Another example can be the tracking of products from the factory to warehouse to the retail outlets. An IoT solution can be implemented to track this supply chain process. By feeding the data from the IoT solution to a back-office application like Dynamics 365 Supply Chain Management, you can build an end- to-end tracking system.

IoT data can also be used from Azure SQL or Azure SQL Data Warehouse to analyze and visualize the results. Another example to utilizing IoT data is to use with Azure Machine Learning to train models along with using the data to train custom models for Azure Cognitive Services.

KEY CHALLENGES OF IOT

There are several challenges which should be considered as you embark on a journey to implement or enable a cloud based intelligent IoT system for your organization. Core challenges include complexity of end-to-end system, cost of the implementing and maintaining, security, and scalability and expansion of your system.

Complexity of an end-to-end system

An IoT system can be complex to setup, manage, and maintain. As discussed previously in the IoT strategy section, it is recommended to consider bringing in cloud provider's partner or a third-party vendor with deep experience to help with this initiative. Introducing edge computing into the mix will further complicate the overall implementation. Depending on the scope of your IoT implantation and availability of cloud developer resources you can always decide to go with a IoT SaaS solution, such as Azure IoT Central, which does not require any development work to setup initially and this solution can be used as is without any development if no further customization is required. If there is already an IoT system which needs to be cloud-enabled or there is a requirement to implement a new customized IoT solution, then it will be prudent to work with the one of the cloud provider's partners.

Taking Microsoft Azure as an example, there are many pieces to a customized solution such as devices, Azure IoT Hub, Azure Digital Twins, storage services, and analytics services that you will have to consider just to get started. To allow edge computing scenarios, edge devices must be procured, build any additional infrastructure, and do additional development to fully realize your edge scenarios.

Costly solution

The complexity of an IoT system with many components also leads to an overall high cost of cloud enabling a current IoT system or setting up a new one. Not only will there be cloud costs for the bundle of services they will provide for your IoT system, there are some additional costs that also need to be considered.

These costs may include IoT devices upgrade or replacement to work with the cloud provider's IoT services. Another cost to consider will be upgrade of the current IoT devices infrastructure if there are already latency issues on the current network. Considering the scope of the IoT system, you may have to bring in cloud provider's partner and advisory experts to help with the initial assessment and implementation of your system. Long term maintenance of the system can be done via in-house expertise but that also means training for the internal resources so they can effectively manage the system in the long run.

If an organization is interested in enabling edge scenarios, cost of edge devices, any new infrastructure costs, and additional development costs will also have to considered. All these costs at the end of the day add up to hefty bill for your organization.

Security

Due to the complexity of an IoT system with several components, the security story of an IoT system is also very complex. What makes it hard is not only the number of components present in an end-to-end IoT system but also the fact that a cloud enabled IoT system may be in a hybrid environment, and at that point you must consider the security of your IoT infrastructure estate, on-premises network, and the cloud IoT services that you are consuming from the cloud provider.

The vast expanse of digital estate of an IoT system spanning from the IoT network to the on-premises network, to the cloud infrastructure does expose a large surface area and digital assets for cyber-attacks.

Security should be considered for all the major components of your end-to-end IoT system including:
- Physical and software security of the IoT devices
- Security of the IoT network
- Infrastructure security of the on-premises network if it is connected in the middle.
- Security of all cloud resources and services

Along with the questions above you want to ensure that all the devices, infrastructure and services have the latest and greatest security updates and patches always installed. Azure IoT Defender is an example of a product you can use from Microsoft Azure to secure all your devices.

Real-time monitoring of your IoT system is also a key element of IoT security. A SIEM (Security Information and Event Management) solution can be utilized for aggregating security events, analyzing them, detecting potential security threats, and then providing insights and recommendations on corrective actions. A SIEM system like Azure Sentinel, works with Azure Defender, and can be used to provide end to end monitoring for an IoT system.

Industry Statistics

47%

Organizations which have been a target of IoT cyberattack and around 26% admitting high to severe impact according to a McKinsey report[298].

---

[297] https://www.linkedin.com/in/johannesdrooghaag/
[298] https://www.mckinsey.com/business-functions/mckinsey-digital/our-insights/ten-trends-shaping-the-internet-of-things-business-landscape

Expertise

As mentioned earlier, IoT is not simple and has many components and pieces associated with it. Due to the breadth of technologies involved, it cannot really be managed and maintained by a single staff member. A customized IoT system, depending on the complexity, may require multiple roles including cloud architects, developers, data scientists, database administrators, and data analysts. Cloud architects to help build an end to end cloud enabled IoT system, developers to assist in building and maintaining a customized IoT system (IoT backends, digital twins, web and mobile applications, etc.) data scientists to train and build machine learning models to be used in the edge infrastructure or in the cloud, database administrators to design databases and data warehouses to store IoT for real-time or future analysis, and data/business analysts to analyze the data and provide business insights and analytics to the organization. As it can be imagined, it is hard to find all this talent easily and retain them for the long run. For implementing a new IoT system, there will be substantial ramp up time and training required for all the roles engaged in the IoT system implementation. As mentioned previously, due to the complex nature of IoT, it is recommended to work with one of the cloud provider's partners to help through the initial assessment and implementation.

FUTURE OF IOT

There are several IoT trends to lookout for and think through for the next couple fo years. There is be going to an increase in organizations adopting edge computing to unlock real-time business scenarios and the edge is going to get more intelligent with additional ML/AI workloads. Due to the complexity and the various components involved, there is going to be a need for a governance framework within an organization along with understanding the IoT data privacy and usage. On the technical front, we are going to see improvements around IoT hardware and software along with satellite and 5G technologies playing a bigger role as wireless networking technologies. All these technical advancements are going to lead to organization creating additional business use cases for IoT.

Increased Edge adoption

As mentioned earlier in this chapter, edge computing supports both nearby processing of data from the IoT devices along with the disconnected scenario.

There is going to be an increased usage and adoption of edge computing as organizations understand its benefits and implementation. The need to trigger real time actions from the edge is going to be one of the key reasons for the adoption of edge computing. Support for edge computing from top cloud providers, availability of smart edge devices and appliances, reduced size of ML models in the edge devices are some of the other factors which will fuel the usage and growth of the edge.

Enhanced intelligent edge

One of the key things built into most of the edge devices, is the ability to process and analyze the IoT data and then trigger actions. This is typically done via embedded ML and AI technology. There are two technical advancements going on that will further enhance this intelligent processing and analysis of data at the edge. First is TinyML where a reduced size machine learning model can be created and provide the same level of capability as a larger ML model. TinyML models can exist on the IoT device itself or in the edge devices.

Second is the ability for deep learning models to be also available in the edge devices and having the capability to run in the low energy requirement edge devices but providing highly accurate results and predictions. Deep learning models typically are more compute-intensive and provide accurate output.

Governance framework

The sheer complexity of an IoT system dictates that there be a proper governance framework setup with an organization. There are several factors which need to be considered in the governance framework, both from technical and business perspective. For business perspective cost, scale, expansion, and privacy of the data being generated from the devices is important. From the technical lens, you should look at IoT devices compatibility, devices upgrades, devices firmware updates, and security configuration for the end-to-end IoT system. The framework should document the best practices and guidelines, which can be used within the IT unit or across other units which may be interested in implementing IoT for their use cases.

Data privacy and usage

As more and more data gets generated from IoT devices, we are going to see heightened concerns around the privacy of the data specially if it contains customer information. Organizations need to consider the existing privacy regulations, its data retention policies, and anonymization of this data before it can be used further within the organizations for insights, analytics, or other purposes.

Non-customer IoT data can also be considered a strategic asset within an organization to be a driver and input for other products and services which can be built by the organization. There may also be an incentive to sell this IoT data to third party organizations which may use it further to build related products and services.

Hardware and software improvements

There are going to be continuous improvements in the hardware and software of the IoT devices, edge devices, infrastructure, and the cloud IoT services. These hardware and software enhancements are going to lead to much more secure components IoT systems.

Security of an overall IoT system is one of the key concerns when deploying or maintaining such a system. Security at the device level, infrastructure level, and cloud service level are all key elements of securing the overall end to end IoT system. The IoT devices not only have to be secured physically but also via the firmware.

New devices are going to available which will enhance the overall device security. One such example of a new and improved hardware and software-based device is Azure Sphere. It is microcontroller unit (MCU) which can be used on IoT device to enhance its security. It contains core Linux operating system and cloud-based security service that can continue to update the device's software security and keep it up to date.

There are going to be similar security and hardware improvements in the edge devices. Newer enhanced edge devices will be made available with low power requirements to support processing and analysis of IoT for longer periods of time.

The sensors on the IoT devices are also going to see enhancements with additional low-cost sensors being available for the IoT devices. These sensors will have low power requirements and will have the ability to operate under harsh weather conditions. All these advancements in hardware and software will unlock additional IoT business use cases.

Emerging wireless technologies

Many top telcos in US, like T-Mobile, AT&T, and Verizon are now offering 5G wireless services in some regions of the US. At the same time smart devices are also extending support for these networks. Currently, the coverage area for 5G mobile network is limited so it will take a few years before the telcos can expand their coverage across their country of operation. 5G networks have many benefits including higher speeds, capacity, and support of additional devices. It will take a couple of years before all the telcos and devices start supporting 5G networks.

Another key wireless technology which is going to be utilized from the edge devices is the satellite network. This will help resolve the issue with disconnected IoT systems. Satellite connections along with the feature of cloud-based satellite ground stations such as Azure Orbital are going to enable some key IoT scenarios for connecting IoT edge devices in remote, rural, or harsh climate places to the cloud.

SUMMARY

IoT is one of the critical technologies being utilized for digital transformation initiatives. This technology is primarily used to reduce costs, improve operational efficiencies along with building new and improved customer experiences. As reviewed and discussed in this chapter, IoT is utilized not only by consumers but also used in the commercial, industrial, and public sector. Some of the key industries benefiting from IoT include manufacturing, energy, healthcare, retail, and transport & logistics.

In the strategy and planning section, we also looked at the key strategy elements to consider including implementing in-house or out-sourcing, choosing the right type of solution, scaling, and expanding the IoT implementation globally. We also reviewed the key challenges for implementing this technology for your organization including complexity, cost, security, and expertise. We wrapped up the chapter with discussing the future trends of this technology.

This technology also has the potential to work with other emerging technologies such as blockchain, for additional use cases.

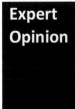

Expert Opinion

"IoT can extend trust to a blockchain network as it expands trust between devices and participants of the blockchain network reducing chances of data-tampering before being added to a blockchain as human intervention is not involved in the flow of the data."

Antonio Figueiredo[299], RVP Salesforce

In next chapter we will be introducing and discussing Blockchain.

CHAPTER 7:

BLOCKCHAIN

BLOCKCHAIN OVERVIEW

According to the Merriam-Webster dictionary, blockchain is "a digital database containing information (such as records of financial transactions) that can be simultaneously used and shared within a large decentralized, publicly accessible network"[300]. The name blockchain is derived from the fact that records are batched together in "blocks" before they are committed to the database. Each block is secure from tampering using cryptographic hashing[301]. The "chain" part of blockchain comes from the fact that the hash value of a block takes both the content of the block as well as the hash value of the previous block before it, to generate the hash for the block, hence "chaining" each block together. Chaining each block to the previous block means that an attempt to alter published blocks on the

---

[300] https://www.merriam-webster.com/dictionary/blockchain
[301] https://en.wikipedia.org/wiki/Cryptographic_hash_function

---

chain would require hacking the hash of all previous blocks which, while technically possible, is practically infeasible.

Figure 7-1

A blockchain network consists of multiple computers (nodes) that each have a copy of the blockchain database. Each node on the network also participates in a process called "network consensus", which means all nodes must agree to the execution of transactions on the network for the transactions to be committed to the chain.

The first blockchain, Bitcoin, was introduced in 2005 with the aim of providing a decentralized and anonymous method for exchanging digital currency (cryptocurrency) between parties without having a centralized authority, such as a bank, as a go-between to facilitate the transfer. This enabled those in the world who do not have access to a bank account or live in a country where the government-issued currency is unstable, to have a secure and cost-effective substitute to traditional banking. Quickly evolving, other blockchains came onto the market, such as Ethereum, that built on top of the premise of Bitcoin by providing both a cryptocurrency, but also the ability to run code on the blockchain, introducing state machine logic enabling conditional events to determine if, when and how much of the cryptocurrency should be transferred.

So why is blockchain considered an important technology for digital transformation? While the idea of using blockchains as a currency transfer system is appealing to many organizations, the primary reason why enterprises are looking to blockchain has more to do with increasing trust and transparency, specifically for multi-party systems. Being able to have a cryptographically secured means to prove non-repudiation of transactions and asset provenance significantly reduces the manual processes that exist today for auditing and dispute resolution.

In this chapter, we'll explore the fundamentals of blockchain technology, different types of blockchains, with a focus on how enterprises are deploying blockchain-based solutions as part of their digital transformation journey.

Expert Opinion	"Blockchain is fundamentally a distributed system at scale. In concert with the drive to networks of value in the market, the technology meets the moment to solve many problems building systems across the boundaries of enterprises."

Yorke E. Rhodes III[302], Director Digital Transformation Cloud Supply Chain, Microsoft
Cofounder Blockchain @Microsoft & Baseline Protocol

---

[302] https://www.linkedin.com/in/yorkerhodes/

ENTERPRISE ATTRACTION TO BLOCKCHAIN

State of the art systems in place today for multi-party business workflows suffer from several challenges. Integration of disparate systems, lack of shared governance and security controls, and data integrity guarantees to name a few. Surprisingly, many legacy processes that exist today are comprised of emailing copies of spreadsheets between parties as the "state of record". As a result, reconciliation of data disputes is manual, time-consuming, and expensive. Blockchain promises to solve many of these challenges through digitizing data on a shared ledger that can be trusted using cryptography. The following four characteristics of blockchain, regardless of the protocol being used, address these concerns.

Industry Statistics

$19B

In 2021, global spending on blockchain solutions is projected to reach 6.6 billion dollars. Forecasts[303] suggest that spending on blockchain solutions will continue to grow in the coming years, reaching almost 19 billion U.S. dollars by 2024.

Immutability

The characteristic of blockchain being an immutable ledger is a fundamental element of the technology that makes it attractive for enterprise use. Ensuring that transactions, once agreed upon through consensus, are not able to be modified once committed to the ledger provides assurance to all parties in the network that the data is an authentic representation of the history of transactions in full. Traditional database systems can also achieve this functionality through audit logging, which provides a history of actions taken on the database, however inspecting the audit log can be time-consuming and more importantly, the audit log itself can be tampered with if not secured properly.

Cryptographically ensuring ledger state allows all parties to 'trust the math' and take for granted that the data being represented is in fact, the final state.

---

[303] https://www.statista.com/statistics/800426/worldwide-blockchain-solutions-spending/

Expert Opinion	"Blockchain has surely touched, if not disrupted, every major industry and is even altering the norms of interaction between people and societies. Blockchain's foundational underpinnings i.e., removal of intermediaries, immutable and cryptographically secure data, transparency to all parties, and frictionless transactions are game-changing in the digital economy. As the expression goes, it is more power to the people. The dust of being a buzzword has fallen off and blockchain-enabled business models are bringing a seismic shift to how business will be conducted in future."
	Priya Guliani[304], Head of Operations, GBA-UK, Senator, WBAF

What if you made an error in a transaction, and need to correct it? For example, if I had sent Sally five dollars but, I owed her six, what would I do? I could simply send her another dollar to settle the balance. While this is a simple example, it is precisely how a blockchain operates. Sending a corresponding correcting transaction would "correct" the ledger state but show the history of originally sending her the incorrect amount of five. This is how a ledger, whether blockchain or not, is intended to work, providing a historical record of all transactions.

Smart contracts

While you can trust the immutability of the data on the blockchain, can you trust the business logic

---

[304] https://www.linkedin.com/in/priyaguliani/

(applications) that produced the data? Smart contracts are applications that run on the blockchain network, making them immutable as well as providing a transparent means for participants in the network to see the execution of the smart contract that produced the data residing on the blockchain. Ethereum was the first blockchain to introduce smart contracts, which are developed in a new programming language, called "Solidity[305]". The power of adding smart contracts to a blockchain is a powerful concept, enabling organizations to implement conditional logic which can execute automatically on the blockchain. In our simple example of above of sending Sally six dollars, a smart contract could be implemented such that the transfer of funds happens only if a pre-condition is first met. For example, you buy a coffee from Sally, send Sally six dollars.

But if the smart contracts, like the data on the blockchain, are immutable, then how do update a smart contract, for example if there are bugs? When a smart contract is deployed, it is assigned a smart contract address that the application using the smart contract refers to, so fixing bugs simply means deploying an updated smart contract and ensuring your application points to the smart contract address of the new contract going forward. The benefit here is an immutable record of smart contract versioning, enabling parties participating in the blockchain to know when the smart contract has been updated, and most importantly, what has been updated.

---

[305] https://en.wikipedia.org/wiki/Solidity

All parties have a copy of the ledger

With systems that use a traditional database where data is shared among multiple parties, one of the biggest challenges is who owns, or hosts, the database. The entity that hosts the database would also have full administrative rights to the database system, including the data residing in the database. This requires the other parties that are consuming the data to trust the entity that hosts the database to not alter the data. Whether through a rogue DBA or DevOps engineer, there exists the possibility that data could be altered without transparency to the other parties of the action. As mentioned earlier, inspections of the audit log could take place, but again this is time consuming and expensive as it would require manual effort.

With blockchain systems, each party has a copy of the ledger. It is not a primary/replica model where other parties have a replicated copy of a primary database, but rather each party has the single source of truth. Because of this, you will often hear blockchain referred to as a "distributed ledger".

How, then, is the copy of the ledger that each party has, updated in a consistent manner? Network consensus is the answer.

Network consensus

Blockchains use a process called network consensus[306] to ensure transactions are correct and subsequently updated on all parties' copy of the ledger. Consensus in computing is not a new concept and has been used for

---

[306] https://en.wikipedia.org/wiki/Consensus_(computer_science)

decades primarily for ensuring system reliability in the event of faulty nodes or processes.

Applicability of consensus for blockchain is tied to the network itself, ensuring that nodes owned by parties participating in the network are not faulty. It's also important to note that the term "faulty" does not just mean system availability (such as high availability), but also applies to nodes that could be acting in a malicious manner. In the case of blockchain, if a node that has been altered to attempt to send false transactions to the network, network consensus ensures that the faulty node's transaction is not committed to the ledger.

It's important to note that there are several different network consensus mechanisms that exist in blockchain networks today. For enterprise blockchain use, the choice narrows down to a select few that are designed specifically for the level of trust that exists between parties participating in the network. Enterprise blockchain networks differ in more ways than just which network consensus mechanism is used, such as privacy and confidentiality models, as well as the ability to execute smart contracts on the blockchain. Public blockchain networks, such as Bitcoin, have been designed specifically for anonymity of participants in the network, assuming zero-trust between participants. As a result, the network consensus mechanism employed in zero-trust public blockchains, called "Proof-of-Work" (PoW), are designed to increase the difficulty of malicious parties in the network to be able to send forged transactions. When a block is mined in PoW, every node on the network is competing for the right to validate the proposed block. When a node successfully "mines" a block, they are rewarded with a portion of the cryptocurrency on the network. However, mining a block is not an easy task. To get the right to mine a

---

block on a public blockchain network, the node must solve an ever-increasingly difficult mathematical puzzle. In simplistic terms, the miner must produce a block that contains a hash value below a determined threshold, called the hash difficulty. The only way to accomplish this is through brute force, which is compute intensive. Since the hash difficulty continues to increase, the amount of computing power to generate a hash that meets the difficulty requirements is ever-increasing, requiring the use of multiple computers (known as mining farms), that may have specialized GPUs designed for such computation.

As such, the need for a blockchain designed specifically for enterprise scenarios surfaced and has been solved through what is called a permissioned blockchain.

Expert Opinion	"In the emergent digital economy, where value is in the connection of everything, blockchain stands as one of the most impactful technologies that organizations will use to transform their businesses and ultimately transform how the global economy operates. While this won't happen overnight, a growing momentum will propel blockchain to a 40-billion-dollar market by 2025." Mike Walker[307], Sr. Director of Applied Innovation, Microsoft

---

[307] https://www.mikejwalk.com/

PUBLIC VS. PERMISSIONED BLOCKCHAINS

Bitcoin and Ethereum are public blockchain networks. This means that any entity, whether a large enterprise or a 14-year-old in his basement, can host a node on the network. A node is a computer, or virtual machine, running the blockchain application stack that is connected to the internet and subsequently connected to all other blockchain nodes on the network. Each node has a copy of the ledger, can send, and receive transactions to the network, as well runs the network consensus mechanism necessary to commit transactions to the network. Since any participant can host a node on a public blockchain network, it is assumed that no single participant can be trusted on the network.

As such, for public blockchain networks, the process for network consensus is highly compute intensive to make it infeasible for a single party to be able to compromise the state of the ledger. In Bitcoin and Ethereum for example, 51% of the entire network would need to collaborate to change the committed state of the ledger.

Permissioned blockchains are blockchain networks that are established for a known set of parties that share a business process with one another. For example, a supply chain network where there are multiple parties that must attest for the state of an asset from producer to consumer. Each member of a permissioned blockchain network has a known identity, with the ability for transactions to be private. Let's take a dairy supply chain as an example, where there is a producer (dairy farm), processor, multiple shipping, and storage parties, and ultimately a retail grocery store. In **Figure 7-2**, we must ensure that the dairy product is at a consistent state for temperature and humidity throughout the product lifecycle.

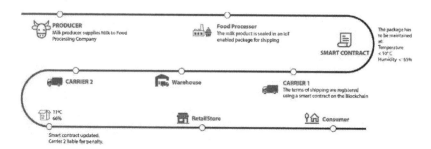

Figure 7-2

Since all parties have a shared interest and existing business processes together, there is semi-trust between all parties on the network. This enables much more efficient network consensus mechanisms that we'll discuss later.

The business process that is being deployed on the blockchain will determine the structure and role of the participants that are on the network. Typically referred to as a consortium, the members that participate in the network may have different privileges assigned to them based on their role in the network. Some members may have rights to perform operations on the network that others do not, such as having the right to add or remove another participant from the network. While public blockchains focus on decentralization, meaning all participants have equal "power" on the network (depending on the number of nodes they host), enterprise blockchains in a consortium are semi-decentralized or centralized.

Let's take our dairy supply chain example above and envision how a consortium would be set up in this case. Likely, the retail store would be considered the "head" of the consortium, as they are the buyer of the dairy products and point of sale of the end-product to the customer. Ultimately, they are responsible for the quality of the goods the customer purchases and subsequently consumes. While the example above is relatively simple, likely there are other contractual requirements the retail store has with members in the consortium, such as time to deliver. If the retail store orders 100 cartons of milk to be delivered by the 10th of the month, if the shipment shows up a day later, the retail store may impose financial penalties to the party responsible for the late shipment.

Let's imagine that a particular shipper continually misses their delivery timelines, and contractual requirements (codified into the smart contracts on the blockchain), state that if the shipper misses a deadline more than three times, the retail store chain has the right to remove the shipper from its supply chain. This would require that the shipper in violation would need to be removed from the blockchain consortium.

Additionally, one shipper in the consortium should not have the ability to remove another shipper from the consortium. So, in this case, the shippers would not have these privileges in the consortium, but rather have participation rights only.

Another important element of permissioned blockchain networks is the requirement for privacy and confidentiality. Some participants on the network should not be privy to the actions and state of other parties. In our dairy example, there are multiple shipping parties. If one of the shipping parties violates the terms of the contract, for example the temperature of one of the trucks exceeds the temperature threshold of 10° C, the other shipping party should not have visibility into this action. The only party that may need to know about this would be the retail grocery store chain as this event may result in penalties to the shipper or worse, cancellation of the shipping contract.

This scenario is a particularly interesting example because it demonstrates two key attributes that in legacy solutions were challenging to achieve.

1. **Attestation of asset responsibility** in real-time with the ability to alert select parties if the dairy product is exceeding certain thresholds of temperature and humidity.
2. **Elimination of manual contract execution**, for example applying financial penalties, if one party violates the contract by exceeding the pre-defined thresholds.

Real-time alerting is incredibly important in this scenario. Without this capability, there is the possibility that the product could be consumed by a customer resulting in the customer becoming ill, or worse, death. Blockchain and IoT enables the ability to detect and alert the appropriate parties such that the shipment can be stopped before ever reaching the customer, thus avoiding the risk of illness.

Certainly, an IoT system alone could accomplish the detection of the environmental conditions of the dairy products and alert parties without blockchain. But what happens on the back end when this happens? In many supply chains today, contracts that impose penalties for failure to comply are executed manually. For example, if one of the shippers violates the contract due to a faulty refrigeration system in a shipping truck, they could recall the truck and subsequently dispose of the contents of the shipment. They would then have to notify the store that the truck is not going to deliver, and the store may impose a financial penalty to the shipper as a result. These all require human interaction – the call, the issuance of the penalty, etc. Again, these can all be automated without blockchain, however where blockchain technologies streamline this process is through the ability to codify the business contract terms into smart contracts on the blockchain itself. These actions can all take place programmatically, but here is where the magic comes in. Since all members of the blockchain network host nodes, they all have the smart contracts executing on their individually owned nodes. There is no dispute with regards to whether the terms of the contract are being interpreted correctly because all parties agreed to the terms when the smart contracts were deployed initially. What blockchain accomplishes in this case is increasing trust and transparency in a manner previously not possible.

Because of these benefits, supply chains are one of the most prevalent use cases for blockchains in development and production today. But the benefits of blockchain extend well beyond supply chains. For examples across

several industries that active blockchain development is
ongoing today, **see Figure 7-3**.

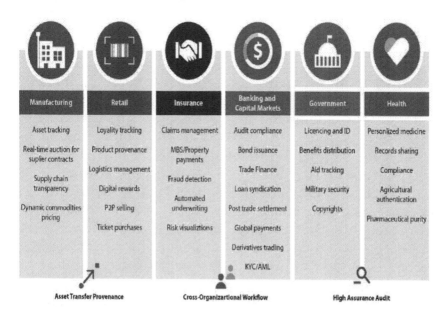

Figure 7-3

Deciding on a blockchain technology

As an emerging technology, the past few years have seen
an explosion of growth and diversity in the types of
blockchain technologies that can be used for enterprise
multi-party applications. Whether a single blockchain
technology will emerge as the primary pattern remains to
be seen, but like database technologies where there are
relational, key-value store and document databases, each
blockchain technology has their place based on what
problems need to be solved by their application. Let's
briefly explore the top blockchain technologies that lead
the market for enterprise adoption and understand what
they have to offer.

Ethereum for the enterprise

Earlier we discussed the differences between public and private blockchains. The power of smart contracts introduced with Ethereum is what gave rise to the interest of blockchain in the enterprise but having your business processes codified in smart contracts on a public blockchain where anyone in the world can see the smart contracts and transactions is not acceptable. This need was discovered early in the history of Ethereum resulting in the formation of the Enterprise Ethereum Alliance[308] (EEA) in 2017. Thirty founding members created the EEA with the mission to "...develop open, blockchain specifications that drive harmonization and interoperability for businesses and consumers worldwide.", working closely with Ethereum Foundation[309]. A primary set of problems to address with the EEA would be to devise a set of specifications[310] that would enable individual entities to create Ethereum-based blockchain clients that would be compatible with one another while still leaving room for innovation. As a result, there are several EEA-compliant Ethereum clients that have emerged onto the market and in use today.

A core difference between public and enterprise Ethereum clients is that the latter does not introduce the concept of a cryptocurrency like Bitcoin or Ether. The intrinsic value of the blockchain itself for enterprise has primarily to do with the business processes being executed on the blockchain rather than the exchange of a cryptocurrency. This has significant impact on the design of enterprise Ethereum clients as the incentive for honest participation in the network has nothing to do

---

[308] https://entethalliance.org/
[309] https://ethereum.foundation/
[310] https://entethalliance.org/technical-documents/

with a currency associated with the network, but rather the participants stake in the network and their ability to benefit from participation in the network itself. As described earlier, by removing unnecessarily compute-intensive consensus algorithms such as PoW in favor of more efficient mechanisms not designed for mining cryptocurrency, increases the speed, and lowers the cost of the network itself. As such, transactions sent on the network do not incur "fees" as they do in public networks, but rather the network being limited to a set of participants that are known, it becomes easy to identify if a participant is spamming a network with transactions to cause a denial-of-service attack.

As the EEA has continued to grow, so have entities that have produced Ethereum clients based on the EEA specification that are optimized for enterprise use cases. We will walk through some of these and discuss their various characteristics.

Hyperledger Besu

Shortly after the formation of Ethereum, one of the founding members of Ethereum, Joe Lubin[311], started ConsenSys[312], a company focused on solution development for Ethereum applications. ConsenSys has since grown, acquiring Quorum from JP Morgan, and investing in a startups funding arm called ConsenSys Labs, which helps seed and grow blockchain technology startups with the goal to enrich the Enterprise Ethereum ecosystem.

ConsenSys created their first Ethereum client in 2018 under the name Pantheon. As an open-source protocol, the intent was to provide an alternative to other

---

[311] https://www.linkedin.com/in/joseph-lubin-48406489/
[312] https://consensys.net/

Ethereum protocols, under the EEA specification. In 2019, PegaSys re-released Pantheon under the name Hyperledger Besu[313], through the Hyperledger Foundation[314]. By making their open-source Ethereum client available through the Hyperledger Foundation as open-source rather than privately making it available through a standard GitHub repository, Consensys accomplished two key goals; a rich open-source community to draw from to further the development of the protocol itself, and gains in credibility and assurance that the future of the protocol is not within the hands of a single company whose motivations may be driven by profitability rather than the advancement of the technology.

Hyperledger Besu provides the core functionality of enabling parties on the blockchain to send private transactions between one another. The Orion transaction manager[315] is the privacy engine for Hyperledger Besu, operating in a very similar fashion to that of Quorum's Tessera transaction manager. One key difference between Orion and Tessera is that Orion supports the concept of privacy groups. Privacy groups enable private transactions to be sent to multiple parties rather than just to a single entity, which can be useful if private state would need to be shared to a group. Going back to our refrigerated dairy example, likely our shipper provides dairy products to more than just a single grocery store. If in fact the shipment is bad, then all retail stores would need to be notified to not accept the shipment as well as impose penalties, if appropriate.

---

[313] https://besu.hyperledger.org/en/stable/
[314] https://www.hyperledger.org/
[315] https://docs.orion.pegasys.tech/en/stable/

ConsenSys Quorum

JP Morgan was one of the early adopters of blockchain technology, so much that they had a team in the financial company focused solely on blockchain technologies. Seeing the enterprise need for blockchain, they built an Ethereum client called Quorum[316], based on the EEA specification. In August of 2020, ConsenSys purchased Quorum from J.P. Morgan, adding it to already existing portfolio of ConsenSys Enterprise Ethereum offerings. Quorum is a fork of the Ethereum Geth[317] client; however, the Quorum team incorporates upstream changes in Geth to Quorum periodically through additional releases. Quorum provides two key things an enterprise needs for using a blockchain – privacy and an efficient consensus mechanism.

Tessera is the name of the privacy engine developed by the Quorum team, otherwise known as the "transaction manager". Tessera is a stateless Java system that provides the encryption, decryption, and distribution of private transactions that enable members of a Quorum network to send private transactions to one another. Using standard public/private key encryption, recipients of a private transaction in Quorum can be assured that the transaction has been sent by the sender as represented in the transaction, and that no other party can view the contents of the transaction itself. The transaction is on the blockchain, which other members can see, but being in an encrypted state means that only the parties involved in the sending/receiving of the transaction can decrypt the transaction.

Another feature of Quorum is the ability to use a traditional database as the storage layer for the

---

[316] https://consensys.net/quorum/
[317] https://geth.ethereum.org/

blockchain. This is an important element of a blockchain solution as the ledger data is as business critical as any other data asset in an organization, so having a highly resilient, scalable data store for the ledger is an important requirement. Managed blockchain solutions, which we'll cover later in the chapter, have other ways to store the ledger data that can achieve this, but for IaaS-based solutions, this is an important capability. In addition to data resiliency, having a performant data store to query the blockchain data will be necessary as the ledger data grows over time, as you will likely want to visualize the data using business intelligence solutions where performance is necessary.

These are just a few of the capabilities of the Quorum protocol. For in-depth resources, check out Quorum's website and associated GitHub repository[318].

Baseline Protocol

The Baseline Protocol isn't a blockchain protocol per se, but rather a technology pattern. The idea of "baselining" disparate enterprise systems across several different parties has been a recent trend in the Ethereum ecosystem. Systems such as CRM or ERP have the need to reconcile state across multiple organizations where a shared business process is in place. Today significant effort is spent to build custom synchronization systems to achieve this goal, or worse, resort to legacy practices such as sending spreadsheets through email. The end-result is inefficiencies resulting in lost inventory, additional capital expenditures, and even regulatory actions that must be reconciled.

While blockchain at its core could address many of these challenges – other challenges surface that need to be

---

[318] https://github.com/consensys/quorum/

addressed. How would a massive permissioned blockchain be deployed and managed that could serve as the system of record for these applications? How is privacy and confidentiality addressed in a scalable way?

The Baseline Protocol[319] is an open-source initiative, originally started by Ernst & Young, ConsenSys, and Microsoft, that has expanded to over 14 companies in joint effort with the EEA and the Ethereum Foundation. Baseline leverages the Ethereum public network as a system of record for shared enterprise systems, while maintaining privacy and confidentiality, and minimizing transactions costs on the network. The core concept behind Baseline is to store the hash of a shared state on the blockchain which the shared systems reference for a given transaction between each other. A zero knowledge microservice runs on a baseline server that runs logic to ensure that the services sharing state have performed the actions with the same result and produces a zero-knowledge proof[320] in the form of a hash (known as the baseline proof) which is then recorded on the Ethereum public network. A smart contract known as the "Shield Contract" holds a Merkle Tree[321] that contains the baseline proofs, storing known states in leaves of the Merkle Tree. This is key to ensuring transaction fees are kept to a minimum as not all transactions between both enterprise systems need to be stored on the Ethereum public network, but rather the top hash of the tree is all that is recorded on-chain.

Baseline is in its early stages as of this writing, however great interest has been shown by large enterprises that

---

[319] https://docs.baseline-protocol.org/
[320] https://decrypt.co/resources/zero-knowledge-proofs-explained-learn-guide
[321] https://en.wikipedia.org/wiki/Merkle_tree

can benefit from a consistent pattern to sharing state across systems.

Hyperledger Fabric

Hyperledger Fabric[322] is a blockchain protocol that was designed from the ground-up specifically for permissioned blockchain networks. Unlike Ethereum, which has its roots in public blockchain networks, the intent with Hyperledger Fabric was to ensure the needs of enterprises were first and foremost in the design, providing flexibility for deployment and development. Hyperledger Fabric, consequently, does not have a cryptocurrency associated with the ledger as the need for a cryptocurrency does not apply to permissioned ledgers. As the name implies, like Hyperledger Besu, Hyperledger Fabric is open source through the Hyperledger Foundation.

Privacy in Hyperledger Fabric is managed in a manner that is a bit different than enterprise Ethereum ledgers through the implementation of "channels", which give the sender the ability to determine which parties should be privy to the transaction being sent. Unlike Ethereum, where each party on the network executes the smart contract, regardless of whether the transaction executing the smart contract is intended for a single party (private transaction), channels in Hyperledger Fabric require only some of the parties the transaction is intended for to execute the smart contract (called chaincode) associated with the transaction. Which parties must endorse the transaction is defined through an "endorsement policy" which is configured ahead of sending transactions to the channel. Parties are authenticated access to specific

---

[322] https://www.hyperledger.org/use/fabric

channels so that transactions sent to those channels do not require private/public key exchange with each transaction, like in Ethereum. While the concept of channels simplifies some aspects of privacy on a blockchain, at the same time the number of channels can grow to a number which can be difficult to manage on a large network.

Hyperledger Fabric has a modular architecture for nodes on the network. "Peer nodes" are individual nodes, typically representing an individual entity such as a company. Peer nodes can send transactions on the network, query the ledger, and execute chaincode. "Orderer nodes" are a consolidated set of clustered nodes responsible for signing transactions on the network through consensus. Think of these as acting in the same role as validators for Ethereum, the key difference being that in Ethereum, the function of the peer nodes and orderer nodes are consolidated into a single node. This configuration enables a much more flexible deployment model allowing for reduced cost for individuals participating on the network as they only need a peer node which does not have to handle the compute burden of both transaction processing and network consensus, the latter being solely executed on the orderer nodes.

Flexibility and ease of development is another goal of Hyperledger Fabric. Rather than introducing a new programming language for the development of smart contracts, developers can write chaincode in languages they already know, such as GoLang and Java. This is an important distinction between Hyperledger Fabric and Ethereum as the developer base of existing GoLang and Java developers is vast, whereas developers familiar with Solidity is much smaller, and largely concentrated in the public Ethereum development community rather than enterprise developers. While Solidity contains elements that are familiar to modern development languages, there is a learning curve to any new language, and development tooling is still in the emerging stage for Solidity, making learning and debugging Solidity code a challenge.

R3 Corda Open Source and Enterprise

In 2014, R3[323] was founded as a company with the intent of providing a distributed ledger technology optimized for the financial sector. Corda is the distributed ledger product that was developed, which has one key distinction from the blockchain protocols discussed thus far – it isn't a blockchain. The terms "blockchain" and "distributed ledger" have been used synonymously with one another as we have been exploring systems that enable trust and transparency for multi-party workflows, and Corda falls into this bucket and as such is widely considered a solution that can be used to achieve the same results that a traditional blockchain solution provides. As such, you'll hear Corda referred to as a blockchain platform based on the merits of functionality it provides, not on the core underlying technology itself.

Corda is offered as two distinct products – Corda[324] Open Source, and Corda Enterprise[325], and is managed in a similar fashion. Corda Open Source is managed by the Corda Foundation[326], which is separate from the company, R3. Corda Enterprise, however, is a licensed product from R3 that comes with additional features and functionality not available in Corda Open Source as well enterprise support. The following additional functionality is available with Corda Enterprise:

---

[323] https://www.r3.com/
[324] https://www.corda.net/
[325] https://www.r3.com/corda-platform/
[326] https://corda.network/

- **Enterprise database support:** SQL Server, CockroachDB, and Oracle databases can be used as ledger stores for Corda Enterprise.
- **Hardware Security Module (HSM) support:** Notary keys can be stored in selected HSMs, further securing notary signing keys.
- **Blockchain application firewall:** Enables Corda Enterprise nodes to be deployed in private clouds behind corporate firewalls while still enabling connectivity to other Corda nodes.
- **High availability:** Notary nodes can be configured in a highly available manner using the Java Persistence API (JPA) to connect to the notary database.

Instead of using validator or orderer nodes to perform consensus on the network, Corda uses what are called "Notaries", which are a clustered set of nodes that perform the function of consensus. It's important to note that in Corda, not all transactions must be processed by a notary. Transactions that do not consume the state of a previous transaction as input, meaning there is no risk of the "double-spend" problem. An example would be an issuance transaction, such as issuing a bond.

Smart contracts in Corda are called "CordApps" and are written in Java or Kotlin. Unlike other blockchains where the smart contract must be deployed to all nodes in the network, CordApps only need to be installed on the nodes that are expected to process transactions related to the CordApp. Ledger state in Corda is subjective based on the state between parties in a Corda network. Rather than all transactions (including private, which are encrypted) being on the ledger, as is the case with Ethereum, members of a Corda network may have state and ledger data that is only persistent between the parties that executed transactions with one-another.

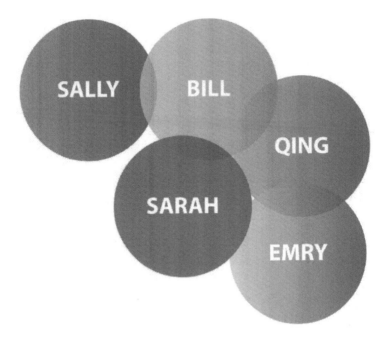

Figure 7-4

For example, in **Figure 7-4**, Sally and Bill share the facts that are known to them. Bill shares only the facts known to him, Sally, Sarah, and Qing, and so on. In the case of Corda, there may be no "single ledger" for an entire network. As such, Corda has the concept of "flows", where transaction processing order is defined into a sequence of steps that specifies how nodes achieve a specific ledger update. For example, if Alice wants to transact with Bob, she must initiate a flow that has been designated for Bob. She then sends a message to Bob with the details of the flow, and Bob will subsequently initiate a counterparty flow (**See Figure 7-5**).

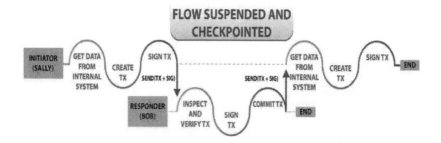

Figure 7-5

As you can see, Corda is very different than other blockchain ledgers while still achieving the same end-goal of providing a distributed, immutable ledger.

Ledger databases

We've discussed blockchain as a method for ensuring that data, once written to the ledger, is immutable through cryptography. A key trait that is shared among all the solutions discussed so far in this chapter is the fact that multiple parties, with some level of trust between one another, can employ a level of decentralization. No single party in the network controls the data source, and consensus among parties must be reached before new records are committed to the chain. But what if decentralization for a shared business process isn't a requirement for a solution, but providing data integrity guarantees that records of transactions have not been tampered with are?

The idea of adding blockchain-like capabilities in traditional database systems is beginning to pick-up in the market, such as Microsoft's Azure SQL Database ledger[327] and Amazon's Quantum Ledger Database[328]

---

[327] https://aka.ms/sql-ledger-docs
[328] https://aws.amazon.com/qldb/

(QLDB). These relatively new offerings are filling a gap that exists where a traditional blockchain solution may be too heavy weight for a system that is fundamentally centralized. Gartner predicted in 2019 that these offerings "...will gain at least twenty percent of the permissioned blockchain market share over the next three years." It's safe to assume that we will continue to see more database offerings come to market with these capabilities over the coming years.

Expert Opinion	"We predict that QLDB and other competitive centralized ledger technology offerings that will eventually emerge will gain at least twenty percent of permissioned blockchain market share over the next three years."

Avivah Litah[329], Gartner[330]

The core design element behind most ledger databases come from borrowing the blockchain architecture related to the hashing of individual rows or tables. Using a merkle tree structure, the root hash is then "published" by the system, which an administrator can then use to later verify the integrity of the database. Though there is a key distinction between ledger databases and traditional blockchains, specifically that ledger databases are not immutable. Rather, they provide tamper-evidence of historical data in the database – known as "forward integrity". As such, there is no protection for the business logic (think stored procedures

[329] https://www.linkedin.com/in/avivahlitan/
[330] https://blogs.gartner.com/avivah-litan/2019/01/21/amazons-qldb-challenges-permissioned-blockchain/

for SQL Server). You must have sufficient trust that the organization hosting the ledger database is not deploying flawed or malicious business logic. So, what protection do you get from a ledger database? Privileged users, such as DBAs, who have malicious intent and attempt to modify the data outside of the API.

So why use a ledger database in place of a blockchain? The answer comes down to what level of trust do you have between the parties that consume the data in your system. There are countless System of Record (SOR) and Security Information and Event Management (SIEM) systems that exist today that can greatly benefit from ledger database technology without having to re-develop a system based on blockchain. Being able to provide auditors, whether internal or external to your organization, that production data has not been maliciously tampered with has unquestionable value.

Choosing the right blockchain
So how do you choose a blockchain technology that's right for you? This isn't a simple question to answer as there is no clear "market leader" from a technology perspective. There are a few key considerations to consider that will help narrow down your decision, though.

Type of application
While all the solutions above can provide trust and transparency capabilities for any type of application, some blockchain technologies have been optimized for specific use cases. R3 Corda was designed specifically for the financial market and as such has found success with several customers whose core business is capital markets and fintech. Ethereum and Hyperledger Fabric, on the other hand, tend to be favored for replacing

traditional supply chain track and trace scenarios. This is not to say that you can't use R3 Corda for supply chain, or Ethereum or Hyperledger Fabric for finance – several companies have successfully. However, it is a dimension to consider.

Cloud platform support

Of the top cloud vendors on the market, all offer blockchain-based solutions based on most, if not all, of the blockchain technologies described above. However, some go the extra-step to provide full-managed PaaS services for specific blockchain technologies, while opting to offer other blockchain technologies as either 3rd-party offerings, or standalone IaaS solutions. The popularity of PaaS-based solutions over IaaS-based solutions with enterprises continues to grow given the benefits of built-in high-availability, patching, and monitoring that PaaS solutions provide. For example, Amazon Web Services offers Amazon Managed Blockchain for Hyperledger Fabric and Ethereum (though the Ethereum offering is for public Ethereum only, not permissioned enterprise blockchains). Amazon also offers Quantum Ledger Database as a ledger database PaaS services. Microsoft Azure, on the other hand, offers Azure Blockchain Service (soon to be replaced by Quorum Blockchain Service), Azure Confidential Ledger and Azure SQL Database ledger.

If your organization has a primary cloud provider strategy, this should play a big part in your decision. Not only is having a PaaS-based solution important to consider, but also consider how well the cloud provider integrates their blockchain solution with other technologies, such as integration with database services, eventing services, as well as robust tooling for development and deployment automation.

Enterprise support

While a cloud provider will provide enterprise support for their blockchain offerings on their platform, what level of support will they provide for the underlying blockchain protocol itself? Having an associated relationship with a company that provides support for the protocol is important should you encounter bugs or need to influence the future roadmap. R3 Corda and Quorum are both supported by R3 and ConsenSys respectively, however Hyperledger Fabric is a project of the Hyperledger Foundation which is an open-source community. Companies such as IBM, Cisco, and Intel have enterprise support offerings for Hyperledger Fabric, but unlike R3 or ConsenSys, do not have direct control over which pull requests are approved and incorporated for bug fixes and features. This isn't necessarily a blocking issue to use Hyperledger Fabric as a blockchain technology, but an important consideration as you think about the long-term investments you make in one blockchain technology versus another.

Development tooling

The developer experience and toolchains are an area where blockchain technologies differ greatly from one another and is a consideration you should investigate deeply before making a choice on which blockchain technology to adopt. Ethereum's Solidity programming language has powerful capabilities but has the drawback of being yet a new language for your development team to learn, master and maintain. ConsenSys has invested deeply here, providing several tools for developing, debugging, and deploying Solidity smart contracts, but it's still early in terms of maturity of these tools and the number of developers in the market that have this skillset. Companies like Microsoft have invested further here, integrating these existing tools with Visual Studio

Code to further ease this technical hurdle, but suffice to say, it is a hurdle. Hyperledger Fabric and R3 Corda, on the other hand, opted to use existing languages for smart contract development to leverage the large number of developers that already have these core skillsets.

Solution provider preference

Solution providers such as Ernst & Young, Accenture, and KPMG have built blockchain practices in their organizations to help companies in their digital transformation journey to blockchain solutions. Many organizations today have a primary solution provider they partner with to help them design and deploy systems in their environments and leveraging an existing partner relationship to blockchain may make sense as you evaluate how to approach your blockchain solution for your organization. However, some of these solution providers have stronger skillsets in one blockchain technology over others as the technology is still nascent. Ernst & Young, for example, is very strong in Ethereum and may sway you into that direction based on their ability to deliver Ethereum very well. This is not a bad thing; in fact, it can play very well in your favor in knowing that your solution provider is deeply invested in the technology they propose for your solution. However, there are blockchain-specific smaller partners that have based their business on a blockchain-agnostic approach to the services they deliver and may be better suited to helping you choose a blockchain protocol that is best suited to your specific applications needs. Envision Blockchain[331] in one such partner, that provides robust support for all three blockchain technologies we have discussed so far.

◆ ◆ ◆ ◆ ◆ ◆ ◆ ◆ ◆ ◆ ◆

---

[331] https://envisionblockchain.com/

MICROSOFT AZURE BLOCKCHAIN

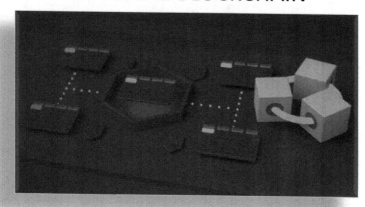

Now that we've established a brief background on blockchain concepts and specific requirements and technologies for the enterprise, the remainder of this chapter will focus on what Microsoft provides regarding blockchain solutions in Microsoft Azure.

In 2015, Microsoft authored its first blog post[332] on blockchain in Azure. Described as "Ethereum Blockchain as a Service", what was announced was bringing a set of Azure Resource Manager (ARM) templates[333] to Azure that enabled customers to easily deploy an Ethereum blockchain network in the cloud. By automating the deployment of the virtual machines, pre-configured for Ethereum, these templates significantly lowered the pain threshold for easily deploying Ethereum in a public cloud.

Why Microsoft got involved early in blockchain and with Ethereum had to do with its customers. Enterprises,

---

[332]https://azure.microsoft.com/blog/ethereum-blockchain-as-a-service-now-on-azure/

[333] https://docs.microsoft.com/azure/azure-resource-manager/templates/overview

specifically in financial sector, were interested in exploring the possibilities that blockchain could unlock for their businesses, given the focus on Ethereum in the enterprise through the EEA. These customers were struggling with the complexities of simply deploying a network and given Microsoft's track-record in providing great automated deployment templates, this was a natural choice. However, alongside responding to customers, Microsoft also took an early approach with getting deeply involved with the blockchain industry, working closely with companies like ConsenSys. Microsoft was also one of the founding members of the EEA in 2017. Clearly, Microsoft identified blockchain as a disruptive technology early and subsequently invested deeply in many areas to make Azure the natural choice for building blockchain-based solutions for the cloud.

When embarking on the journey of a blockchain-based solution, Microsoft breaks down the core areas of technical work into three buckets:

1. Launch and manage the network.
2. Model smart contracts
3. Build and extend the application.

Different personas will work on each area, with some overlap in development between 2 and 3. The core intent here is that you need infrastructure in place before you can develop smart contracts, which you need before you can develop an application layer on top of for customers to interact with. We'll explore each of these areas, with a focus on what Microsoft provides to make each of these steps easier.

Launch and manage the network

Building a blockchain network is not for the faint of heart. While traditional systems usually consist of a centralized back-end system with an application layer that users interact with, a blockchain-based system will consist of a back-end system that is distributed, with all parties involved in the network hosting their own infrastructure that communicates with one another to reach consensus on incoming transactions, as well as synchronizing the ledger state across all nodes. While ARM deployment templates remove much of the burden when it comes to deploying the network, what it does not address are the DevOps associated with managing the network once it's been deployed. How are updates managed seamlessly between nodes for host OS or ledger software stack updates? How is high availability configured for both the virtual machines and associated storage hosting the ledger. Microsoft has been a leader in providing Platform as a Service (PaaS) offerings for complex systems. For example, prior to the availability of Azure SQL Database, one needed a Database Administrator (DBA) to design, deploy, and manage the complexity of SQL Server deployed in a virtual machine or bare metal. Blockchain was no exception, in fact you can argue that due to the multi-party aspect of blockchain, it was even more necessary than other software systems to be built as a PaaS offering.

Azure Blockchain Service & Quorum Blockchain Service

At the annual Microsoft Build conference[334] in 2018, Microsoft made available Azure Blockchain Service[335], a fully-managed PaaS blockchain offering. Based on the Quorum Ethereum ledger, Microsoft provides a service

---

[334] https://mybuild.microsoft.com/
[335] https://aka.ms/abservice

---

that not only has all the benefits of a typical PaaS service with automatic updates, high-availability, and simple deployment, but also provides built-in governance controls which make adding and removing other members to your consortium easy.

Customer Story	Xbox game publishers access royalties statements even faster now that Microsoft uses Azure Blockchain Service Read the entire story[336]

It's important to note that at the time of this writing, Microsoft has announced the retirement of Azure Blockchain Service[337]. Specifically, that Azure Blockchain Service will transition from a Microsoft-provided service to a partner-offered service, provided by ConsenSys. While on the surface this may appear that Microsoft is de-vesting in blockchain technologies, quite the opposite is true. As an emerging technology, blockchain is rapidly evolving with new releases of the Quorum blockchain protocol happening very frequently (as in months). For Microsoft to keep up to date with new releases of Quorum, they must validate not only the new releases of the protocol, but also must re-validate the underlying platform architecture responsible for the hosting of the protocol. This can result in Azure Blockchain Service being out of date at times with regard to being able to provide customers with the latest features and capabilities in the rapidly evolving

---

[336] https://customers.microsoft.com/story/microsoft-financial-operations-professional-services-azure
[337] https://docs.microsoft.com/en-us/azure/blockchain/service/migration-guide

blockchain market. Instead, Microsoft and ConsenSys are working together to bring forward a new service provided by ConsenSys, Quorum Blockchain Service[338]. This means Microsoft can do what it does best – provide world-class cloud infrastructure enabling ConsenSys to focus on what it does best – provide world-class blockchain software for enterprises. In addition to enabling an agile approach to bringing the latest and greatest Quorum offering to customers, customers will now have a "one stop shop" for support should they have issues with their blockchain network. Instead of wrangling between Microsoft and ConsenSys, customers will have the leader in enterprise Ethereum (ConsenSys), supporting their blockchain deployments. Customers currently on Azure Blockchain Service will be able to easily migrate over to the new ConsenSys offering.

Customer Story	Given that issues such as traceability, sustainability and authenticity are common to all luxury brands, it made sense for these competitors to work together to drive change and develop a shared solution. LVMH thus joined forces with Prada and Richemont to design **Aura** Blockchain Consortium, a multi-nodal, private blockchain secured by ConsenSys technology and Microsoft. **Aura** is open to all luxury brands, not just the founders, and offers flexibility to support companies of varying sizes and adapt to individual needs. Read the entire story[339]

---

[338] https://consensys.net/QBS
[339] https://www.lvmh.com/news-documents/news/lvmh-partners-with-other-major-luxury-companies-on-aura-the-first-global-luxury-blockchain/

This shift demonstrates Microsoft's commitment to blockchain technologies in Azure, as Microsoft is a customer of the technology itself. The Microsoft Cloud Sourcing and Supply Chain organization has built a blockchain-based solution for track and trace of components vital to the rapid expansion of its Microsoft Azure Cloud. Yorke E. Rhodes III, Director of Digital Transformation at Microsoft, led the journey that Microsoft embarked upon to digitize the sourcing of hardware components for the Microsoft Azure Cloud.

Expert Opinion	"In Microsoft's cloud hardware supply chain, we've built a system that is secure by design across a value chain of suppliers that transcends enterprises to form a network. This sets the foundation for Digital Transformation by enabling immutable and trusted n-party transactions across the supplier base on shared atomic objects in the shared ledger. Captured is the lineage and provenance of serialized goods, the transactional business objects controlling them such as purchase orders, invoices, and loans. This establishes corporate financial controls with supply chain operational agility and financial integrity linking value of goods transactions on them and financial flows."
	Yorke E. Rhodes III[340], Director Digital Transformation Cloud Supply Chain, Microsoft Cofounder Blockchain @Microsoft & Baseline Protocol

---

[340] https://www.linkedin.com/in/yorkerhodes/

For more information on the system that Microsoft built for Azure Supply Chain, see Yorke's blog[341] where he outlines the problems Microsoft was facing in their supply chain, and how adopting a blockchain-based solution on Azure has increased operational efficiency while increasing trust between parties on the network.

Model smart contracts

Now that we have covered the basics of how to launch and manage a blockchain network in Azure, interacting with the blockchain through applications is the logical next step. We'll cover primarily Ethereum-based development as Microsoft has most of their development tools based on Ethereum.

With Azure Blockchain, there are two ways to get started down the blockchain journey once the network has been deployed. There is overlap between these two, however we'll take them one at a time, focused more on developers and non-developers.

Azure Blockchain Workbench

If you want to start deploying smart contracts to an existing Azure Blockchain Service network with a focus on modeling and visualizing how smart contract flows actually operate, Microsoft has an offering called Azure Blockchain Workbench[342] that is focused on getting started quickly. Azure Blockchain Workbench is a solution template that provisions several Azure services **(See Figure 7-6)**.

---

[341] https://cloudblogs.microsoft.com/industry-blog/manufacturing/2020/12/17/improve-supply-chain-resiliency-traceability-and-predictability-with-blockchain/

[342] https://azure.microsoft.com/features/blockchain-workbench/

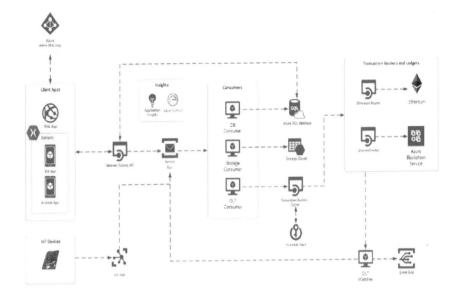

Figure 7-6

Once deployed, the user interacts with a Web App (**See Figure 7-7**) that provides you a visual experience for deploying smart contracts, interacting with the smart contracts, as well as seeing the flow of contract state through the process.

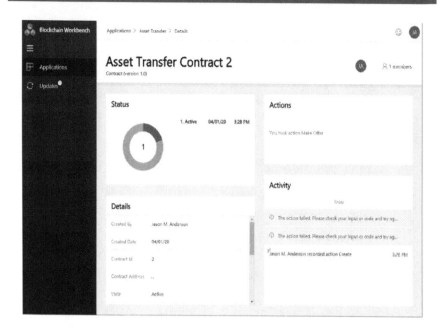

Figure 7-7

Workbench is incredibly helpful when beginning your blockchain journey as it helps to quickly understand how a blockchain works, as well as can be a very useful tool in prototyping smart contract logic for your use case. The initial IaaS deployment templates that Microsoft provided starting in 2015, helped greatly in setting-up the initial blockchain network for customers. However, customers were struggling with developing blockchain solutions for their businesses. In many cases, these customers would hire Solution Integrators to help, spending upwards of $500K on development only to result in having a demo that showed scrolling text, rather than something an executive could easily grasp and realize how blockchain could benefit their business. By removing the burden of up-front development (and associated costs), Workbench enabled customers to quickly get to proof-of-concept (POC) in a way that could be easily communicated to executives or customers, while using the funds that would have been previously spent on early POC development for use in producing the final solution.

Azure Blockchain Development Kit

If you are a developer and already familiar with Microsoft development tools such as Visual Studio and Visual Studio Code, the Azure Blockchain Development Kit[343] is the other great way to get started building applications for blockchain in Azure. As highlighted earlier in the chapter, developing for Ethereum can be challenging as Solidity is a new programming language, designed for codifying business logic on a blockchain. Microsoft has invested in tools for developers that do not replace existing Ethereum development tools such as Truffle and Ganache, but rather incorporates these tools into Visual Studio Code as an extension, providing a familiar GUI "wrapper" for these existing command-line tools.

The Visual Studio extension for Azure Blockchain enables developers to do several things when developing for blockchain:

- Develop, debug, deploy and interact with Solidity smart contracts.
- Connects natively to Azure Blockchain Service, public Ethereum networks through Infura[344], or to a local development environment.
- Access to several sample Solidity smart contracts as well as Truffle boxes[345].

---

[343] https://github.com/Microsoft/vscode-azure-blockchain-ethereum/wiki
[344] https://infura.io/
[345] https://www.trufflesuite.com/boxes

If you are familiar with Visual Studio Code, you can easily install the Azure Blockchain Development Kit through the Extensions tab. Rather than outlining these steps in this chapter, I highly recommend following the tutorial[346] Microsoft has published which walks you through how to download the sample, build and deploy it to Azure Blockchain Service, as well as interacting with the contract once deployed. No knowledge of blockchain is needed to follow this tutorial and using this tutorial will help you as we progress into the section the following section on extending your application using Logic App connectors and Microsoft PowerApps.

By embracing open source in the development of the Azure Blockchain Development Kit, Microsoft did not re-invent the wheel, but rather provides an interface to easily use the development tools that already exist for Ethereum development, such as Truffle and Ganache. Additionally, and the Solidity Visual Studio Code extension, created by Juan Blanco.

Expert Opinion	"The blockchain dev kit coupled with the Solidity vscode extension enables Ethereum developers to have a one-stop shop for developing, testing and deploy smart-contracts to work with the Azure blockchain and public chain." Juan Blanco[347], Director at OBJECTSPACES LTD Nethereum Founder & Solidity VSCode Extension Creator

---

[346] https://docs.microsoft.com/azure/blockchain/service/send-transaction
[347] https://www.linkedin.com/in/juanfranblanco/

Extending the application

Once smart contracts have been deployed on your network, you need an application interface to interact with the smart contracts on the blockchain. Traditional applications such as Web Apps or Azure Blockchain Workbench can be used to accomplish this. However, Microsoft has gone a step further by leveraging the low-code Azure Logic Apps and Microsoft Power Platform to enable rapid application development for blockchain-based applications.

Ethereum Blockchain Connector with Azure Logic Apps

The Azure Logic App[348] platform provides the ability to automate workflows in Azure with writing low, to no, actual code depending on your workflow. One way to think about Logic Apps is that they are "if this, then that" logic to deterministically act based on event criteria that you configure. The flexibility enabled with Logic Apps is vast, enabling you to create your own custom logic for input and output, or leverage a broad set of existing connectors that reduce the amount of code needed to integrate with your application.

Microsoft published a Logic App connector for Ethereum[349] enabling you to easily interact with either the public Ethereum network, or a private Ethereum network, such as Azure Blockchain Service, with little to no code necessary to plumb it together. You can use Azure Logic App connectors in tandem with one another, providing a rich set of services that can communicate with your blockchain network. For example, if you want a select set of SQL Server transactions to be copied to your Ethereum blockchain, you can use the SQL Server

---

[348] https://azure.microsoft.com/services/logic-apps/
[349] https://docs.microsoft.com/azure/blockchain/service/ethereum-logic-app

Logic App connector in conjunction with the Logic App connector for Ethereum to do so – without writing a single line of code.

Microsoft Power Platform

The investments in low-code development for the "Citizen Developer" has been a tremendous focus of Microsoft over the past few years. Citizen developers are defined as individuals, not formally in a development role and may not have formal development training, who create business applications for use in an IT-approved environment. In many cases, these developers are close to the business and therefore deeply understand the requirements for applications that can be used to increase efficiency and solve business challenges that otherwise would be difficult to get approved and completed through traditional development lifecycles. The Microsoft Power Platform[350] provides a rich set of tools and resources for these citizen developers to create a vast array of applications, leveraging integration solutions such as Logic App connectors and Power Automate Flows to connect to various back-end systems. The Microsoft Power Platform consists of several different products, but for the purpose of this chapter we'll focus integration with blockchain through Power Apps and Power Automate.

Power Automate Flows use the same codebase as Logic App Connectors, enabling to Microsoft to leverage investments across both Azure and application front ends like Power Apps. Power Apps are a development environment that uses GUI controls as the primary interface for creating application logic. Anyone who has used tools such as Visual Basic or Visual Basic for

---

[350] https://powerplatform.microsoft.com/

Applications (VBA), would be very comfortable using Power Apps. Using Power Apps and Power Automate Flows together, you can quickly create applications to interface with blockchain for use as proof-of-concept, pilot and even for production systems. To demonstrate the simplicity of how to build a Power App that connects to blockchain, specifically Azure Blockchain Service, this Microsoft Ignite 2019 video[351] (start at 22:30) shows how to use Visual Studio Code and Power Apps and Power Automate Flows to build a simple blockchain application.

Confidential Consortium Framework

Encryption technologies are designed to ensure confidential data stays confidential. Encryption-in-transit is something we use every day when we connect to a website with an https: address, ensuring that data passed from the client to the server is protected on the internet. Encryption-at-rest refers to ensuring that your data, when in storage, is encrypted and subsequently protected. What's relatively new in cloud computing is the concept of encryption-in-use, which refers to data being encrypted when it is read from storage and subsequently executed on the systems CPU. With new technologies, such as Intel SGX[352], a region of silicon in the process is dedicated to this function, known as a trusted execution environment.

Seeing the potential of this technology, Microsoft has developed an open-source framework, called the

---

[351] https://youtu.be/oww1ZtIbX2Q?t=1325
[352] https://www.intel.com/content/www/us/en/architecture-and-technology/software-guard-extensions.html

---

Confidential Consortium Framework[353] (CCF), which is a software stack that interfaces with the trusted execution environment, making it easy for developers to build applications that can support encryption-in-use.

Azure Confidential Ledger

So how does blockchain tie into encryption-in-use scenarios? One of the drawbacks of traditional blockchains we explored earlier is the fact that network consensus mechanisms, by design, have a relatively low transaction throughput. The process of multiple nodes validating a transaction has inherent network latency, limiting transactions per second in the 1,000's. By leveraging trusted execution environments for consensus, transaction throughput can achieve near-database speeds.

Seeing this possibility, Microsoft provides a tamper-proof storage service, called Azure Confidential Ledger[354] (ACL). ACL provides the ledger functionality of a blockchain, but rather than storing state data, it can be used to store any types of files that need to be protected from tampering. Unlike other protected storage services such as Azure immutable Blob Storage[355], ACL leverages CCF which ensures that data stored in the ledger is confidential and impossible to access without the appropriate keys – including Microsoft. ACL is a powerful service which can be used for protection of any type of blob data, such as audit logs, but extends even further as being a great add-on to a blockchain network. Since blockchains are designed to store state data rather than files, in situations where the state of a business process on the blockchain is linked to

---

[353]https://www.microsoft.com/research/project/confidential-consortium-framework/
[354] https://aka.ms/confidentialledger
[355] https://docs.microsoft.com/azure/storage/blobs/storage-blob-immutable-storage

a file, such as a contract in .PDF format, the file can be stored in ACL with a hash of the file linked to the blockchain. This provides end to end protection of both state and the file itself.

Azure SQL Database ledger

Earlier in the chapter we briefly touched on the emerging trend of ledger databases. At the Microsoft's annual BUILD[356] 2021 developer conference, Microsoft announced the availability of Azure SQL Database ledger[357]. The ledger capability of Azure SQL Database is a feature rather than a separate Azure service. Unlike Amazon's QLDB service, the ledger in Azure SQL Database can be enabled for existing databases, requires no changes to existing applications or stored procedures, and no need to learn a new SQL-like API.

All transactions processed by Azure SQL Database ledger are cryptographically linked to one-another, just like a traditional blockchain. Hashes of the database are then stored externally in Azure Storage immutable blobs, or Azure Confidential Ledger. By doing so, any tampering at the data layer of the SQL Server can be detected by comparing the hashes stored in tamper-proof storage against the real-time calculations of the hashes in the database through a process called database verification. This novel approach eliminates the need for a decentralized network, adopting instead a "trust, but verify" model for centrally stored data, enabling other parties to verify the database without having to host the database themselves.

---

[356] https://mybuild.microsoft.com/
[357] https://aka.ms/sql-ledger

The ledger feature of Azure SQL Database supports 2 types of application patterns – updatable and append-only.

Updatable ledger tables

As implied in the name, updatable ledger tables offer the ability to support updates and deletes, in addition to inserts in the database. While this may seem counter-intuitive for a tamper-evident solution, it's an important scenario to cover as most existing System of Record (SOR) applications today have insert/update/delete patterns.

How, then, is tamper-evidence achieved when one can change or delete records? Each update or delete is captured in a shadow "history" table in the system. This ensures that a full chronicle of the rows modified over time are preserved. In addition to preserving the previous values of rows, updatable ledger tables also track the transactions that made the changes to these rows, along with capturing the user identity of who issued the transaction. This additional metadata provides data lineage capabilities that are useful for forensics purposes, particularly when privileged users attempt to modify or delete data by issuing malicious transactions.

As a simple example, let's take a bank account balance using a simple schema of customer ID, first and last name, and balance (**See Figure 7-8**). If we look at Nick, he started with an initial balance of $50 (a). His balance is later updated to $100. When this happens, the transaction is recorded as a delete of the original insert of $50, with an insert of a new value of $100 (b).

CustomerID	LastName	FirstName	Balance	ledger_transaction_id	ledger_sequence_number	ledger_operation_type_id	ledger_operation_type_desc
1	Jones	Nick	50.00	999	0	1	INSERT
2	Smith	John	500.00	1002	0	1	INSERT
3	Smith	Joe	30.00	1002	1	1	INSERT
4	Michaels	Mary	200.00	1002	2	1	INSERT
1	Jones	Nick	50.00	1055	1	2	DELETE
1	Jones	Nick	100.00	1055	0	1	INSERT

Figure 7-8

Of course, a real-world bank ledger would have a much more complicated schema with normalized tables, but the key concept here is that delete operations are captured and preserved, such that they can be traced later if necessary.

Append-only ledger tables

Append-only ledger tables block the ability to issue update or delete transactions at the SQL Server, further protecting the data from tampering in comparison to updatable ledger tables. The append-only pattern is ideal for Security Information and Event Management (SIEM) systems, such as a facility entry tracking system, where only inserts occur. Append-only ledger tables act the same way as updatable ledger tables, though there is no associated history table as there are no previous versions of rows to store with the append-only pattern.

Another useful pattern for append-only ledger tables is for off-chain storage of blockchain data. Traditional blockchains, like Ethereum, are not optimized for high read query throughput, like traditional databases. As such, querying blockchain data for business intelligence, and being able to transform that data into useful relational models, means you need to copy the data on the blockchain to a database. The problem with this approach is that once the data leaves the blockchain, you cannot fully trust the data's integrity as it could be tampered. Using Azure SQL Database ledger as the off-chain store would maintain data integrity from the blockchain to the database, eliminating this concern.

BLOCKCHAIN CHALLENGES

Certainly, blockchain isn't a panacea that will solve all challenges in multi-party business workflows. As mentioned earlier, blockchain is yet to achieve the level of transaction throughput that traditional database technologies can offer. So, when is a blockchain solution appropriate? The first question you should ask yourself is whether a blockchain is even the right technology for your business process.

Is blockchain right for your business process?

There are four considerations to consider when evaluating whether a blockchain solution is right for your business process.

1. **Business process that crosses a trust boundary:**
   A trust boundary in this case is normally defined
   as multiple companies but could be defined as
   multiple organizations or subsidiaries in a single
   company. The key point to consider here is
   whether there is a trust challenge in these
   boundaries. Only you can answer this question,
   but ultimately if your business process can be
   grounded in allotting trust to a single party in the
   process, then blockchain may not be the best
   solution.

2. **Multiple parties working off the same data:**
   Closely tied to question one above, if the data
   source the multi-party business process consumes
   is from a single source, the question is "who owns
   and controls that data source?" A single party
   hosting the database has full administrative control
   over the data source, and while hopefully not
   likely, would have the ability to alter the data
   without the knowledge of other parties
   participating in the business process.

3. **Intermediaries control the single source of the
   truth:** A way to solve questions one and two is to
   have a non-biased, third-party host the single
   source of truth that all parties use for the shared
   business process. This puts all parties on the same
   level regarding access to the data and eliminates
   the risk of a single party having the ability to alter
   the data without other parties knowing. However,
   this comes with some drawbacks. Giving-up
   control to another party is one as there needs to be
   sufficient confidence in the security infrastructure

of the third party hosting the data. Cost is another as the third-party is likely hired to manage the data source. These concerns may be acceptable for the parties involved to bear, but it can lead to another challenge outlined in the next question.

4. **Low-value, manual verification, and audit processes:** Most systems deployed today rely on manual auditing processes to ensure data integrity. These manual inspections of data sources, DevOps practices, and evaluation of audit logs are time-consuming to complete, and do not guarantee data has not been tampered. An auditing party can be a member of the blockchain network as an observer, having full read capabilities of the ledger avoiding the costly and time-consuming process of on-site audits.

If the four points above apply to your business process, then a blockchain may be a good candidate to add the digital trust you are looking for. But one should be aware that of challenges associated with blockchain that may not become evident until you've started down the blockchain journey.

Technology

While adopting any new technology will have inherent challenges associated with a learning curve, blockchain introduces a complexity that should be considered before adopting. By its decentralized nature, blockchain requires all parties who plan to participate in the network to host infrastructure (nodes). The nodes must be running the same versions of the underlying protocol, must have the appropriate security controls employed to keep out intruders, while allowing communication to other nodes, as well having high availability properly employed. While platform-as-a-service (PaaS) offerings orchestrate much of this configuration, it does require each party in the network to pay for the associated costs of the infrastructure and DevOps needed to keep it running.

The next technology challenge is integrating the blockchain with your existing applications, such as providing business intelligence (BI) dashboards which provide insight into the data on the blockchain. While blockchains are essentially databases, they are not optimized for high-throughput queries. As such, a typical practice for providing analysis of blockchain systems is to stream the data from the blockchain to a database management system, such as SQL Server. Data ingestion into the database needs to be configured to pull only the data your business needs and transform the data to the relational or other format needed based on the database destination chosen. You then need to consider whether the data, once replicated to the off-chain database, can be trusted. What stops a privileged user from tampering with the data in the database once it has been replicated to the database? Using a ledger database in conjunction with the blockchain can solve this off-chain integrity concern, as the data can then detect any potential tampering once the data has been replicated. This begs the question of whether a ledger database may, in fact, be a better solution rather than a decentralized blockchain? If the participants in the network can trust a central authority to host a database but can verify the data has not been tampered with, then a ledger database may be a much simpler, and ultimately cheaper, solution.

Business

Technology challenges exist in any new system to be implemented. However, with blockchain, another challenge arises which in many cases is not apparent until the project has progressed from a proof-of-concept to a pilot – how and who will operate the network?

Blockchains digitize trust of the data between parties that jointly interact with the data in question. However, the parties that will ultimately participate in the network will have to jointly agree to the governance models associated with the technology which automates the business logic in the blockchain. While network dynamics will vary, networks where trust is low between parties (such as the dairy example earlier in the chapter), there may be participants in the network who are competitors with one another. These parties have no trust with one another. Bringing these parties together to jointly agree on the rules to participate in the network, while in principle seem simple, in practice have historically taken months, if not years, to realize.

Having an un-biased third-party orchestrate the formation of the network, and ultimately operating the network, is one approach to remove the concerns of having one of the parties participating in the network take this challenge on. Typically, blockchain projects start with one party of the network, typically called the "anchor party", start the project. They have identified a business case where blockchain can automate and digitize the process, and subsequently begin to build a solution as a proof-of-concept. When transitioning from proof-of-concept to pilot is when bringing in a third party makes sense, as this will likely allay concerns of other parties joining of the potential trust issues of a competitor running the network

BLOCKCHAIN FUTURE

As a rapidly evolving landscape, blockchain, and related ledger technologies such as ledger databases and confidential computing, enterprises have the luxury of choice when determining which technology best suits their business needs. Unlike a few years ago, when the future of whether blockchain would emerge as a lasting digital transformation technology was in question, it's clear that blockchain is here to stay. Gartner predicts that "2021 is the year enterprise (permissioned) blockchain begins its long climb out of the 'trough of disillusionment'."

Expert Opinion	"2021 is the year enterprise (permissioned) blockchain begins its long climb out of the 'trough of disillusionment'." Avivah Litah[358], Gartner[359]

---

[358] https://www.linkedin.com/in/avivahlitan/
[359] https://blogs.gartner.com/avivah-litan/2021/01/13/3-blockbuster-blockchain-trends-in-2021/

Public network interoperability

While private blockchain networks are, and will continue to be, the primary enterprise use for blockchain technology, the ability to interoperate with public networks like Ethereum, is gaining momentum. Much of this has been fueled by the recent excitement over non-fungible tokens (NFTs). Though much of this NFT excitement has been questionable, such as the sale of a piece of digital art from the relatively unknown artist Beeple for $69 million[360] which was the largest sale of a piece of art for a living artist. What NFTs have shown is the power of being able to assign non-repudiable ownership of an asset, either digital or physical, in a transparent and immutable manner. The applicability of tokenization in the enterprise space has been evident for private blockchains but use cases of token assignment from private networks which are subsequently attested for on public networks can provide transparency for parties who do not participate in the private blockchain.

One example of this would be the emerging space of carbon credits[361]. Tokenizing these credits from private blockchains between energy consortiums that are then attested for publicly on Ethereum drives transparency that anyone can view, not just the participants and regulatory bodies involved in the carbon credit trading network. But doesn't the energy consumption on public networks defeat the purpose of what carbon credits, for example, are trying to achieve?

---

[360] https://www.theverge.com/2021/3/11/22325054/beeple-christies-nft-sale-cost-everydays-69-million
[361] https://globalcarbonfund.com/blockchain-for-carbon-markets/

Energy consumption

As described earlier in this chapter, public blockchains are intentionally compute-intensive to mitigate the risk attacks. According to one estimate, the mining of Bitcoin for one year uses about as much electricity as the entire Czech Republic[362], or 67.88 TWh (terawatt-hours).

The Ethereum Foundation recognizes this challenge and have been on a journey to change how Ethereum works to solve this problem. Ethereum 2.0 will move the network from PoW to Proof-of-Stake (PoS). Rather than all nodes competing for the right to mine a block in the network, PoS selects a subset of nodes on the network, based on their "stake" in the network (Ether holdings), for this right. According to Ethereum creator Vitalik Buterin[363], this change will reduce power consumption on Ethereum by up to 10,000 times[364]. Suffice to say, this will significantly change the economics for using the public Ethereum network in conjunction with private Ethereum networks.

---

362 https://digiconomist.net/bitcoin-energy-consumption
363 https://www.linkedin.com/in/vitalik-buterin-267a7450/
364 https://heraldsheets.com/vitalik-buterin-ethereum-2-0s-pos-can-reduce-the-chains-energy-consumption-by-over-10000x/

SUMMARY

Blockchain is a very powerful technology that has taken the industry by storm. Fueled in 2017 by the "ICO boom"[365], in 2019 we began to see the focus shift from crypto to enterprise use cases being actively developed and deployed. While enabling trust and transparency for legacy systems such as supply-chain, blockchain opens-up a new set of business opportunities not previously possible. For example, Starbucks is using Azure Blockchain to provide visibility into where a coffee-drinker's coffee comes from[366]. While novel and interesting, the real power in this solution is that by attesting for the coffee's distribution on a blockchain, a rural farmer in Rwanda can discover that his coffee is of export quality[367]. This enables him to achieve a level of credit with banks that previously was not possible.

We explored not only the fundamentals of blockchain technology, but how Microsoft has swiftly developed a set of services and tools to make a developer's blockchain journey as easy as possible. What once took six months and $500K to develop a proof-of-concept with a solution integrator can now be done with Azure Blockchain, the Azure Blockchain Development Kit and the Microsoft Power Platform in minutes.

For enterprises looking to add blockchain capabilities to existing systems or are looking for solutions where a decentralized blockchain may be too heavy for their needs, using solutions such as Azure SQL Database ledger enables you to use the skills you already have

---

[365] https://www.gemini.com/cryptopedia/initial-coin-offering-explained-ethereum-ico#section-initial-coin-offerings-on-ethereum
[366] https://traceability.starbucks.com/#/
[367] https://stories.starbucks.com/stories/2019/knowledge-is-valuable-coffee-journey-going-digital-for-customers-farmers/

with a familiar system with strong query capabilities to gain digital trust.

If you haven't yet started your journey in evaluating whether a blockchain-based approach will help in your digital transformation journey, you aren't too late. In fact, the time is ripe now as the technology is beginning to emerge and take hold across the globe.

Made in the USA
Coppell, TX
06 May 2023

16501664R00254